About Pfeiffer

Pfeiffer serves the professional development and hands-on resource needs of training and human resource practitioners and gives them products to do their jobs better. We deliver proven ideas and solutions from experts in HR development and HR management, and we offer effective and customizable tools to improve workplace performance. From novice to seasoned professional, Pfeiffer is the source you can trust to make yourself and your organization more successful.

Essential Knowledge Pfeiffer produces insightful, practical, and comprehensive materials on topics that matter the most to training and HR professionals. Our Essential Knowledge resources translate the expertise of seasoned professionals into practical, how-to guidance on critical workplace issues and problems. These resources are supported by case studies, worksheets, and job aids and are frequently supplemented with CD-ROMs, websites, and other means of making the content easier to read, understand, and use.

Essential Tools Pfeiffer's Essential Tools resources save time and expense by offering proven, ready-to-use materials—including exercises, activities, games, instruments, and assessments—for use during a training or team-learning event. These resources are frequently offered in looseleaf or CD-ROM format to facilitate copying and customization of the material.

Pfeiffer also recognizes the remarkable power of new technologies in expanding the reach and effectiveness of training. While e-hype has often created whizbang solutions in search of a problem, we are dedicated to bringing convenience and enhancements to proven training solutions. All our e-tools comply with rigorous functionality standards. The most appropriate technology wrapped around essential content yields the perfect solution for today's on-the-go trainers and human resource professionals.

Pfeiffer
www.pfeiffer.com

Essential resources for training and HR professionals

Thanks to my wife, best friend, spouse, and life partner, M.J., who gives me purpose and is always there to support me in my endeavors.

Special appreciation goes to my mom, Rosie, who has provided inspiration and support throughout my life.

Training **Workshop Essentials**

Designing, Developing, and Delivering Learning Events That Get Results

ROBERT W. LUCAS

Pfeiffer

A Wiley Imprint

www.pfeiffer.com

Published by Pfeiffer
An Imprint of Wiley
989 Market Street, San Francisco, CA 94103-1741
www.pfeiffer.com

For additional copies/bulk purchases of this book in the U.S. please contact 800-274-4434.

Pfeiffer books and products are available through most bookstores. To contact Pfeiffer directly call our Customer Care Department within the U.S. at 800-274-4434, outside the U.S. at 317-572-3985, fax 317-572-4002, or visit www.pfeiffer.com.

Pfeiffer also publishes its books in a variety of electronic formats. Some content that appears in print may not be available in electronic books.

Library of Congress Cataloging-in-Publication Data

Lucas, Robert W.
    Training workshop essentials : designing, developing, and delivering learning events that get results / Robert W. Lucas.
      p. cm.
    Includes bibliographical references and index.
    ISBN 978-0-470-38545-6 (pbk.)
      1. Workshops (Adult education)   2. Employees -Training of.   I. Title.
LC6562.L83 2009
658.3'124 -dc22

2009004213

Acquiring Editor: Matthew Davis
Director of Development: Kathleen Dolan Davies
Production Editor: Dawn Kilgore

Editor: Rebecca Taff
Editorial Assistant: Lindsay Morton
Manufacturing Supervisor: Becky Morgan

Printed in the United States of America

Printing   10 9 8 7 6 5 4 3 2 1

CONTENTS

LIST OF FIGURES, EXHIBITS, AND TABLES

This book is an important tool for helping resolve your workshop design and delivery conundrums!

If you are

An internal organizational trainer;

An external training consultant;

A professional speaker;

An educator in a secondary, post-secondary, or career school responsible for staff development or training other adults;

A meeting planner; or

A counselor, accountant, financial advisor, or other professional who conducts informational seminars for your clients; or an entrepreneur

then you will find valuable advice and answers to your questions regarding how to create and run a creative and effective training workshop.

How This Book Will Help

Training Workshop Essentials lays out the process of preparing and delivering information in a formal group setting through the use of strategies based on how your learners' brains best process information. It can be helpful for:

Sharing your knowledge on virtually any topic;

Inspiring others through motivational techniques and strategies;

Generating enthusiasm for new processes, procedures, policies, or concepts;

Expanding your current client base by updating existing customers on exciting new products or services; and

Bringing in new clients or customers through informational seminars.

No matter in what setting you find a need for sharing valuable ideas and information, this book can help you by making the event more successful and adding value to your learners' investment of time.

What You Will Find in the Book

Through almost four decades of experience in various industries training and educating adults on dozens of different topic areas, I have gained some valuable and unique insights into what works and what does not related to training. That is not to say that I am the definitive source in the field; however, I do have a toolbox full of proven techniques and strategies to share with you. Sharing is my goal with this book, since I did not have access to one like it when I started my career. Thus, as the old saying goes, "I learned the hard way." My objective in writing this book is to be a resource to you and to, I hope, save you time and frustration and help increase the effectiveness of your workshops and learning events.

Many of the things that you will read in this book translate easily to virtually any industry or organization. They provide a blueprint for the effective design, development, and delivery of a training workshop. Specifically, you will find tips and techniques, charts, lists, recommended resources, processes, procedures, and guidance on how to create a learning event that will help WOW your audiences while positioning you as a dedicated and practiced professional.

Should you need additional resources, please contact me directly at blucas@robertwlucas.com or visit www.robert-wlucas.com, where you can sign up from my free monthly e-newsletter. In it you will find more games, activities, and resources that you can add to your own toolbox of strategies.

Happy Training!

Bob Lucas

ACKNOWLEDGMENTS

y special thanks go to my senior editor, Matthew Davis at Pfeiffer, for his belief in and support for making this project possible.

Also, thanks to the following folks at Pfeiffer who brought this book to fruition. Without their knowledge, skills, and dedication, these words would be nothing but coverage on a page: Lindsay Morton, Dawn Kilgore, and Rebecca Taff.

INTRODUCTION

Relationship Between Training and a Workshop

The word "training" is often used interchangeably with synonyms like "coaching," "instructing," "lecturing," "tutoring," "teaching," and "instructing."

The focus of training is typically to provide a structured learning event in which people can access information and strategies to develop new knowledge, skills, and attitudes. It is normally more effective if a systematic and analytical process is applied. In many training programs, activities are designed to aid learning and to facilitate the development and expansion of new or existing behaviors.

Workshops can be delivered in a variety of formats these days. Some of the more common are

Audio-based—where content is delivered in an audio file (e.g., CD, MP3 file [podcasts], or cassette) and often has an accompanying written participant guide. Learners can purchase and/or download information, then progress through material at their own pace.

Blended learning—in which learners do a knowledge pre-assessment online and develop a specific learning plan for themselves followed by participation in a live instructor-led online workshop. They then take a post-assessment to measure their level of learning and if necessary can take follow-up content workshops to fine-tune areas in which they have deficits or desire to expand their knowledge.

Computer-based training (CBT)—training content is pre-packaged in software that includes animation, graphics, text, audio, and video components. Learners can progress through material at their own pace.

Self-study courses—materials are written, often in a workbook format through which learners can progress at their own pace. Often there is a final test that can be submitted for a certificate (see American Management Association in Resources section).

Teleseminars or teleclasses—in which learners call in to a designated number and are linked together through a central number and receive workshop content from you or another expert. These events can be recorded for later downloads or to create a package of material that can be handed out in future workshops or sold to generate residual income.

Video-based—content is delivered via a video/DVD format and typically has an accompanying written participant guide. Learners can progress through material at their own pace.

Webinars—in which material is delivered live through use of a combination of telephones and graphics, slide shows, or videos via the Internet.

Website seminars—graphics, audio, video, and text can be posted on your website for e-learners to access. You can set up special pages on your website that are accessed with a password given to people as they register. Learners can progress through material at their own pace.

For the purposes of this book, we will focus on more traditional live classroom workshops. These are typically comprised of a single interactive educational learning events or series of events or meetings in which a small number of participants meet to exchange ideas and information and to focus on specific issues, techniques, or skills in a given field or area of expertise (e.g., accounting, human resources, education, or management). In such programs, participants strive to find solutions, solve workplace issues, or gain hands-on practice in using their skills. Activities are designed to help facilitate and improve performance. Role plays, simulation games, brainstorming, small group discussions, and other similar interactive group strategies are often used, along with multi-media (e.g., DVD, CD-ROM, or videos) or audiovisual aids.

I have combined many of the elements above in the text of this book in order to better coincide with what researchers now know about how the brain best processes, stores, retries, and applies information. Because we know that the brain works best when it is engaged on a variety of levels and through various means, an interactive training experience in a workshop setting makes perfect sense.

The Role of Instructional System Design (ISD)

Have you ever attended a workshop or learning event led by a "talking head" or someone who just drones on with little participant involvement? If so, you know the value of a learner-centric event that actively engages participants in the learning at various points during the event.

Many books have been written about the instructional system design (ISD) process in which the five steps for addressing performance needs are met. In that process, also known as ADDIE (Analysis, Design, Development, Implementation, and Evaluation), a thorough analysis is conducted by trainers or others who must determine the underlying causes of a performance gap (the difference between expected and actual performance). Once a determination is made that there are true learning needs to be met, a workshop or learning event is designed, materials are developed, content is delivered (implemented), and the program is later evaluated for effectiveness using the steps of the ISD process.

In this book, you will read about the ADDIE process, with a focus on creating and delivering a creative, efficient, and interactive workshop that incorporates much of what researchers have found to be effective in training adults. Using concepts related to how adults learn differently from children and how the brain best processes information (brain-based learning) and is able to gain, retain, recall, and use information, *Training Workshop Essentials* will show you how to create dynamic, fun, and effective learning events.

Anyone responsible for creating and delivering information in a group setting can benefit from the ideas and tools provided in this book. Throughout the book, you will learn the basics of workshop design, development, and delivery from a whole-brain perspective. In other words, you will learn how to address the three different learning modalities (auditory, visual, and kinesthetic), tap into brain-based or accelerated learning strategies, address the needs of different generations and diverse learners, and employ learner-tested techniques that will make your events memorable.

Why Worry About Workshop Format?

The outcome of any learning event is determined by the amount of forethought and effort that you put into it. If you fail to think about crucial elements like audience makeup and numbers, environment, support materials, equipment, facilitator expertise, and other aspects that influence learning, you could doom your session before it starts. As the Greek philosopher Plato once said, "The beginning is the most important part of any work."

By taking the time to assess learning needs before undertaking any training project, you can save yourself a lot of wasted time and effort and make it more valuable for participants. Once you have determined that training needs exist, there is much to do in your design process. The first, and most important, step is to accurately identify who your audience will be. This is true of an internal program that is targeted at members of your own organization, as well as an event that will be offered to the general public. It is crucial that you address the specific needs of your learners in order to ensure that they take away information and ideas that they can immediately apply in their lives. This is one aspect of adult learning that many trainers, consultants, and educators often overlook. With training time being a precious commodity in today's harried world of doing more with less, you cannot afford to take this step lightly. This book will provide a detailed roadmap to help ensure that your design journey is successful.

How Does Development Impact the Workshop?

Most trainers, teachers, and consultants can prepare a period of instruction that follows the traditional model of instruction of "Tell 'em what you are going to tell them. Tell 'em. Tell 'em what you told them" (Introduction, Body, and Conclusion of a lesson plan). The key to a more successful exchange of knowledge and transfer of learning back to the workplace is to stimulate the brains of your learners and actively engage them. This can be done through the development of creative visual aids and activities that reinforce your verbal message and help learners remember what they experienced.

The experience that most adult learners recall about class-room events is that they sit and take copious notes while the trainer, teacher, or speaker spews volumes of "important" information. In academic settings, this knowledge is typically tested to make sure that "learning" has occurred. In reality, such follow-up only causes learners to cram and commit information to short-term memory long enough to answer test questions; only to forget it immediately afterward.

The strategies and techniques provided in this book go beyond this basic approach in order to reach out and pull learners into the session content and allow them to truly experience and retain it for later use.

What Makes Your Delivery So Important?

Once you have successfully designed and developed your workshop, you must turn your attention to making sure that you create an environment in which the information is delivered in a creative and effective manner. Because adults are just basically kids with big bodies and more experience, you can often incorporate many of the same techniques that teachers use to enthuse your learners and make their learning fun. This can include strategies such as the use of music, color, light, motion, games, props, and much more. You are limited only by your imagination in what you do in your workshop. The key is to always remember that anything that you do or use must ultimately be tied to your learning objectives in order to prevent your learners' perception that they wasted time.

How This Book Is Structured

Throughout the book you will read about strategies and tools that can make your workshops a creative learning utopia. After you go through all the chapters, you will have everything that you need to design, develop, deliver, and evaluate any learning event. You will also have a sound grasp of a variety to techniques and tools that tie to current brain research on ways to enhance your learning environment, stimulate the brains of learners, and present information in a manner that gains and holds the interest of your participants in order to maximize their learning.

I have scattered classroom-tested shortcuts and techniques that I have used in training adults for almost four decades throughout the book. I have also offered specific examples of techniques that I have used over the years, called "Strategy for Success" interspersed with other information in the chapters.

In the first chapter of the book we will delve into some of the models and theories related to effective training and education and take a look at how these concepts can play an important role in developing your workshops and learning events. To do this, we will examine the research of important contributors to the adult learning field—people like Abraham Maslow, Frederick Herzberg, Clayton Alderfer, Georgi Lozanov, Malcolm Knowles, and Howard Gardner. We will also look at popular learning-related models and processes, such as adult learning principles, multiple intelligences, instructional systems design (ADDIE), brain-based learning, and learning modalities.

Chapter 2 focuses on ways to help identify your learners, their wants and expectations, and strategies for analyzing their needs. We will also examine strategies for providing an environment in which people with special needs and those from other cultural backgrounds can maximize their learning experience.

In Chapter 3, you will learn the importance of creating a dynamic learning experience for participants. We will start by examining factors that influence your workshop success (title, day, date, month, time, staffing, facility, equipment, training aids, and much more). You will learn effective marketing strategies that can help fill the seats in your workshop as well as how to structure your content, set valid learning objectives, apply the instructional systems design process, and evaluate the success of your function.

Chapter 4 will open the door to brain-based research. We will examine recent research on how the human brain best processes information so that you can create a more stimulating learning environment—one in which learners are free to explore and become involved to their level of comfort and capability. Included in this journey through the brain, you will read about how environmental factors such as light, sound, music, motion, color, novelty, and other mechanisms stimulate brain neurons to help learners gain, retain, and use what they experience.

Chapter 5 will provide you with strategies and for effectively engaging learners. You will learn how to establish rapport with learners, gain, and maintain their interest and how to incorporate many learner-centric techniques.

Chapter 6 gets into the nitty-gritty details of how to present information in a dynamic and professional manner by mastering communication skills and presenting information like a pro. You will experience strategies for dealing with a variety of learning situations, effectively asking and responding to questions, and generally preparing yourself to project an image of confidence and capability when in front of your learners.

Chapter 7 will prepare you to jazz up your audiovisual aids and training materials so that you can better attract and hold learner attention while sharing important workshop concepts with them. You will learn how to better use static and electronic aids that you have designed in a manner that best capitalizes on the way the brain grasps information.

In Chapter 8, you will find strategies for planning a more successful learning outcome by giving participants a heads up on what to expect before they even arrive at the workshop. Discussion centers on topics like creating a positive emotional environment for learning, making the first few minutes count, empowering learners, and leading by example.

Chapter 9 gets into strategies for ensuring that attendees are ready to learn. You will learn to address learner needs, connect with them, give and receive feedback, and present information in a manner that aids learner memory. Techniques such as icebreakers, interim reviews, and energizers will also be discussed.

The final chapter of this book brings everything together. In Chapter 10, the importance of closure and how to end your workshop on a high note will be covered. As you read about strategies for helping aid transfer of training, you will find techniques and strategies for reinforcing key concepts and reviewing session material in a positive, fun, and upbeat manner. You will also explore ways to end your sessions with the use of props, music, games, activities, and other memorable techniques that will help cement concepts in the minds of your learners.

PART 1

Building a Powerful Workshop

CHAPTER 1

Making Learning Effective

After reading this chapter, and when applying what you learn, you will be able to:

1. Explain the role of a facilitator.

2. Discuss the six adult learning principles.

3. Identify Gardner's eight multiple intelligences and describe ways to address them in training.

4. Describe the three learning modalities and how they affect information acquisition.

5. Select strategies to address each learning modality in a learning environment.

6. Determine accelerated and brain-based learning strategies to enhance your learning initiatives.

"Education is what remains after one has forgotten everything one learned in school."

Albert Einstein

Identifying Your Role

Your role as a facilitator of knowledge exchange is to ensure that your learners "get it." Anything less means that you failed to meet their learning needs. You can have all the knowledge in the world between your ears; however, if you cannot effectively communicate it in a way that allows your learners to "gain it, retain it, recognize and recall it, and use it," they will likely leave the room feeling cheated. To ensure that there is a transfer of learning from you to them and ultimately to the workplace, you must act as a conduit. Your challenge is to make everything you do learner-centered, since your participants are your purpose for being there. Without your learners, you are not needed. To accomplish all this, actively engage learners from the beginning of the workshop and continue to do so at various points throughout the session. Give them information, let them experience and apply it, then review the information or concepts periodically. The key is to not only provide information, but also to tell learners how to apply it outside the classroom. Do not assume that they will "get it" on their own, as they might be distracted, confused by your approach or explanation, or simply may not understand a key point. Give examples, build in activities where they can discuss and process information (small group discussion, problem solving, role play, demonstrations, and open-ended question forums) to draw them in and verify that they grasp your meaning.

A simple technique to help verify understanding is to build in interim reviews through which you can test recognition and comprehension of information. This strategy will be discussed later in the book, but is nothing more than quick, fun activities where key concepts presented to that point in the session are reviewed. You can accomplish this by the use of small group energizer activities that focus on key concepts. For example, games, word search, or crossword puzzles.

Adult Learning Principles

The ways that adults learn (andragogy) have been studied for over one hundred years in Europe; however, Malcolm Knowles is often credited with introducing the concept in the United States in the 1970s. Following that period, many people have debated the validity of Knowles' theory, while others have applauded the simplicity and logic of it. Knowles identified six core adult learning principles in his 1973 book *The Adult Learner: A Neglected Species*. In that publication, he described how the principles could be applied in any adult learning environment. The core principles are

1. *Adults have a need to know why they should learn something.* Since time is so precious in today's harried world, you must take the time at the beginning of your workshop to gain learner buy-in. You can do this through discussion of learning objectives that outline key outcomes that learners will take away and be able to

apply following the session. Another approach is to tell learners ways in which they can use the information. Remember, this may not be as obvious as you think to some people. For example, in describing these six core principles to a group of trainers in a train-the-trainer workshop, you could build in an activity in which learners work in small groups to discuss why each of these concepts is important and how they might be used in their own training sessions.

2. *Adults have a need to be self-directing.* Unlike children, adults have many life experiences that are used to make their own decisions. For this reason, they typically expect that they will have some degree of control over their life situations and be responsible for decisions they make. Use this concept to build problem-solving and decision-making activities into your workshop and to allow plenty of opportunity for participants to respond to and ask questions. For example, in your workshop, make sure that there is ample time for learners to work in small groups on topic-related issues. When forming groups, ask or assign group leaders to keep track of time, control group direction, and act as spokespersons during an activity debriefing at the end.

3. *Adults have a greater volume and different quality of life experience than children do.* Because of their life experiences, adult learners will bring new ideas, skills, and questions to your workshop environment. This can be a double-edged sword. On the positive side, you can tap into their previous knowledge and experience to add more meaning and real-world flavor to the content that you provide. Use learners as coaches, experts, leaders, and co-presenters at various points based on their

expertise level. On the negative side, some people may be more challenging or pessimistic about ideas that you present because of their previous learning and knowledge. You can counter the latter by being thoroughly prepared, having a sound understanding of how to deal with different participant behavior, and maintaining a non-defensive posture when questions do arise (see People Strategies for Trainers in the Resource section for additional ideas on the topic of handling difficult classroom situations). For example, to bring learners together and tap into their expertise, try doing an icebreaker activity at the beginning of the workshop in which learners exchange information and identify what they believe are their strengths and weaknesses related to the topic to be presented. Use this information to pair people in the session so that an exchange of ideas and coaching can occur. This allows more knowledgeable people to feel productive, valued, and important, while those needing information gain a new resource and possibly bond with other learners.

4. *Adults become ready to learn in order to perform more effectively and satisfyingly when they experience a need to know or are able to do so.* As the old adage goes, "Necessity is the mother of invention." When adults feels the pain of not being able to perform well enough in their jobs or they receive negative feedback on performance, they often rush (or are rushed) off to training to "fix" their deficits. Unfortunately, this approach often masks organizational issues that are causing the performance breakdown. Examples of this include poor supervision or management skills on the part of their bosses, policies that inhibit effective job performance, or an environment

that does not adequately prepare and support employees. Still, when such learners show up in your session, your task is to try to enhance their knowledge, skills, and attitude (KSA).

By focusing on this core adult learning principle, you can tap into their desire to learn. You can also engage them in the learning event to allow maximum transfer of knowledge. For example, you may have learners whose organization has shifted to a team environment and some employees are having trouble working effectively with others. They may attend your workshop on effective interpersonal communication or on team building that teaches roles and expectations and skills for building better work relationships.

5. *Adults enter a learning experience with a task-, problem-, or life-centered orientation to learning.* Children focus on learning knowledge in order to pass tests and graduate. Adults focus on gaining new knowledge, skills, and attitudes (KSAs) that will allow them to transfer what is learned back to a life situation immediately and resolve issues that they have. For example, if someone is working in an environment in which he or she interacts with many customers from the Hispanic community and does not speak the language, the person might attend a Spanish language workshop.

6. *Adults are motivated to learn by both extrinsic (external) and intrinsic (internal) motivators.* Researchers have developed many theories of motivation over the last century to try to explain how to deal with such motivators. For example, Abraham Maslow's Hierarchy of Needs theory, Frederick Herzberg's Two-Factor theory, and

Clayton Alderfer's Existence Relatedness Growth theory, any of which you can apply to a learning environment.

By better understanding the premise behind motivation theories, you will be better able to create a learning environment that addresses both intrinsic and extrinsic needs of your learners. One simple way to do this is to use small incentive prizes that relate to your session topic for volunteers, people who arrive and return from breaks on time, and those who accomplish certain tasks. Such rewards address extrinsic learner needs. You can end the session early or recognize individual performance through applause or appointment to specific leadership roles in order to provide for intrinsic needs. Even though rewards are often short-term motivators, if you use them in conjunction with other brain-based learning strategies, you can create an environment that is more conducive to learning. Just do not rely solely on rewards, props, and other "gimmicks" to support a lack of knowledge or poor delivery style. It will not work. You still have to excel in your role as facilitator and/or subject-matter expert (SME).

The key in selecting motivational strategies is to realize that what motivates one person does not motivate all. Use a variety or techniques and, if you realize that something is not working, switch to an alternate strategy immediately. Also consider who is in your audience and the topic of your workshop. For example, while smiley face toys and funny props would work well for a group of front-line employees in a workshop on customer service, it would probably not be a good idea to use them in a session on handling grief to friends and family of deceased people.

Strategy for Success

To ensure that you are addressing the core adult learning principles, make a list of all six and, as you design your workshop content, list each activity, strategy, and technique that you will use next to the principle to which they apply. Items may be listed beside more than one principle if they apply. When your program design is complete, you should have something listed next to each principle. If you do not, go back and modify accordingly. For example, you might use a problem-solving activity in which learners first identify their personal strengths and areas for improvement related to the challenge based on previous experience. This could apply to all six principles, depending on how you introduce the activity.

Multiple Intelligences

Since the release of Howard Gardner's groundbreaking research on multiple intelligences in 1983, he and other researchers have conducted numerous studies on the human brain's ability to learn in various ways. In his original study, Gardner proposed that people have seven intelligences. This is opposed to the standard intelligence quotient (IQ) test areas and verbal and performance sub-areas normally measured by more popular adult intelligence tests, such as the Wechsler Adult Intelligence Scale. He later revised his theory to add an eighth intelligence (naturalist) and continues to speculate about a possible ninth (existential). Research continues in the area of multiple intelligences. Many other people now believe that there are actually additional intelligences that will be identified in the future. By focusing on Gardner's eight areas, facilitators and trainers can enhance the learning opportunity for participants by offering something that will capture and hold the interest of all learners. To do this, workshop activities, content, and

Figure 1.1. Gardner's Eight Multiple Intelligences

materials should include elements that will address the eight intelligences shown in Figure 1.1.

1. Musical/Rhythmic Intelligence

This intelligence allows someone to create or compose music and to understand, interpret, and appreciate it. In your workshop, you can address this intelligence by engaging learners through the use of music before the session, during breaks, and as background during small group activities. You can also have them work individually or as teams to create music-based songs or skits that tie to your session topic or event and are based on well-known music.

Strategy for Success

   A way to create a sense of camaraderie and built to a creative and fun closing activity is to have learners work on their skits throughout the session as they obtain new information or learn additional concepts. They can then incorporate these into their team skit that they would perform at the end of the workshop. The skits could be videotaped and a copy given to each learner on CD-ROM following the session, along with a follow-up questionnaire about the workshop, completion certificate, or additional resource material. All of this would remind participants about and reinforce the workshop content.

2. Bodily-Kinesthetic Intelligence

A second intelligence gives learners the ability to solve problems or manipulate items using their own bodies or parts of the body. To tap this intelligence during learning events, use physical activity to engage brain neurons and help stimulate learning. You can do this through activities in which learners are actually creating a product, problem solving, being creative, or using learning skills like interpersonal communication and team building, or simply moving to get blood flowing to carry oxygen to energize the brain. You can accomplish the latter through Brain Gym activities that you will read about later in the book. Using such activities you can get learners up and moving in order to increase the energy levels during a program.

Additionally, you can place toys or other props on tables and allow learners to manipulate them quietly throughout the session. This can help them address their kinesthetic need. A secondary advantage of such items is that when you see multiple people manipulating their toys or props, you have a non-verbal cue that it is time for a break or change of pace.

3. Logical-Mathematical Intelligence

This intelligence involves the ability to reason, calculate, think in a logical manner, and process information.

To address the need of people with this intelligence, use problem-solving and decision-making activities to engage learners individually or in groups. This allows them to build on previous knowledge or experience and taps into the core adult learning principles that you read about earlier. Many times, learhners have the answers to their own workplace and life issues. They simply need structure and the chance to focus on those solutions. Building such activities into your workshop will provide them with such opportunities.

4. Linguistic Intelligence

The fourth intelligence relates to the ability to read, write, and communicate effectively in a variety of ways.

In order to engage learners with this type of intelligence, provide occasions in which learners have to read, analyze, discuss, and present their thoughts and ideas about issues posed in the session. You can also use tools such as word games, storytelling, rap songs, or journal writing. Use these types of techniques throughout your learning event.

Such activities offer opportunities for learners to network and share ideas while practicing interpersonal communication skills like listening, speaking, and reading non-verbal cues.

5. Visual/Spatial Intelligence

The ability to think in pictures and to visualize a conclusion or result is Gardner's fifth intelligence.

There are many ways to tap into this intelligence. You can build in visualization activities in which you play soft background music while learners close their eyes and visualize situations that you describe. The mental images that you encourage should tie directly to your learning objectives and can be followed by a summation in which you ask open-ended questions, such as who, what, when, how, and why. For example, following a period in which participants visualize themselves being successful in a specific situation, you might ask something like:

♦ "What knowledge or skills made you successful in your vision?"

♦ "In what ways did performing in that manner aid your success?"

♦ "What additional knowledge or skills could have improved the situation you envisioned?"

Such questions help learners focus in on key knowledge and skills that they can use in the future when they face similar situations to the one described in real life.

You can also address this intelligence by using jigsaw puzzles or images related to your session topic to assist learners in recognizing and understanding key concepts.

For example, you might make a jigsaw puzzle from a photo of a piece of equipment used on the job and allow people to work together within a specified time period to assemble it, then discuss its functions. You could also create a flip-chart page with session learning objectives and cut it into jigsaw pieces that you distribute as learners enter the room. Let participants work in small teams to assemble them as a way to introduce key session elements.

6. Interpersonal Intelligence

This intelligence is crucial for understanding others, their emotions, traits, and abilities, and how best to interact with people.

Team-building activities that allow learners to share information, solve problems, and make decisions all provide opportunity for learners to work together and exchange ideas and information. Such activities strengthen potential bonds among learners, help expand their resource network, and allow them to practice their communication skills. All of these can be beneficial to aid learners in improving relationships and becoming more proficient in working with others.

You can also use friendly competition such as timed events in which learners solve puzzles, answer questions, or accomplish a task in small groups. Give small session-related prizes to volunteers and winners in such events in order to add fun and address some of the motivational needs of learners.

7. Intrapersonal Intelligence

The seventh intelligence provides learners the ability to form accurate self-perceptions and use the knowledge to function effectively throughout life. Many people have not had the opportunity think about their own strengths and areas for improvement related to their behavior, beliefs, skills, and other personal aspects that impact the way in which others perceive them.

Build in self-assessment activities that include the use of professional behavioral style instruments such as, the Personal Profile System (PPS) or Myers-Briggs Type Indicator (MBTI). These tools help learners identify key personality or behavioral styles. Through them, you can provide a chance for participants to identify personal factors, improve self-esteem, recognize how their characteristics affect relationships and their level of success, and get to know others better. The more learners know and understand themselves, the more likely it is that they will be able to understand others.

Another strategy that can help with this intelligence is to allow learners to journal thoughts or ideas and describe how they feel about certain issues or events.

8. Naturalistic Intelligence

Gardner's last intelligence involves the ability to observe, understand, and classify patterns in nature and to become more aware of one's natural environment. People with this intelligence interact well with nature, in environments in which they grow and nurture things and animals. They learn best through gathering and analyzing items prominent in nature. Being outside and engaging in kinesthetic activities are motivators for such learners.

You can tap this intelligence of your learners by providing opportunities in which they explore their natural environment. For example, you might hold a scavenger hunt for clues to a session-related situation or challenge that you present. Before the workshop begins, hide the clues in different areas of the room and outside in a garden atrium or patio area. Allow a timed period in which learners search for them individually or as a team. To do this, hide strips of flip-chart paper with the session learning objectives on them and allow learners to find them. Once learners find all the paper strips, ask finders to post them on a flip chart and read them aloud to others while you explain how each objective will be addressed in the session. You can reward people who find the objectives.

Additionally, have everyone give a round of applause for the group's effort in order to reward all learners. This avoids the perception that there will be losers in the workshop.

Another way to include everyone and provide rewards to them is to have those finding the strips reward other finders, then have them give their objectives to others who did not find one. These people come to the board to post and read the objectives. You can then reward those people also. Give anyone not involved to that point small prizes so that there are not losers.

You can also address this intelligence by placing plants in the room and providing plenty of natural light for the environment. You could also allow small groups of learners to assemble outside on a nice day to brainstorm a topic or issue.

Learning Modalities

Simply stated, learning modalities (styles) are differing approaches that people use to learn. Each adult learner is unique and has one or more preferred sensory sources through which information is accessed based on age, experience, ability, gender, and a variety of other factors. These sensory preferences are often called "learning modalities" and involve receiving information through *auditory* (hearing), *visual* (seeing, mental imagery, spatial awareness), or *kinesthetic* (physically experiencing) means.

In any given hour of consciousness, the brain collects, analyzes, and stores thousands of bits of information. As part of this data assimilation and comprehension, your learners use their preferred learning modalities (senses) to gain input. Most people have a preferred primary, as well as a secondary sensory preference that they use most often. Because of this, you should consider these three primary ways that people access information or learn when designing your workshop.

It is important for you to recognize your own preferred style as well as be able to recognize others' styles so that you can successfully facilitate learning and share information in a manner that is most effective. The reason for this is that, if you are not aware of your own preferences, you may unconsciously design and deliver information primarily in a format with which you are most comfortable. In such instances, you might ignore the learning needs of a portion of your learners and ultimately cause a breakdown in the learning cycle.

Exhibit 1.1 is provided to help you identify your own learning preferences. You can also use it to assess the preferences of your learners when needed. Before taking the assessment yourself, make blank copies of the survey to give to your learners in future learning events. This can help ensure that you are building training workshops that are truly effective and from which learners benefit most.

EXHIBIT 1.1. Learning Modalities Self-Assessment

Take a few minutes to read each of the statements below.

In the Preferred Behavior column, place a check (✓) in the space by statements that best describe your learning preference. Once you have selected applicable statements, follow the instructions at the end of the survey in order to determine your preferred style(s).

Style Category	*Preferred Behavior*
_____ 1.	_____ Like to touch or handle things when looking at them
_____ 2.	_____ Spell well
_____ 3.	_____ Like to listen to books on tape
_____ 4.	_____ Enjoy reading books
_____ 5.	_____ Verbal directions alone confuse me
_____ 6.	_____ Enjoy background music while working on a project or an activity
_____ 7.	_____ Would rather spend time discussing a topic than reading about it
_____ 8.	_____ Prefer the use of colors and colored paper on handouts
_____ 9.	_____ Enjoy writing
_____ 10.	_____ Often talk to myself
_____ 11.	_____ Enjoy working with my hands
_____ 12.	_____ Am a good athlete
_____ 13.	_____ Enjoy jigsaw puzzles
_____ 14.	_____ Have a lot of nervous energy (e.g., manipulating objects or change in pockets, tapping pencils, etc.)

(continued)

EXHIBIT 1.1. (Continued)

Style Category	Preferred Behavior
_____ 15.	_____ Remember jokes, stories, and conversations
_____ 16.	_____ Collect things
_____ 17.	_____ Comprehend information better if reading aloud
_____ 18.	_____ Can read maps well
_____ 19.	_____ Doodle or draw pictures
_____ 20.	_____ Use finger as pointer when reading
_____ 21.	_____ Like games, role plays, and simulation activities
_____ 22.	_____ Use rhymes and jingles to remember things
_____ 23.	_____ Get meaning from someone's body language and facial expressions
_____ 24.	_____ Good at locating things or places
_____ 25.	_____ Take many notes during a lecture
_____ 26.	_____ Interpret and understand graphs and diagrams well
_____ 27.	_____ Follow written instructions well
_____ 28.	_____ Talk rapidly and use hands to communicate
_____ 29.	_____ Like to take things apart and put them together
_____ 30.	_____ Enjoy talking to others on the telephone

TOTAL A _____ V _____ K _____

After rating all statements, go back and place an A (Auditory), V (Visual), or K (Kinesthetic) in the Style Category column before the appropriate statements, based on the following:

A = Numbers 3, 7, 9, 10, 15, 17, 20, 22, 26, and 30

V = Numbers 2, 4, 5, 8, 13, 18, 19, 23, 25, and 27

K = Numbers 1, 6, 11, 12, 14, 16, 21, 24, 28, and 29

Finally, count the number of check marks next to statements, by Style Categories, and put those totals by the appropriate letter on the **Total** line. For example, if the total number of checks next to statements labeled "A" was 5, you'd put a 5 next to the "A" on the **Total** line. Do likewise for totals next to "V" and "K."

The letter with the highest Total next to it is likely your primary learning modality or style, while the second-highest score indicates your backup or secondary preference. If you have equally rated styles, you likely shift between them, depending on the situation and learning function in which you are involved.

Source: R.W. Lucas, *The Creative Training Idea Book: Inspired Tips and Techniques for Engaging and Effective Learning.* New York: AMACOM, 2003. p. 17.

Strategy for Success

To demonstrate how you might address each learning modality in a workshop if you were conducting a workshop on that topic, here are some strategies that you could incorporate to address each preferred style:

Auditory—Have learners participate in a group activity in which they create and sing a rap song about the three different modalities.

Visual—Show a flip chart or PowerPoint slides of the three modalities listed, along with graphic images illustrating all three. For example, use an image of an ear for the auditory, an eye for the visual, and a hand touching something for the kinesthetic.

Kinesthetic—Have your learners form teams and demonstrate each type of intelligence in a small group activity. For example, the team assigned the auditory modality might act out a skit in which one learner is coaching another.

Identifying Auditory Learners

Using your voice, small group activities, sounds, and various audible mechanisms can enrich the learning environment for your auditory learners.

Learners who have a preference to the auditory modality typically:

♦ Enjoy participating in listening-based activities (e.g., discussions or lectures)

♦ Can often be easily distracted by other people and sounds around them

♦ Lose interest during visual demonstrations, especially ones that are detailed

♦ Uses self-talk when reviewing information, problem solving, or making decisions

♦ Read aloud (their lips move)

♦ Gain the most value from information gathered in verbal lectures or presentations, small group discussions, and in listening to audiotapes or other people

♦ Like listening to music while studying or working on a project

♦ Participate readily in small group discussions and activities

♦ Extract emotional meaning and intent from vocal nuances, such as rate of speech (words spoken per minute), inflection or pitch (high/low), voice tone, volume (loudness/softness), voice quality (pleasant/unpleasant), and articulation or enunciation of words

(clearly pronouncing words without cutting off endings or slurring)

♦ Tend to be more extroverted

♦ Are often able to recall conversations, jokes, and stories and to attribute them accurately to the person from whom they heard the information

♦ Benefit from learning activities involving verbal interaction. Math, spelling, writing, or complicated written tasks may be difficult.

In some instances, the language used by learners can help in identifying their preferred learning modality. Auditory learners might use statements such as:

♦ It's clear as a bell.

♦ I hear what you are saying.

♦ It sounds to me as if. . . .

♦ That sounds good to me.

♦ What you are saying is music to my ears.

♦ If I am hearing you correctly. . . .

♦ Sounds like a good idea. . . .

♦ That has a familiar ring to it.

♦ It sounds like you are saying. . . .

In order to enhance learning opportunities for your auditory learners, make sure to build in a number of activities in which there is verbal exchange in small and large groups. You can also incorporate a variety of aural stimulation, such as, instructor-led discussion, music, debates, panel discussions, role plays, interactive

CD-ROM, reading text aloud, use of tape recorders, or demonstrations involving verbal explanations.

Identifying Visual Learners

By providing a variety of visual stimulus in your workshop environment, you will better engage learners who use their eyes to gather data and information.

Learners who have a preference to the visual modality typically:

♦ Gain understanding from stimuli received through their eyes and envisioned in their minds

♦ Memorize by seeing pictures, diagrams, or lists

♦ Sit in a location where their view is unobstructed, for example, in the front of the room, on an aisle, or at the end of a table

♦ Extract interpersonal message meaning by observing a person's body language, facial expressions, gestures, and dress

♦ Read directions thoroughly (often multiple times) and then match them to pictures or drawings before they begin working on projects

♦ Are prone to daydreaming or imagining during verbal activities or lectures

♦ Are often introspective, shy, quiet, or reserved

♦ Comprehend more by reading something rather than having someone else read to them or verbally communicate information

♦ Visualize concepts of theory and content received through patterns or pictures in their mind

- Doodle or draw images during lectures or when listening for extended periods

- Are often good spellers

- Learn best from visual stimulus (e.g., slides, transparencies, handouts, flip charts, posters, or videos)

- Take numerous notes to reinforce what they experience and for reference later

- Have a subconscious, emotional reaction to color and light

- Often have trouble following verbal instructions or directions

In some instances, the language used by learners can help in identifying their preferred learning modality. Visual learners might use statements such as:

- I see what you are saying.

- I get the picture.

- I believe I see what you mean.

- The picture is clear to me.

- I see your point.

- I have a good picture of the situation now.

- As I see it. . . .

- That conjures up images for me.

- I can see light at the end of the tunnel.

In order to enhance learning opportunities for your visual learners, make sure to build in a number of activities and materials that are rich in color and images and that appeal to the visual sense. You can also incorporate a variety of visually stimuli through learning aids, for example, flip charts, posters, video, handouts, and slides.

Identifying Kinesthetic Learners

To help ensure that you have addressed the needs of your kinesthetic participants, design programs and activities in which movement is a regular part of the learning. Have people move to other locations in order to participate in activities at various points during your workshop. Encourage activities in which learners have to handle things, interact, or physically move. For example, use stretching or cross-lateral activities to stimulate the brain. Additionally, have actual items available for touching or exploration when possible. When this is not possible, use mockups or models that look like the real object, simulators, or other substitutes for reality.

Using activity, you can engage learners who have a preference for more active learning and who grasp concepts best when they are part of the learning experience.

Learners who have a preference to the kinesthetic modality typically:

♦ Gather information and gain maximum understanding by being involved in an activity or by performing a task

♦ Gesture and make physical contact with others while talking

♦ Learn best through explaining, exploring, manipulating, and assembling or disassembling ideas or objects

♦ Ignore directions and simply jump right in to an assignment or project in order to try to gain understanding

♦ Have body parts in motion while listening, studying, or taking a test, for example, tapping a pencil or their feet

♦ Do not like to read or work on research-based assignments

♦ Become bored of fidgety during lectures or periods of inactivity

♦ Appear disorganized

♦ Have trouble memorizing lists or details

♦ Extract meaning and comprehension through touching, doing, and interacting with others or items

♦ Prefer physical face-to-face input

♦ Exhibit extroverted and outgoing behavior

♦ Enjoy activity but often leave a mess when working on projects

♦ Are mentally stimulated by movement (their own and others')

♦ Enjoy hands-on problem-solving activities

♦ Use strong gesturing and enthusiastic vocal quality in conjunction with interpersonal communication

In some instances, the language used by learners can help in identifying their preferred learning modality. Kinesthetic learners might use statements such as:

♦ I'm moved by what you said.

♦ Let's roll our sleeves up and get started.

♦ I think I have a handle on what you mean.

- ♦ I can't quite grasp your point.

- ♦ It feels right to me.

- ♦ Let's pick the problem apart and see what we are dealing with.

- ♦ Let's jump in and get started.

- ♦ It feels to me as if. . . .

- ♦ Actions speak louder than words.

- ♦ Let me handle this.

- ♦ I've got a grip on what you are saying.

- ♦ Let's do it!

Addressing Learning Modalities

Once you have identified the learning modalities of your participants, there are many strategies available to address them. For the best possible outcome, plan a variety of approaches to learning. Build in segments in which all participants are involved, then break out and conduct small group discussions, partnering activities, and opportunities for individuals to work alone periodically.

Use the indicators that you read about above to help identify the learning modalities of your participants in order to help decide what approaches to take in delivering information. Once you have done so, think of ways to address the needs of all learners. When trying to decide modalities based on some of the elements indicated, look for several combined signals (clusters), rather than just taking one indicator as being definitive of modality preference. Also keep in mind that each learner is a unique combination of experiences, needs, and learning modality preferences. For that reason, the behaviors you read about are simply common indicators of preference. You should not view them as absolutes. Always ask participants for their input or needs, rather than assume.

The following are some tools for effectively addressing the different learning modalities that you will encounter in your workshops.

Strategies for Engaging Visual Learners

Animation. If you use multimedia presentations, include animation. For example, you can download animated clip art at www.microsoft.com to enhance your written messages on your PowerPoint slides. Just make sure that the graphics tie to the concepts in your text so that they reinforce rather than detract from your meaning.

Color Code Key Concepts. This idea ties into the concept of using color to stimulate the brain, as you will read later. Include brightly colored papers (for handouts), assorted colored markers, and posters with content that ties to the session topic and previous concepts that learners have experienced. When selecting colors to use on flip charts and slides, it is best to limit the number of colors to one for the title line and no more that two alternating colors for lines of text. Follow the same color scheme on all similar visuals. This allows learners to anticipate upcoming colors mentally and limits possible "surprises" or distractions that might take their focus from what you are saying. It also allows them to form mental images to connect content while providing reinforcement of key program elements.

Demonstrations. To illustrate a process or concept before learners attempt to replicate it, give a demonstration with an actual item or a model of the item to the group. This allows them to see operational functions and potential applications, and encourages them to ask questions.

Flash Cards. Have learners create flash cards (small strips of cardboard or poster board) with images or key concepts written on them. You can use these in a small group activity, as a review of material, or in a presentation that groups give to others to reinforce verbal messages while adding visual stimulus. Use various colors of poster board to add additional visual enhancement. You can put masking tape on the back to post them to a wall or flip chart or small magnetic strips to attach them to a metal writing surface.

Graphics. You can also add simple, colorful cartoon characters, graphics, and caricatures to handouts, flip charts, and other visual aids to add a splash of color. When using these items, be conservative rather than adding too many images. You should not cause visual distractions or draw attention from your written message.

Mind Maps. Use mind maps (graphic displays of key concepts that branch out from a central idea) to visually indicate the flow and connection of key session components. You can draw these on a handout or writing surface, project them on a slide or on a transparency. Have learners create their own mind maps as they take notes from a lecture or discussion in order to help cement the concepts in their minds.

Note-Taking. Have learners fill in the blank spaces in workbooks with key concepts that you cover or take notes on handouts provided to them at the beginning of the session.

Paint Mental Pictures. Offer quotes, stories, analogies, and examples that are relative to points made in the session in order to help generate mental images of a key concept or theme. This allows learners to relate to previous experiences and thereby better grasp and retain what was said.

Photographs. Use photos of actual items or that illustrate a concept that you are trying to convey. For example, a picture can help a viewer extract emotional messages from the photo subject's facial cues.

Tables/Charts. Organize lists, key concepts, models, or other information into a table or chart format and either display it on a slide or flip-chart page or give handouts of it to learners.

Video Clips. Show a brief portion of a popular movie in which concepts related to the workshop topic are illustrated; then follow that with an activity in which learners discuss what they saw.

Visualization Activities. Include activities in which you ask participants to close their eyes and envision how certain situations might appear if they applied content discussed in the session. You can also play classical, new age, or other slow tempo music to help the auditory learners. For example, in a workshop on interpersonal communication, have learners imagine how customer service would improve if they applied effective listening skills learned during the program. Ask a series of questions to stimulate their thinking while they have their eyes closed. After a designated period, stop the music, and have them open their eyes and discuss their ideas in small groups to exchange thoughts. Ask learners to capture their thoughts on flip charts for large group discussion and action.

Strategy for Success

To appeal to your visual learners, prepare a series of flip-chart pages with quotes (similar to the ones at the beginning of each chapter of this book) by famous people. Include cartoons or other graphic images and use an assortment of marker colors. Make sure that the quotes tie to your workshop content.

Strategies for Engaging Auditory Learners

Audiotapes or CDs. Use recorded music and recorded information segments from authorities on your topic to reinforce what you have shared or to make a key point and add more depth.

Guest Speakers. Bring in an outside "expert" to share views, ideas, and information that can support and supplement what you have offered while adding additional content to the workshop. This is especially helpful if the person is well-known.

Lecture. Lectures are relatively easy to prepare and deliver and can be used to provide large amounts of information in a short period. They can be effective for providing policy and procedure or regulatory information, for example, if you are covering policies, laws, or safety standards. Even in those cases, try to build in short, interactive questioning and small group discussion to help learners better internalize the information that you give them.

Lectures are often referred to as "information dumps." While they are one of the oldest means of relaying information to learners, they are also probably one of the least effective when used exclusively. This is because researchers have found that the brain processes information best through multiple senses and in a variety of ways. To capitalize on this research, use lectures sparingly and supplement them with interactive strategies that engage your learners.

Mnemonic Devices. Use memory aids called mnemonics to help people gain, retain, and recall information later. Either you can provide these aids or have learners create their own. Examples of mnemonic devices include:

♦ *Acronyms*, which are words formed from the first letters of words. For example, many students in the United States memorize and recall the names of the U.S. Great Lakes with the acronym HOMES (Huron, Ontario, Michigan, Erie, and Superior).

♦ *Rhymes.* Rhymes are familiar to most learners and tap into a person's musical intelligence area. For example, A traditional mariner's rhyme for weather forecasting reminds sailors that "Red sky in the morning, sailor take warning; red sky at night, sailor's delight."

♦ *Acrostics.* By stringing together a series of names, items, or terms, you form an acrostic. The first or last letter of these words together makes a sentence or represents a group of well-known items or names. For example, the following acrostic was used to teach children the nine planets (before recent discoveries that brought Pluto into contention): My (Mercury) Very (Venus) Educated (Earth) Mother (Mars) Just (Jupiter) Sent (Saturn) Us (Uranus) Nine (Neptune) Pizzas (Pluto).

Oral Instructions. Give instructions orally, but also provide a visual copy (e.g., slide, transparency, writing surface, or handout) so that learners can refer back to them if needed. This aids your visual learners and ties into the brain-based learning concept of repetition that you will read about later.

Storytelling. This is an ancient technique for sharing information. It is still effective today for engaging listeners and changing the pace of the workshop. You can tell your own stories and share real-world examples related to the session topic, or you can elicit stories from your learners.

Rhythmic Sounds. Build group activities which rhythmic sounds and instruments (e.g. drums, cymbals, sound sticks, and others) into your learning events. These exercises can act as an energizer in which learners create a song around key session topics. This taps into Musical Intelligence identified by Howard Gardner and into brain-based learning research that suggests that sound and music helps stimulate the brain.

Small Group Discussions. Have learners periodically form random small groups to discuss key session concepts, problem solve, make decisions, and practice skills learned.

Word Association. Use activities in which learners use word association to review key session concepts. These might be in the form of an opening icebreaker or an interim review activity.

Strategy for Success

To appeal to your auditory learners, incorporate a variety of noisemakers and sounds, (whistles, gongs, bells, and music) into your workshop design. For example, you can integrate sounds that are heard each time you transition from one slide to the next in PowerPoint.

Strategies for Engaging Kinesthetic Learners

Discussions. Get kinesthetic learners more involved in the learning process by forming small groups and having everyone participate in discussions throughout your workshop. You can have people physically relocate to other areas of the room in order to incorporate physical movement.

Energizer Activities. There are hundreds of books and articles available that provide games and other activities that can be used to gain and hold learner attention and to re-energize them when they have been in a workshop for a while and need a quick mental break. Use such activities periodically, but make sure that you select ones that tie to your session content and teach or reinforce key concepts. Doing that potentially prevents learners from viewing the activities as a frivolous waste of time.

Games. Fun and novelty are two elements of brain-based learning. Build in opportunities for learners to play. After all, adults are just kids with big bodies. They learn behaviors as children and repeat them as adults. Since many of their early learning experiences involved playing games, allow them to revisit those fun times and gain new knowledge or reinforce what they know. You can modify popular board and dice games or create your own to share key concepts or to allow learners to practice knowledge and skills learned.

In-Basket Activities. Develop activities in which you give a stack of items (e.g., memos, forms, letters, and other materials) that would often show up in a workplace in-box to learners. Give a specified period for them to sort through materials and make decisions on any action they need to take on each item. This is a great activity for teaching and reinforcing workplace skills like time management, problem solving, decision making, delegation, and resource management. You can use them in sessions for supervisors and managers or other decision-makers.

Note-Taking. The simple act of note-taking requires focus and mental and physical exertion on the part of learners. Encourage everyone to take notes so that they customize handout materials to their needs and that they capture key ideas that they can refer to later.

Plays or Acting Out Skits. Include interactive strategies such as these to actively engage learners, to allow them to practice skills, and to help them teach others in the group. Such events can often be memorable and help reinforce learning while introducing a bit of fun into your workshop.

Problem Solving. Form small groups and allow learners to work collectively toward solving real-world issues that they can associate with their own workplace and lives. They can then transfer their solutions to their own situations.

Props. Use a variety of props that tie to your theme or that you can use to grab and hold attention during various portions of your program. For example, you might use masks, Groucho Marx glasses/nose, hats, wands or other magic items, movie clapboards, or jumbo playing cards (see Creative Presentation Resources in the Resources section at the end of this book). These types of items tie to concepts of brain-based learning related to adding novelty and fun to aid processing of information by the brain.

Role Play. Have learners assume various roles in hypothetical situations in order to practice skills and use knowledge gained in the workshop. This can be a sound learning strategy if you appropriately explain expectations, objectives, and roles up-front, monitor the interaction, and effectively debrief at the end to allow learners to explain their perceptions of what occurred and what they learned from the activity. An important element is to make the scenarios as realistic as possible without drawing attention to a specific workplace issue or person whom people in the room would recognize.

Simulations. Use activities that you design around real-world situations. These can teach important moral and value lessons as well as help people gain knowledge and skills that they can transfer to their own environments. One such simulation, created in the mid-1960s, is known as SimSoc (Simulated Society). Participants in leadership and other programs form groups, but are not told which sector of society they represent. Throughout an all-day event, they must accomplish tasks that result in rewards and penalties while the rules keep changing or are adapted (to simulate real-life occurrences). At the end-of-day debriefing, the facilitator asks participants to share their experiences and their emotions. The latter can be quite dramatic based on whether people found themselves in the upper class, middle class, or lower class of society during the day.

Stretching. You can use simple stretching exercises during periods in which learner energy level seems to be dropping to re-engage and stimulate them. These can be as simple as having everyone stand behind chairs for support while you walk learners through some low-stress movements. For example, have learners touch their left index fingers to their noses, then have them touch their right index fingers to their noses. Have them raise their left feet and pat their heels with their right hands five times. Have them continue doing similar tasks using different body parts for a minute or so. Such activities can cause learners to think about the instructions and become more physically involved. In doing so, they increase the blood flow that carries oxygen to the brain and refreshes it, making them more alert. When doing such activities, always tell learners to participate to their level of comfort. Give the group to permission modify any exercise or movement so that you do not embarrass someone who might have a disability, injury, or limited mobility.

Strategy for Success

To appeal to your kinesthetic learners, place colorful, soft, manipulative toys on learner tables for them to play quietly with as they listen. Examples of manipulatives include foam squeeze toys in various shapes, stress balls (latex filled with sand or powder), Puffer balls (aid filled latex balls), Koosh® balls, mini Hobeman Spheres®, Silly Putty®, or PlayFoam® (see Creative Presentation Resources in the Resources section).

Accelerated Learning

Accelerated learning was developed in the 1970s and is based on research by a professor of psychiatry and psychotherapy from Bulgaria, Dr. Georgi Lozanov. In his early programs, Lozanov taught a foreign language though the use of visual arts, classical music, and activities. He called his methodology "Suggestology" (based on the theory that suggestions affect learning outcomes). Through his strategies, students were able to retain from 100 to 1,000 vocabulary words a day with a 98 percent or better retention rate.

According to Lozanov, his approach to learning simply supplements the way that the brain naturally learns and retains information and allows people to learn more efficiently and effectively. He believed that, by emulating a more natural learning process, the learning of his students was accelerated, thus allowing better comprehension and retention of information and skills learned. It is this basis that lead to the evolution of accelerated learning, as many trainers and educators know it. (See International Alliance for Learning [IAL] in the Resources section.)

In an accelerated learning environment, the facilitator helps create a positive environment for learning by focusing on positive feedback and avoiding negative reinforcement. There are multiple opportunities provided for learners to grasp information individually and in groups in order for them to capitalize on their full learning potential and minimize and limit beliefs that they may have related to their ability to learn or master knowledge or skills. The three elements that will determine success are the facilitator, the environment, and the learning process design.

Typically, an accelerated learning environment includes such things as:

♦   A facilitator who addresses the individual needs of learners

♦ An environment that is aesthetically pleasing, interaction-rich, and appealing to all learners

♦ An atmosphere in which learners are physically and emotionally safe and can experiment and grow

♦ Colorful peripherals on the walls

♦ Classical (baroque) or upbeat music tied to the session theme or activities

♦ Learners working collaboratively in groups while playing board, memory, or other games

♦ Individuals and groups using their creativity to put together collages, skits, and musical songs tied to the session topic

♦ Opportunities for learners to integrate the learning into their real world, to reflect on the learning and its relevance to them, and to celebrate success

♦ Techniques and activities that involve different learning styles

♦ A multitude of other whole-brain strategies that engage learners throughout the event

Brain-Based Learning

Brain-based or brain-compatible (active) learning theory focuses on creating an opportunity in which attainment and retention of information are maximized. This concept incorporates the latest research on how the brain learns best and encourages application of findings to training and educational learning environments.

A key to the successful application of brain-based learning theory precepts is for everyone involved in the learning process (program designers, managers, trainers/educators, and learners) to first understand how the brain functions. They must then identify personal strengths and areas for improvement related to the theory concepts and modify their approach to learning accordingly. They must also consciously focus on learner needs and learning modalities to ensure that format and program delivery are effective.

According to the brain-based theory, learning is an active process. Challenges, ambiguity, and creativity are incorporated and encouraged by using accelerated learning strategies. Facilitators actively engage participants in their own learning. Participants are prompted to think outside the box related to examining information and issues. Problem solving, questioning, ongoing interaction, and feedback are important elements in the absorption process, and they are used freely. Learners are also provided with many opportunities to make associations with knowledge and skills that they already possess while forming new patterns and making additional connections. The use of analogies, simulations, metaphors, jokes, stories, examples, and various interactive techniques strengthen connections to workshop content.

In brain-based learning environments, materials and instruction must be learner-centered and delivered in a manner that is fun, meaningful, and personally enriching. There must also be opportunities for participants to have time to process what they experience in order for them to make mental connections and master content. In doing so, learners can increase personal comprehension and better grasp meaning and potential opportunities for application.

Strategy for Success

One way to ensure that you are adequately addressing true learner needs when creating program content is to take the time to do an advance analysis of what participants already know related to your intended session topic(s). You can accomplish this by mailing a questionnaire to participants and their supervisors a couple of weeks before scheduled training.

If you are an internal trainer or consultant, you can also conduct face-to-face or telephone interviews, hold focus groups involving those who will be attending and/or their supervisors, or make visits to work sites to observe on-the-job behavior of participants related to the program topic. Take the information gained into account as you design your workshop content.

If advance analysis is not possible, post closed-ended questions written on flip-chart paper and related to program content on the training room wall. Examples of such questions include, "How much experience do you have in _____?" or "How many times have you _____?" Have participants respond to the questions as they enter the room. Then tabulate and incorporate their responses into your session content, if possible. You can also hand out 3-by-5 cards or blank paper. Have learners either respond to questions and collect answers or discuss them in small groups. Following collection of responses, you can share them with the entire class.

Brain-based learning offers many opportunities for enhanced learning and retention of information and skills if used properly. There are many books and articles on the market that address brain-based learning concepts (see Resources section). You will learn more about brain-based learning throughout this book. You can also get started on learning more about the topic by searching the Internet. That will result in a wealth of valuable resources that can lead to the creation of more effective learning experiences for your learners. A number of additional resources and references can be found at the end of this book and by visiting the author's website (www.robertwlucas.com).

Personalizing What You Have Learned

- What are the most important things that you read in this chapter? Why?

- What are some ways that you can immediately apply concepts covered in this chapter?

- What additional resources or topics do you want to research based on what you read?

Addressing the Needs of Your Learners

A fter reading this chapter, and when applying what you learn, you will be able to:

1. Recognize the different generational differences in your audience.

2. Develop training success strategies to address learner needs, wants, and expectations.

3. Create a learner profile that can better help you serve the needs of your participants.

4. Analyze learner needs in a variety of ways.

5. Meet the needs of a diverse audience of learners.

"Creative minds have always been known to survive any kind of bad training."

Anna Freud

Identifying Your Audience

So much has been written about ways to determine who your audience will be and what they want or expect from your presentation that it seems redundant to spend a lot of time covering the topic here. Instead, I want to share with you some ideas for identifying important values and needs of potential learners based on their generation. When you first focus on who might be best-suited to attend your workshop or what you might plan for them in the session, consider the following general information about generations within society.

The Challenge of Generations in the Learning Environment

For the first time in history, there are four major age groups or generations in the workforce of the United States and many other countries. These people work side-by-side and supervise one another. The challenge is that they bring with them distinct beliefs and values that influence their needs and expectations in the workplace and in the training environment.

The Builder Generation (1901–1945)

This group is the oldest living generation in North America and consists of two generations, spanning over forty years, as opposed to the other generations, which span approximately twenty years. The reason that many researchers combine two eras is that these groups share similar values and beliefs. Different names (Mature, Silent, Traditional, or Veteran) are used to refer to members of this generation. They worked hard throughout their lives, often struggling to make ends meet and feed their families due to fewer opportunities and lack of formal education. Since they are dependable, members of this generation can be counted on to show up on time, do what they are paid to do, and work toward the common good of the group.

Many Builders, who were often the children of poor immigrants, view education and training as a luxury. They focus on gaining technical job skills to comply with their value of working hard in order to achieve a goal. Since they did not grow up with a lot of technology, they may need more time to complete tasks involving it. They might also need additional instruction before they master complex technology-based tasks. Their approach to learning is often more traditional, instructor-led format in which learners take a more passive role. Creative small-group activities (e.g., team building and group problem solving or decision making) may be a challenge for some members of this generation.

Strategy for Success

To meet the needs of the Builders, create a learning environment in which you deliver information in a formal manner (instructor-led) and include activities, which are clearly defined, well-structured, purposeful, and not predominantly technology-based.

Baby Boomers (1946–1964)

Demographically, this group dominates the workforce. The Baby Boomers differ from any other generational groups in that they are a transition group. They were the last generation before the end of the industrial age and the first to experience the technology age. This fact gives them opportunity to have the knowledge of how life was before technology dominated daily life and the workplace. Being part of a transition group further provides the opportunity to tap into the evolving technological innovations that can make life more efficient and better connect people. Boomers often feel an entitlement because of opportunities provided to them by their parents who, in many cases, often went without to provide opportunities for their children. They also tend to challenge the status quo of society, government, and the workplace.

In a learning environment, they may adapt and accept technology well (depending on whether they were on the front or back end of the generation), welcome opportunities to take an active role and assume control of their learning, yet may challenge and question you. They want answers to real-world issues and need to understand how what they learn will immediately apply and help them move ahead in the workplace and the world.

Boomers saw their parents toil on the farm and in blue-collar jobs only to barely get by. They recognized the importance of gaining an education in order to advance professionally and to increase their opportunities for prosperity. As a result, Boomers were the first generation to flock to college and higher education. Many of the group are very competitive and are often noted for their efficiency, teamwork, quality, and service approach to the workplace.

Strategy for Success

Provide a learning environment for the Boomers in which they can assume leadership roles, work toward creative attaining real-world skills, and where small group activities are used in order to allow idea sharing and collaboration. Blended learning (a combination of instructor-led and technology-based) works well for most Boomers.

Generation Xers (1965–1980)

This generation grew up in the shadow of their over-achieving Boomer parents. They are skeptical about the future, and to some extent feel cheated out of the opportunities that many Boomers had. Xers' frustrations are due in part to the fact that Boomers continue to dominate the workplace, thereby locking the Xers out of key positions.

Xers have a lot to offer the workplace of today. They multi-task well compared to the Builders and Boomers, who did not grow up with technology as their primary means of information and entertainment. Their technical capabilities tie directly into the needs of organizations desiring to position themselves as globally competitive and cutting-edge. Because of their propensity for challenging the status quo and not accepting "because" types of responses to questions, they bring an out-of-the-box way of looking at things differently.

Xers are often referred to as the why generation because they typically exhibit extreme pessimism about many things; this is the generation that believes that something must be proven valuable before they buy into it. They grew up witnessing their parents' misplaced trust in the system and feeling that they would not inherit the opportunities that the Boomers had. One true value that this generation brings to the workplace, and to the world, is their acceptance of diversity. They have grown up in a period in which gays and lesbians, single women, ethnic groups, and people of all races were recognized as adding value in their own right.

This is a generation that was around at the start of the technology revolution. They grew up playing Pac-Man® and other simplistic (by today's standards) electronic games. They ultimately moved onto the personal computer, where they spent countless hours entertaining themselves while their parents worked. They have often learned by trial-and-error. They mastered the technology while they learned how to process information and deal with issues in a non-linear and fast-moving fashion. The result is that they now view things and process information differently than their predecessors in the workplace. In a learning environment, they are comfortable with technology-based as well as instructor-led activities. They have the ability to see big-picture results following a decision process and have also developed the patience and attitude that helps them focus on getting to an end result.

Strategy for Success

Create learning environments for the Xers that include ample use of technology and opportunity to creatively problem solve. Be prepared with answers to questions related to workshop topics and explain how to apply what they learn effectively to the real world.

Millennials (1981–1999)

Millennials are often referred to with monikers such as, Generation Y, Nexters, or Generation Why and "baby busters" or "echo boomers" (because they are descendents of Baby Boomers and early Gen-Xers). There are nearly eighty million of them, and they are having a huge impact on entire segments of the economy. As they age, they already make up one-third of the U.S. population and will be become the next dominant generation of Americans.

Members of this multi-tasking group grew up with computers at home, a 500-channel television selection, instant messaging, music downloads, and the Internet. As a result, their brains move at a rapid pace and attention spans can be shorter when faced with lecture or tedious, time-consuming activities and processes. Learning needs to be delivered at a rapid pace with little down time in order to hold their interest. Engagement through use of multi-media, individual and group activities, and a smorgasbord of learning strategies is the way to keep this group focused.

Millennials often focus on helping others, changing society for the future, giving back through volunteerism, and working in groups. In all aspects of their lives, they seek to have time for relationships and extreme fun (e.g., trick biking, snowboarding, rock climbing, skateboarding, and air surfing). They relish opportunities for group activity and want the flexibility to spend time on projects that they enjoy. Influenced by parents who value education and a workplace that demands it, most Gen-Yers recognize that the key to their success lies in advanced learning opportunities.

The members of this generation often take an informal approach in everything from how they dress (casual clothing) to the way that they accomplish tasks. They are smart and want work that is challenging and meaningful. They also want clearly defined tasks, regular interaction with their supervisors, timely answers to questions, and patience on the part of project or team leaders. Because they are smart and have had broad exposure to information through the Internet, they often tend to question things. They do not do this from an antagonistic standpoint; but out of true interest and a desire to learn how and why things are as they are.

Strategy for Success

Create a fun, informal environment in which learners have plenty of opportunity for exposure to technology and where they get to work closely with their peers to share ideas and information.

Learner Needs, Wants, and Expectations

In Chapter 1, you read about adult learning principles and how learners come with experience and knowledge that can be tied to your workshop content. They also have an expectation that they will walk away with solid knowledge and skills at the end of the session. Your goal should be to ensure that you identify and fulfill their needs, wants, and expectations.

What Learners Need

With some exceptions (their supervisor directs them to attend or mandatory legal, organizational, or regulatory training), most adult learners typically volunteer to attend training. They do this out of a desire to attain new knowledge and skills or in some cases for self-improvement related to their attitudes or opinions. As a result, they will normally become active participants in the learning process if you give them an opportunity.

To help your learners meet their needs, design the workshop in a manner that allows frequent involvement and that allows participants to interact with you and others while sharing ideas, opinions, questions, and issues. This format makes the content come alive and is more meaningful to your learners, while providing you with continuing feedback on how well the session is progressing. For example, if learners are taking a more inactive or passive role, even though you have built in activities and exercises, perhaps they need more information, better directions, or something to inspire or motivate them toward engagement. Some things to encourage the latter include rewards, incentives, a break, or an energizer activity to get the blood and oxygen flowing to the brain.

The easiest way to ensure that you are meeting expectations is to identify their needs in an opening activity or a pre-session questionnaire. Throughout the workshop, do interim reviews and activities that provide you with feedback on whether you are addressing their needs adequately.

What Learners Want

Researchers have done numerous studies over the years related to what drives people and what they want when they purchase something (in this case training). Marketing and sales professionals have focused on the results of such research for years in order to maximize revenue generation. By applying what we know about people and following the approach of marketers you can also help create a situation in which the desires of your learners are met. The key is to focus on the benefits that learners will derive from the training, such as more knowledge, enhanced skills, an opportunity to make more money, or a chance to be promoted. Do not just try to show them the features of the training. For example, do tell them that during the training video scenarios will be used, networking opportunities will be provided, participant workbooks will be given for future reference, or training will be held at a convenient location. These are features, not benefits.

The following are some of the things that learners often want and some that they want to avoid. Use these in your workshop marketing efforts and in the design of workshop content and materials whenever possible to motivate learners, enhance the overall learning experience, and to get them to come to future sessions.

What People Want

♦   To achieve success

♦   To be healthy

♦   To be comfortable

♦   To be loved

♦   To experience pleasure

- To feel safe and secure
- To gain recognition
- To have fun
- To make money
- To maintain positive self-esteem
- To save time
- An opportunity for self-improvement
- To win peer support and admiration

What People Want to Avoid

- Death
- Insecurity
- Loneliness
- Pain
- Loss of money
- Wasted time

What Learners Expect

As you will read in Chapter 6 related to presenting yourself and the workshop effectively, learners expect that you will come prepared and deliver a meaningful workshop. They also expect that you will conduct yourself professionally and that you will manage the learning process and classroom efficiently to ensure that all attendees have a positive learning experience.

Much of what learners expect is based on their prior learning environment experiences. If they are relatively young and have not attended many adult training events, they will base expectations on their experiences through high school and perhaps college. In those environments, they likely sat in rows or tiers of desks and had someone lecture them for most of their classes. Interaction or active involvement might have been limited and not encouraged due to the large numbers of students and limited timeframes.

If your learners are older and more experienced in the workplace, they have potentially had a wide range of experience in observing different facilitator styles. As a result, they may have formed opinions and expectations on what is good or bad. Depending on your experience, knowledge, and skills, and how effectively you deliver your workshop content, this can help or hurt you,.

To further compound the array of expectations, you may have a number of people who come from other cultures and who were taught to respect trainers and educators because of their expertise. The logic in such instances is that, if you are in front of them speaking, you must be an expert. In many cultures (Asian in particular), they have probably learned not to question the instructor, since this would cause him or her to lose "face" (esteem) and cause embarrassment. This is something upon which people from such cultures frown.

Before you can effectively manage all the expectations in your training room, you have to try to identify them early in your workshop. Do this through some type of fun, non-threatening activity.

Strategy for Success

To help identify trainee expectations, you might use an icebreaker in which learners introduce themselves and then share what is important to them in a learning environment. The following activity can accomplish this while engaging learners and tying in to brain-based learning concepts while introducing a bit of novelty and fun into the workshop.

Prior to the session starting, create slides, transparencies, or flip-chart pages with the following questions on them. Determine the appropriate media format based on the size of your group. Use color and humorous graphic images or borders to enhance the text and to add a bit more levity while attracting attention.

What is your name?

What one thing do you most want to learn today?

What one thing do you hope does not happen in this workshop?

What are you thinking now?

When time to start the session comes, either have someone else introduce you while you enter from behind learners or enter from behind them using some form of noise or attention-getter, for example, a train or coach's whistle, bike horn, hand clappers, or something else to draw attention to you. You should also be wearing some outlandish prop, such as Groucho Marx nose and glasses, rubber animal nose, Cheese Head top hat and bowtie, or trick nail through the head.

Do not say a word as you proceed to the front of the room; smile and wave and proceed to turn on the projector or turn the flip chart to display the first prepared question.

Turn, smile, and gesture to someone in the front row and then gesture to the question on the slide, transparency, or flip chart to indicate that the person should answer the displayed question.

Randomly select four or five other learners, one at a time, to have them introduce themselves in the same fashion. Keep smiling and remain silent as they do so.

(continued)

Repeat the process while presenting the next two questions, until three to five minutes have passed.

At that time you should project the final question: "What are you thinking right now?" And, with open arms, gesture to the entire group to indicate that anyone should respond.

Typically at this point, someone will say something like, "This is different" or "This *is* strange." They might also ask, "Are you ever going to speak?"

If the question *is* asked, remove the prop, and state, "I was wondering whether you wanted me to talk." Introduce yourself and explain that, while you do not take yourself seriously, you take the topic seriously. Then debrief the activity.

If the question *is not* asked, remove the prop(s) introduce yourself, explain that, while you do not take yourself seriously, you take the topic seriously. Then debrief the activity.

Next, have learners spend five minutes discussing what they hope to learn during the workshop and why it is important that they do so.

After five minutes, have each person do a self-introduction and share his or her goal for the session with the entire group as you capture their needs on a flip-chart page.

Post the page for future reference and have all learners give a round of applause for their contributions.

If you are using incentives, give a piece of candy to each person. Tell them it is to replenish all the brain cells they killed during the activity!

The source of this activity (and others) is R.W. Lucas, *Creative Learning: Activities and Games That REALLY Engage Learners*. San Francisco: Pfeiffer, 2007, available at www.presentationresources.net

Focus on Your Learners

You must never forget that your learners are the most important element of your workshop. If learners do not show up, you have no reason to be there or to have the event. Everything that you do should be focused on identifying and meeting the desires, needs, and expectations of your learners.

Develop a Learner Profile

Once you have determined what your session content will deal with based on your needs analysis, part of your planning process should include deciding who would most benefit from attendance. In other words, whom should you target with your marketing efforts? Further, the more you know about your learners, the more likely you are to have a successful learning outcome and meet their needs. You can try to identify learner characteristics during your analysis process or in an activity at the beginning of your workshop. Of course, if you wait until the workshop, you will not be able to incorporate what you find into the original session design.

There are formal, commercial profiles available that can be used to determine more specific information about individual learners. For example, are they more like thinker versus intuitive type personalities? In some instances, like a workshop on team building or interpersonal relationships, where you want people to get to know one another more intimately, such information would be useful. However, for general learning events, a demographic overview and some of your learners' preferences should suffice.

Whatever approach you take to identifying learners, you should probably gather as much information in advance as possible about the people who are likely to attend your workshop . This will allow you to better prepare to meet their needs and send an unstated message to learners that you are interested in helping them achieve their goals.

You can gather some helpful information about your learners by answering the following questions:

♦ To what generational category do they belong?

♦ What is the gender makeup of the group?

♦ What is the average education level?

♦ What are their job titles or positions?

♦ What level of responsibility (how many people do they supervise) do they have?

♦ Did they volunteer or were they required to attend?

♦ What are their expectations of the session?

♦ With what common problems or performance issues do they deal?

♦ What are some of their passions or motivators related to learning? For example, what is most important in a learning environment?

♦ What are their pet peeves related to learning?

To determine some of the above characteristics, create a short questionnaire that can be sent to workshop attendees when they register or that can be handed out as they arrive in class.

Strategy for Success

To quickly learn a bit of information about your learners and their expectations or needs once they arrive, create a list of learner profile questions. Then form small equal-sized groups and have each group select a leader and scribe. Next have them spend time discussing the questions, brainstorming, and charting responses. Then have small groups share their responses with the entire group.

Some possible questions might include:

♦ If you were facilitating the program, what would you be sure to include? Why?

♦ What things most contribute to your learning?

♦ What things detract from your learning?

♦ What do you hope does not occur during the training?

♦ What attributes would an ideal facilitator possess or exhibit?

♦ In a typical learning environment, what gets you actively involved?

♦ Related to the training topic, what would help you better perform your job?

♦ From a growth perspective, what do you hope to learn during the training?

♦ What do you least like to do in a learning workshop?

♦ What do you most like to do during a learning event?

♦ What training techniques do you find to be most effective? Why?

♦ What training techniques do you find to be least effective? Why?

♦ At the end of a training session, how do you know it was a successful learning event for you?

At the end of the activity, reward leaders and scribes with small prizes or candy. Have everyone give a round of applause for group participation so that everyone is recognized for his or her contributions and there are no "losers."

Training Needs Analysis

There are typically three scenarios related to your position and ability to perform a training needs analysis.

Internal Practitioner

If you work within an organization, you have the added benefit of being able to access key people or stakeholders.

These include people who have a stake in ensuring the successful outcome of training endeavors, such as human resource staff, supervisors, and managers at different levels in the organization. These people can provide important information during a needs analysis. You also likely have access to employees who will participate in any training programs and you can observe them on the job in order to collect information directly.

The key to an effective analysis is to collect data from multiple sources to double-check suspected or identified needs. Use these people and any other viable sources of information available in order to determine the content from which your learners will most benefit.

External Practitioner

If you are outside the organizational chain (educator, consultant, facilitator, coach, or trainer), but work with clients, your success in designing and delivering an effective workshop also depends on accurately predicting learner needs and expectations. This becomes a bit more challenging because you often do not have the access to needed data. For example, you probably will not be able to view some internal human resource reports, performance appraisals, sales and productivity reports or have direct performance observation opportunities. You also may not enjoy the same level of trust as those within the organization. Still, you must ultimately deliver a training program and materials that will satisfy those learners and organizational stakeholders. You will need to work closely with workshop sponsors or stakeholders if you are conducting a session for a single organization. To the best extent possible, you will need to get an accurate picture of performance issues.

Public Workshop Provider

If you are scheduling a public workshop, one that people from several organizations will attend (for example, a train-the-trainer workshop to certify trainers to deliver a workshop package that you have developed), you should attempt to gather any information possible from potential attendees. The challenge when you are soliciting attendees from mailings or other marketing initiatives is that you may not know much about the actual people who register for your workshop. As a result, you will have to create more generic content on a topic. This is not as desirable as delivering a more targeted workshop.

Even if you do not have a lot of advance access to information about the group, try to gather anything that would allow you to customize elements of the content to learner needs. If time permits, you might contact people as they register via telephone, e-mail, or mail and attempt to find out their needs, expectations, and issues related to the workshop topic. If this is not possible, consider gathering information from other sources. For example, prior to designing your workshop, you might hold focus groups and invite people who make up your target demographic audience (gender, age, race, or ethnic background). Ask them questions related to the planned session topic. Examples of questions that you might ask include:

♦ What would be important to you in such a session?

♦ What type of activities or format would you prefer?

♦ What similar training programs have you attended in the past and what types of information did you receive?

♦ How many people should attend such a session?

You could also send out questionnaires or do telephone interviews.

Traditional Needs Analysis Strategies

As you will read in Chapter 3, the first stage of the ISD process revolves around gathering information to help make a determination about whether training is appropriate and/or even needed. If so, you must determine what type of specific learning needs exist. To help accomplish that, the following strategies will help you determine what your learners will need so that you will have tools for conducting your own analysis when necessary.

The basic purpose of a training needs analysis is to determine what employee "performance gap" (PG) exists. Once this gap has been determined, you can create learning objectives and session content to address it. To determine the performance gap for employees, you have to figure out the difference between expected performance (EP) (the level that the job requires) and current performance (CP) (the level at which they currently perform). The gap might be in terms of employee KSAs. The formula for this is:

$$EP - CP = \text{Performance Gap}$$

Some traditional tools for analyzing employee performance are listed below.

To collect information during a person performance analysis, you can use the following strategies:

Performance Appraisals. By reviewing employee performance appraisals from the target workshop demographic group, you might be able to spot trends or patterns related to needs in the area of KSAs. Even though appraisals can be beneficial, it is best to look at other indicators of performance. This is because, in many instances, these documents can contain subjective perspectives from supervisors instead of quantifiable or measurable observations. The latter often occurs because supervisors are not adequately trained to evaluate performance, forms are poorly designed, or the supervisor did not have adequate time to observe employee behavior before writing the report. An example of a situation in which this might occur would be a new supervisor coming into a department shortly before appraisals are due.

Performance Data or Reports. Productivity, sales, or other measurable organizational data sources can offer insights into overall individual and organizational performance. They might also point to specific training needs or a performance trend that you might need to research further and correlate against other data sources. For example, customer complaints may be on the rise.

On-the-Job Observation of Performance. If you have the luxury of being able to observe potential attendees as they perform their job tasks related to your session content, you may gain some valuable insights into their needs. For example, a meaningful example for a customer service workshop might stem from an observation of a pattern of employees not following standards of service. If you reference such events, make sure that you do so anonymously and do not draw attention to specific employees or groups. The latter could cause embarrassment and resentment from those involved, as well as from other participants, who may fear that you will likewise put them on the spot. In either case, some learners might withdraw and not actively participate.

Interviews. Taking time to speak to potential attendees on the telephone or in person can result in a wealth of valuable information that will assist you in effectively designing a workshop that will truly meet your learners' needs.

Questionnaires. If possible, send out a questionnaire in advance to gather input on workplace issues that learners are experiencing and that relate to the session topic and expectations.

Focus Groups. Use small groups of eight to ten prospective learners to gather information based on pre-written questions.

Attitude Surveys. If the organization has conducted attitude surveys, try to obtain results to see what patterns, trends, or issues exist that you might need to address through workshop content.

360-Degree Surveys. Where possible, use surveys through which participants provide feedback on themselves and where supervisors, peers, customers, or other persons with knowledge of the employee's performance also give input.

Strategy for Success

To help ensure that you are meeting the needs of your learners, get them actively involved in an opening activity in which they self-disclose information as part of a quick in-class analysis. To do this:

Tape sheets of flip-chart paper with closed-ended questions (short answer) around the walls of your workshop room.

Divide responses into columns under each question and separate with a long line (T-chart) for ease of tabulation later.

As learners enter, instruct them to move between sheets and answer all the questions by putting a check mark below their preferred response in each case.

Hint: Hand out colored stickers to each learner or use various colored, water-based markers as participants enter the room. If you do the latter, make sure that you tape an additional sheet of paper under each one or the question sheets. This will help ensure that the ink does not bleed through onto the wall.

Base some in-class assessment questions on specific session content and include other generic ones. The following are sample questions. Put each one on a separate flip chart page and leave space to respond under the questions.

What one thing do you want to get from this session?

What one thing do you hope does NOT happen in this session?

How many times have you attended a workshop on a similar topic?

Never   1 to 3   4+

What type of learning environment do you most prefer?

Lecture   Instructor-led discussion   Small group activity _____ Combination _____

In what way do you prefer to learn new information or skills?

Seeing   Hearing   Doing

Additional Analysis Information Sources

Another way of gathering content information involves conducting a literature scan of competing workshop or seminar marketing materials. To obtain this information, identify competing companies or individuals who offer workshops on your topic, visit their websites, and get onto their e-mail or mail distribution list. There materials will give you ideas for naming your program, creating learning objectives, pricing the event, selecting locations, and developing content. Why recreate the wheel when many of these organizations have been successfully developing and marketing workshops worldwide for years. You can find some of the larger organizations that offer a wide array of workshop topics in the Resources section of this book under Seminar Companies.

Meeting Needs of Diverse Learners

Diversity is a standard factor in most workplaces today. As the world grows closer through globalization and the influx of people from other cultures, you cannot overlook the needs that any person brings to the learning environment. Many trainers and educators fail to prepare themselves or plan for the instance in which they encounter learners who are culturally or otherwise different from them. This is a big mistake because their role is to ensure that all learners have equal access to information.

By learning about various cultures and people with special needs, any trainer can successfully integrate strategies into his or her learning events that will help ensure a richer outcome for everyone. You can accomplish this by researching various disabilities and learning as much as possible about people, their beliefs, values, and needs. Do this before trying to conduct training programs and you will be able to provide an inclusive learning environment for everyone.

Instead of focusing on how some people are different, explore the subtle elements that make everyone unique, yet similar. The facets of diversity have just as big an impact on learning ability as with the various learning modalities, intelligences, and other brain-based factors that you read about in Chapter 1.

There are many advocacy groups, organizations, websites, written materials, and other resources that address various categories of people and their needs (see Disability Advocacy Groups and Organizations in the Resources section). Such groups can help you better prepare for the task of integrating all learners into the learning process. Many of these sources offer useful tips that you can incorporate into your programs.

Do not lose sight of the fact that each learner is unique and has individual needs based on his or her own situation and preferences, even though they are all part of a larger diverse group. For this reason, the best way to determine what learning needs your participants have is to ask them.

Learners with Special Needs

A greater awareness of the needs for people with disabilities worldwide in the past two decades has led to many advances in opportunities, especially in the area of learning. As a trainer, you should educate yourself on the legal requirements and special needs of various groups of persons with disabilities. This will allow you to design and deliver program content that meets the needs of all your learners. Remember that you cannot let your personal beliefs or prejudices limit the opportunity of anyone to learn in your workshops.

The first step in creating a positive learning environment for people with disabilities is to ensure that your language, and that of other trainers and participants, and your learning materials are not offensive or discriminatory. Never single out or embarrass any learner for his or her disability or any other diversity factor. Instead, simply address people by name or a generic term (e.g., man or woman). Additionally, avoid the potentially offensive word *handicapped*, since this often attributed to old English language when referring to a beggar or someone who traditionally was disabled and stood on corners with "cap in hand."

Persons with disabilities typically just want the same opportunities to learn as others in a session. This might require some special accommodations, but need not be distracting or cause any hardships for you or other learners. In most cases, learners who sign up for your workshops have learned to adapt to their environment and simply need minor adjustments in order to be successful in a workshop. Depending on their level and the type of disability, this might involve sitting closer to the front of the room or a light source in order to see or hear what you say. It might also mean sitting next to an exit or large aisle to enable mobility during activities and breaks.

Keep in mind that the law in a number of countries requires you to make accommodations to allow learners with disabilities access to the same opportunities in the workplace as other participants. To better understand how to accommodate learners, research various disabilities and employment laws of your country by doing an Internet search. Specifically look for materials and information on ways to create a learning environment that meets the needs of such learners. You can also look in the phone book for agencies that support people with disabilities and even volunteer time to work with such groups. By doing so, your knowledge and empathy will likely increase.

By becoming aware of some of the needs of people in various categories of disabilities, you can enhance the learning experience for all. The following are some strategies for success with some of the typical disabilities that you may find in your workshops. As the population ages, the likelihood of having one or more participants with these conditions will increase.

Strategy for Success

In many instances, some learners who have disabilities (vision, mobility, or hearing deficits) have learned how to optimize their own learning experience. They may not tell you that they have a disability. In other cases, they may fear you will single them out or embarrass them by special treatment. For that reason, they will not identify their disability. A simple way to help in either instance is to be alert to situations in which some people seem to exhibit special needs and accommodate them if possible without drawing attention to them.

There are several ways to plan for and accommodate potential instances of non-disclosure. One strategy is to ensure that room always exists between tables and rows of chairs to allow anyone with limited mobility (wheelchair, cane, or crutch) easy access. A second technique is to ensure that you provide a variety of nutritional opportunities for learners and encourage everyone to take personal breaks quietly, as they need them. This allows people with medical conditions such as diabetes (need to eat at specified times) or back

(continued)

problems (sometimes need to stand or change positions) to move about and take care of their own needs as they arise without disturbing others or drawing attention to themselves. Additionally, because people with sight and hearing impairments will often sit close to the front of the room or near lighting, if you have learners participate in activities in which they get up and relocate to other places, allow them to return to their original seats once the activity is concluded. This precludes you from inadvertently moving learners to a position that limits their ability to see or hear effectively once you resume your session.

To determine whether anyone needs special accommodations in your workshop, put a statement on your registration form related to that issue. You can simply add a statement that says something like, "In order to ensure that we meet the needs of all our learners, we ask that you contact us immediately if you have special nutritional or environmental needs. This will allow us to discuss possible accommodations before the day of the program."

Strategies for Accommodating Learners with Disabilities

Remember that your goal is not to treat learners with disabilities as special, but to treat them as equal. The following general suggestions can help make your workshop more professional and help meet the needs of all learners, not just those who need accommodations.

Never Assume. Instead of thinking that you know the best approach for effectively interacting with persons with disabilities, privately ask them what you can do to help enhance their learning experience and that of others in the workshop. Keep in mind that two people with a similar disability may have different needs. Do not make the mistake of taking a blanket approach and trying to address all needs with one strategy.

Accommodate Individual Needs. Make whatever accommodations are possible when selecting facilities and designing materials, classroom layout, activities, and other facets of learning. For example, ensure that doorways are at least 36 inches wide (914.4 mm) in order to accommodate standard-size wheelchairs and that water fountains, restrooms, elevators, and other facilities and structures are accessible when choosing a workshop venue. Also make sure that tables are accessible for learners in wheelchairs. Knee spaces should be at least 28 inches (711.2 mm) high, 32 inches (812.8 mm) wide, and 20 inches (508 mm) deep and the tabletops of accessible tables and counters should be from 28 inches to 34 inches (710 mm to 865 mm) above the floor. You can find more specific guidelines for compliance with the Americans with Disabilities Act (ADA) at www.access-board.gov/adaag/html/adaag.htm#4.2.4.

Monitor the Physical Environment. As part of your planning process, check to ensure that you have included accommodations for learners who have disclosed disabilities or have special needs. This includes elements such as heating, lighting, noise levels, seating arrangements, and the types of food and refreshments served.

Help Facilitate Learning. Provide a safe, comfortable, accessible learning environment in which discrimination and the exclusion of people with disabilities is not tolerated. This includes being on guard not to use, or allow others to use, language that might be offensive. This could include comments, stories, or jokes that might focus attention on individuals or groups who have some type of disability or special need.

Build in Adequate Breaks. Make sure that you plan enough breaks for personal comfort (at least once every sixty to ninety minutes), even if you just allow learners time to get more refreshments and take a quick stretch and bathroom break. To set up this expectation, let learners know in your opening remarks that it is okay for them to quietly get up and take a personal break if they need to. This will ultimately contribute to the success of the workshop, since the mind tends to wander when it focuses on other things.

Provide Opportunities for Small Group Learning. Building small group activities into your session can increase effectiveness for participants who have disabilities, speak English as a second language, or are simply more comfortable in small group settings. For a variety of reasons, some people are reluctant to offer opinions, ask questions, or become involved in learning activities in large group. When provided with small-group or one-on-one opportunities, these learners will become active participants.

Accommodating Vision Impairments

You are likely to encounter learners who have total or partial vision loss in your workshops. Some people have assistance dogs, while others have corrective devices or have had surgery that allows some vision. You may also have some learners who are "legally blind" and have very limited vision under certain circumstances (bright or reduced lighting).

In order to maximize the learning experience for all participants in your workshop, you should become familiar with the different types of vision loss and make an effort to accommodate where possible. To assist in your efforts, you can try the following strategies:

◆   Try to determine the level of sight impairment. For example, does the learner have loss of some vision or is he or she legally blind?

♦ Ensure that your training environment can be easily navigated by all learners and that there are not any obstacles or barriers.

♦ Focus on the abilities of all learners and be positive about their accomplishments. Praise even partially completed or accurate tasks.

♦ Encourage learners with sight impairments to select a location that maximizes their learning. Often, this is in the front of the room or near a bright light source.

♦ Point out things and areas of which the learners need to be aware. For example, indicate potential obstacles or hazards, doors, materials, and refreshment and restroom locations.

♦ Use common language and do not be afraid to use words like "look" or "see."

♦ Speak in a normal tone of voice. Just because a learner has a sight impairment does not mean that he or she cannot hear well.

♦ Give details slowly, specifically, and concisely and allow time to complete tasks before moving on.

♦ If a learner has a working dog, ask permission before attempting to touch or otherwise interact with it. Also, do not forget to build in time to allow the dog to be taken outside occasionally.

♦ If necessary and appropriate, print materials in larger font sizes on white, non-glare paper or have the type on computer screens enlarged.

♦ Allow plenty of time for learners to process information and instructions and to follow through on tasks.

Accommodating Hearing Impairments

Just as with vision impairments, many people have difficulty hearing with one or both ears. In some cases, they may not acknowledge or even recognize their own hearing loss since it has been a gradual loss over time.

There are a number of things that you can do to better enhance learning opportunities for participants who have hearing loss. Try the following:

♦ Try to determine the level of impairment prior to training. For example, is it mild, intermediate, or total? And is the loss is in one ear or both?

♦ Ask the participant(s) what accommodations might increase their learning effectiveness.

♦ Encourage the learner to locate to a position that maximizes hearing effectiveness. Typically, will be in the front of the room and near any audiovisual aids you will be using.

♦ If you have participants move for an activity, allow them the option of returning to their original preferential seating locations.

♦ If you are going to use audiovisual aids, you may want to inform the participant prior to class so that they can adjust any hearing aid volume, if necessary.

♦ Keep background noise to a minimum if participants are using hearing aids or have only partial hearing. Such sounds can distort what they hear.

♦ If an interpreter is present, position the person where he or she can effectively see and hear you and where you can see both the participant and the interpreter.

♦ When an interpreter is used, address comments and questions directly to the learner, not to the interpreter. Remember that the interpreter is a tool through which the learner communicates. Additionally, do not have side conversations with the interpreter in the presence of the learner. Ethically, interpreters are bound to share messages received with the learner.

♦ Face participants when speaking.

♦ Speak slowly, clearly, and concisely.

♦ Keep hands and other objects away from your mouth. This includes bushy facial hair that might obscure your lips.

♦ Use facial expressions and gestures freely to emphasize points.

♦ You can use hand and arm gestures to get participant attention or you can lightly touch someone on the shoulder if he or she is looking away.

♦ Ensure that only one person in the group speaks at a time. This is important if an interpreter is present to capture and translate what others say to the learner.

♦ Provide materials and instructions in writing as you communicate verbally so that the learner can refer to them and potentially catch anything that was not heard clearly without having to ask for someone to repeat it.

♦ Use diagrams, charts, posters, flip charts, and other types of graphic and visual images when possible. These help maximize receipt of information.

♦ Ask the learner if he or she would like someone to take notes for him or her. You can also give out copies of your leader's guide so that people can focus on discussion and conversation instead of having to look down.

♦ Repeat any questions or comments from other participants to ensure that the learner heard or got the message.

♦ When learners are required to read material, allow plenty of time before speaking again. Get the participant's attention before you do start speaking.

Accommodating Mobility Impairments

Millions of people have various forms of motion or mobility impairments (spinal cord injuries, arthritis, amputations, muscular dystrophy, multiple sclerosis, or cerebral palsy). Each of these disabilities can create pain and loss of the ability to navigate or move easily or at all. To assist in providing access to learners with such impairments you should become aware of their causes, symptoms, and strategies for accommodating. The following can help in a learning environment.

♦ Try to determine the level of impairment prior to training (mild, intermediate or total).

♦ Ask the participant what accommodations might increase his or her learning effectiveness.

♦ Allow learners with impairments to locate wherever they are most comfortable and can have the maximum mobility, for example, near exits, restrooms, or aisles.

♦ Design room layouts that provide easy access for assistive devices such as canes, crutches, wheelchairs, or prosthetics. Typically, freestanding chairs or tables that can be moved easily are best. U-shaped and theater-style seating can limit access and mobility.

♦ Design activities in which participants can interact equally with others. Be careful of requiring excessive relocation within the room or timed events requiring movement.

♦ Post materials on the wall at a height that does not require excessive neck strain by looking up to view them.

♦ Allow plenty of time for activity and task completion.

♦ Be careful of competitive activities in which participants must complete tasks and be compared to others based on their physical accomplishments.

♦ When speaking one-on-one to someone in a wheelchair during individual coaching, explanation or discussion, think about your location. Sit at eye level with the learner or stand at a distance that does not require prolonged looking up at your face.

Learners from Other Cultures

The population expansion of the United States and throughout the world continues each day. With this growth comes the challenge of people who speak different languages coming together in training. For you and other trainers, the opportunity is to design and deliver programs and materials that will be understood and successful.

The following are some strategies for creating a learning environment in which those from other cultures or who speak a language other than English can achieve maximum learning potential.

Respect Personal Preferences. Each culture has its own "rules" of what is acceptable. Until your learners give permission or the group agrees on rules of conduct, be cautious when interacting with learners. Do not assume familiarity by addressing people by their first names until you have established that type of informal environment or relationship.

Strategy for Success

To ensure that the right tone and same expectations regarding conduct in the classroom exist for all learners, create some ground rules early in your workshop. To do this, introduce yourself as people enter a session or at the beginning of the session and explain that the program will be in a relaxed and informal format. Have learners print their preferred names on their name tents. You should use whatever they write unless you inform them early in the session that everyone will be going by first names to encourage more camaraderie and networking. For example, if someone writes Mr., Ms., or Dr. Nyugen, then address him or her as such.

You are likely to find that even though you tell learners to call you by your first name in your introduction, some will still use the more formal Mr. or Ms. _____ or professor, if in an academic setting. This is a cultural show of respect. Unlike North Americans, who tend to be more informal, people in many cultures covet and respect titles and academic credentials. Failure to recognize and honor this value could cause a learning and relationship breakdown.

Speak Clearly and Slowly. Many Americans speak rather quickly. As a result, someone who speaks English as a second language and who is trying to comprehend and translate your message into his or her own language, or someone with a learning disability, will struggle. Speak at a rate slow enough to allow for understanding without being insulting.

Speak at a Normal Volume and Tone. Just because someone speaks another language does not make him or her deaf. Yelling or changing tone does nothing to enhance understanding. Many times, people unconsciously raise their voices in an effort to try to increase comprehension. You will not enhance communication by increasing your volume and will likely offend the learner to whom you are speaking.

Use Open-Ended Questions. If your goal is to gauge understanding and increase communication, try using open-ended (start with who, what, when, how, why) to encourage participants to voice opinions and increase dialog. Closed-ended questions get little information and may actually allow a person to mask his or her inability to communicate in English. In fact, a question like "Do you understand?" can be very offensive. The learner might interpret your intent as you believing that he or she is not smart enough to comprehend your message.

Use Non-Verbal Cues Cautiously. As a trainer in a global world, you would be wise to learn as much as you can about other cultures and subcultures and the ways that people within them communicate. Once you have done so, incorporate findings into to your training and work to educate others around you. Many common non-verbal cues have many different, even offensive or rude, meanings in other cultures.

Use Inclusive Language. Avoid terminology that could potentially exclude, isolate, or discriminate. For example, instead of using language such as, "You guys or gals/ fellows have found out . . .," try referring to participants generically as, "Many of you have found out. . . . " This is a more inclusive approach and not likely to offend anyone.

Listen Patiently. Take your time and focus on what your learner is saying. Try to understand the intent of what the person is saying. You may be frustrated, but imagine how the learner feels with others looking on.

Avoid Offensive or Discriminatory Jokes or Remarks. Humor often does not easily transcend cultural boundaries. Additionally, some people have hidden sensitivities. Jokes or comments that center on race, culture, politics, religion, sexual orientation, height, weight, or other personal characteristics can offend and have no place in a learning environment or workplace. Participants have personal preferences and define social acceptability in different ways based on their own value systems. While you do not have to agree with the views of others, you should respect them in order to maintain credibility and not potentially alienate learners.

Watch Terminology. Just as titles, jokes, and remarks can offend, so too can certain words or terms. Terms that some people might find offensive include handicapped or crippled, retard, boy, girl, idiot, ladies and gentlemen, and ma'am. Any of these may conjure up negative stereotypes or project condescension to some participants, depending on your audience and training location.

Use Standard English. Technical terms, contractions (didn't, can't, shouldn't), slang (like, you know, dis, whoopee, rubberneck) or broken English (sentences that are imperfectly spoken or that fail to follow standard rules of grammar or syntax) can be obstacles to someone who does not speak English well.

Some participants may not speak a language, especially in public forums, because they are either self-conscious about their ability or choose not to. An additional factor to consider is that, unlike Western cultures, some cultures value and use silence as an important aspect to communication. Many trainers might interpret this to mean that the learners do not understand what you told them.

Avoid the Word No. Unlike many North Americans, people from some cultures (parts of Asia, especially) are careful not to offend or cause someone embarrassment or to loose esteem or "face" in the eyes of others. For that reason, some languages do not even have a word for *no*. In some instances, people from such cultures might say "yes" or something like, "That may be difficult or impossible" or they may even tacitly agree, with no intention of following through or complying, rather than simply saying "no" and hurting feelings or offending. Being conscious of this cultural variation can help you to prevent frustration and potential animosity within your learning environment.

Use Care When Giving Constructive Feedback. Any time that feedback on performance is given, it should be in a positive, assertive, and friendly manner. This is especially important when dealing with participants from other cultures. If you must make corrections or give constructive feedback, try language that you direct at the behavior or performance and not at the learner. You may even want to take responsibility for the error upon yourself. For example, if someone fails to perform a task correctly or fill out a form, you might say, "Maybe I wasn't clear about what I wanted you to do." Then repeat your instructions.

Repeat Information When Necessary. Repeat information if someone requests it. Take your time and do so without appearing irritated or distracted. Remember that people who speak English as a second language, and those with certain types of disabilities, may not get every word spoken or may not fully comprehend the first time they hear something. This is where written information can also help.

Strategy for Success

To help enhance communication and comprehension with all learners, give verbal information supplemented by written materials. Also use a variety of audiovisual aids to reinforce your message.

Remember that the more times that learners see, hear, taste, touch, and feel something the more likely they are to gain, retain, recognize, recall, and use it later.

Personalizing What You Have Learned

- What are the most important things that you read in this chapter? Why?

- What are some ways that you can immediately apply concepts covered in this chapter?

- What additional resources or topics do you want to research based on what you read?

Creating a Dynamic Workshop Design

fter reading this chapter, and when applying what you learn, you will be able to:

1. Identify the elements of a successful workshop.

2. Remember important factors to consider when designing and developing your workshop.

3. Write effective behavioral learning objectives.

4. Explain the five phases of the Instructional System Design Process.

5. Use the Four Levels of Evaluation to track training results.

6. Develop an effective learning plan.

"Success depends upon previous preparation. Without such preparation there is sure to be failure."

Confucius

Elements of a Successful Workshop

The obvious goal of any learning event is to provide or enhance the knowledge, skills, and attitudes of attendees. In preparing to do this, you will need to do your homework and decide many things related to the format, content, delivery, location, materials needed, and much more. As you read in the last chapter, you also need to spend a great deal of time discovering your learners and their needs.

When designing your learning event, you must consider various elements. In this chapter, you will examine a multitude of factors related to successfully planning your workshop. The following are typical elements to include in your thinking as you design your workshop.

Select a Powerful Workshop Title

Your first step is to determine the appropriate session topic and a workshop title. Keep in mind that the title you choose will be a key factor in attracting the attention of potential attendees.

Many other materials and e-mails cross the desks of potential workshop attendees and their supervisors each day. You need to find a title that is concise, adequately describes the workshop's focus, and grabs their attention. A good rule of thumb is to make the title pertinent to key concepts to be covered and to keep it short and simple. For example, instead of "Developing Effective Management:

Skills That Will Meet the Needs of Your Organization and Help Employees Grow," try something like "Management Skills That Work" or "Management Skills That Get Results." You should also consider a "tag" line that goes under the title to further entice or explain the content. For example, "Proven Tips and Techniques That Improve Productivity" or "Ten Guaranteed Strategies That Enhance Workplace Performance." In your session description, you can add additional information and bulleted learning objectives that will help explain what you mean.

Scheduling

Through trial and error, many trainers have learned that some days of the week and time periods work better than others for a learning event. Consider the following when choosing when to hold your workshop(s).

Day of the Week

In many cases a learner's attendance at a workshop will be influenced by his or her job, position, work environment (whether management supports training), job responsibilities, and a multitude of other issues. Even so, some days of the week typically work better than others for people to attend.

Monday is a day when people are returning to work from the weekend, vacation or a business trip. This day tends to be stressful and packed with tasks or catch-up work and responsibilities. For these reasons, Mondays should be avoided when scheduling your workshop.

Tuesday, Wednesday, and Thursday are typically safe days to schedule learning events. Attendees have often caught up on work assignments on Monday and are not yet focused on taking off for the weekend. In the latter instance, many people take three- and four-day weekends and use Mondays and Fridays as part of that event.

Fridays are often good days for workshops because many people get all their work caught up during the week in preparation for being gone on Friday. This is especially true when you are holding the workshop offsite in a desirable location, such as near a resort or tourist area where families can accompany your attendees. Further, if a Friday session ends early, attendees either go back to their offices to finish last-minute items or can get a bit of extra time for their weekend.

Saturdays work well for self-development workshops or business retreats that are followed by a social gathering. If the workshop is at a remote location, people can arrive early, relax, spend the night, then make a weekend of the event with their families or friends following the workshop. One drawback for Saturday sessions is that some religions hold services on that day.

Sunday is sometimes used for personal development workshops, but Saturday tends to work better for most people. Many people reserve Sunday to spend time with their family and friends or to attend religious services. Business meetings work better on other days of the week.

Time of Day

When selecting the time period, do not forget to consider factors over which you have no control. These might include traffic patterns (rush hours), your audience (professionals who normally start work at 8:00 to 9:00 A.M., shift workers, or work-at-home people who have flexible schedules), or other organizational commitments (planned events like picnics, celebrations, large sales meetings, or annual conferences) that would require attendance by potential attendees.

Half-day workshops are normally scheduled between 8 A.M. and 12:00 or 12:30 P.M. and 4:30 or 5:00 P.M. Full-day sessions are typically scheduled between 8:30 or 9:00 A.M. and 4:30 or 5:00 P.M., with lunch and breaks included. Keep in mind that trainers who conduct afternoon sessions often encounter learners who are mentally winding down around 4 or 4:30 P.M. and starting to think about packing up to leave in order to beat traffic and get home.

If you are conducting multi-day workshops, consider when to start and end, especially if attendees will be traveling to the meeting. It is often good to start a bit later on the first day and end a bit early on the last day. This will allow people who are commuting from a distance or using public transportation to make arrangements that will get them to the workshop on the morning of the session, rather than incurring the expense of overnight accommodations. They can also catch early transportation to arrive at home and not have to spend an extra night after the session ends. Otherwise, they would incur additional expenses and lost productivity time that might dissuade them from attending.

If you are planning an evening workshop, consider the fact that rush hour traffic may delay attendee arrival. Additionally, unless you are providing food, people will need to grab something to eat on their way or to bring to the session. Such sessions typically start between 5:30 and 6:00 P.M. and end between 9:30 and 10:00 P.M.

An alternative is to conduct a noontime "lunch and learn" event for which people arrive at 11:30 and leave at 1:00 and either bring their lunches or have them provided. This is often a good time slot for quick refresher content, short presentations on a given topic, or to introduce concepts, policies, products, procedures, or regulatory information.

Your topic focus will drive your schedule in many cases. For example, personal development or self-help type workshops are best as evening events following work or in some cases on a weekend. Since many people are reluctant to give up their weekends with family and friends, the latter might not be the best choice.

A final consideration is that, rather than doing three days consisting of six-hour days, you may want to consider two nine-hour days. This saves expense because you do not have to pay staff, purchase food, and rent a facility for three days. Additionally, learners are not away from their offices as long and can save travel expenses.

Month

Various times of the year are more conducive to better attendance than others. The time of year selected for your workshop is important to its success. Additionally, it can determine where you hold it. For example, if you are holding your workshop in the winter, you may want to consider a warm climate location to which people can get easy transportation or access.

In deciding when to hold your event, consider the following points:

January through May are typically good months to hold a workshop except for the first couple of weeks of January. This is because January follows the holiday season and many people are getting ready for the New Year and getting back into a routine after being out of the office for extended periods. In addition, if you are in colder areas of the country or world, travel could be an issue for people. As for any other months, you should avoid major public and religious holidays.

June through August might clash with vacation schedules while children are out of school. Depending in what part of the world you are holding the workshop, the weather can be hot during this period.

September through early November are often good months for workshops since travel is not impacted by weather and there are not many major holidays during the period. In the United States, the end of November is not good due to Thanksgiving, when many families travel or vacation.

Early December works well, but after the middle of the month, you should avoid scheduling a session because of conflicts with the major religious holiday seasons.

Staff

The person(s) who stand in front of the room to deliver your workshop content and those with whom learners come into contact can create either a perception of success or failure in the minds of your learners. Because of this, selection of the workshop staff is an important factor. Anyone who has contact with learners or potential learners is representing you and your organization. The person must be trained in positive customer service skills and have a sound knowledge of your program(s), processes, policies, procedures, and how to access and transmit information to those interested in your workshop(s). If someone contacts a registrar and does not receive good customer service or the correct information, that person will likely not register for a workshop and will tell others about the negative experience. Similarly, if an attendee gets a bad impression of you (or of other facilitators) or the way you conduct the session, learner needs and expectations will not be met.

Facility

The appearance, size, and functionality of your venue are all important to learners and to the level of workshop success. If you choose a room or training area that is inadequate in size, features, accessibility, and necessary equipment and convenience, planned activities could fail. If the maintenance of the facility is faulty or other aspects of the area are restrictive, learners could be inconvenienced and could view the event as a failure or waste of time. Cutting corners to save money is not always a good idea when booking a workshop site.

Consider the size of the facility. A room that is too large and has a lot of empty tables or space will look deserted and could send a message that many people did not show up for the workshop. This could leave attendees wondering what those people know about the session that they do not. On the other hand if the room is too small, learners will feel cramped, activities may not work as planned, and you may have to modify planned events.

Strategy for Success

Visit available venues to decide where to hold your session. Make site visits after you have planned your workshop content and know what equipment, space, accessories, and support you will need. Think about all the associated factors that you will read about at various points in this book such as accessibility, training aids, access to electrical power, Internet connections, and catering. Do not forget to consider things such as the ability of learners to get to and from the event in a timely manner and having adequate space for planned activities.

Equipment

Availability, type, and technical support for the equipment that you will use are important considerations. Make sure that everything you plan to use in the workshop is present, in good working order, and that there is someone on call if something malfunctions or you need assistance with the operation of a piece of equipment.

Training Aids

Use training aids that can support and enhance your verbal message. Make sure that you have professionally designed anything that you will be using, such as posters, slides, flip charts, or handouts. Also make sure that all these items are present before learners arrive. If possible, remove or cover anything that does not support your session content or that might distract or confuse learners. Examples are generic pictures, posters, or decorations on the walls.

Strategies or Methods

You can get your message across to learners and effect learning outcomes while meeting planned objectives in many different ways. Based on what researchers have found about brain functioning, learning, and memory, it is best to choose a variety of strategies and techniques that will engage and stimulate your learners. Later in the book, you will find an entire chapter dedicated to this topic.

Format

Many training workshops are conducted in the traditional classroom style; however, depending on your intended learning outcomes, group makeup, location, availability of staff and resources, budget, and organizational culture, a number of options are available for information delivery. The following are some of the typical formats in use today.

Typical Workshop Format Options

♦ Single one-day workshop

♦ Two one-half day sessions

♦ Several short lunchtime "brown bag" events where people meet for each session over lunch

♦ A combination one-half day content event followed by online or teleconference follow-ups

♦ Online courses offered through an organization's intranet

♦ Tele-seminar in which learners call in to ask questions or hear a short lecture

♦ Webinar in which learners log onto your website to view slides or other information and call a specified telephone number to participate in an interactive discussion and hear instructor-led content.

♦ Blended learning through which you use a combination of classroom instruction and technology-based format in multiple sessions. Learners might attend an instructor-led session in a classroom, then log onto a website for a follow-up webinar, or participate in a teleconference. Alternately, learners might log onto a website on their organization's intranet to take a self-paced course or do preliminary assessments or pre-work and later attend a classroom session.

Food and Refreshments

The human brain works best when it is well-nourished with the right foods and has been adequately hydrated. Researchers have done numerous studies to determine which types of foods and beverages stimulate brain neurons and which ones hinder their effectiveness. They have also explored the impact of water and various beverages on learning. As a trainer or educator, the more you know about these subjects, the better you can prepare to aid learning outcomes.

Accommodations

You will have to think about staff and attendee accommodations when holding multiple-day workshops offsite at a hotel or conference center. Typically, if you are holding a function in a hotel, you can negotiate with the sales staff to reserve a block of reduced-price rooms for attendees. Learners who make a reservation by a designated date can take advantage of the discounted rate. Such arrangements often allow you discounted or free use of a meeting or conference room or a discount on catering. Do not be bashful about asking for such an arrangement.

Travel Arrangements

Travel arrangements should be handled as soon as you have decided on a definite workshop date. You are likely to get cheaper rates when you book hotels, car rentals, accommodations, and meeting space early. Additionally, when you determine your venue and hotels early, you can alert registrants so that they can budget and plan their own trips. This often helps increase registration numbers.

Marketing

Effectively marketing workshop offering(s) is an area with which many trainers struggle. Most typically do not have a business or marketing background and are unsure of how to go about getting information about their program out to their target audience. Many organizations and resources can provide information on effective marketing. For example, the American Management Association (www.amanet.org/seminars/) offers a series of live and technology-based seminars on the topic. An Internet search for resources on marketing training workshops or seminars will produce a treasure chest of information. Searching the major booksellers for books on the seminar business is also useful.

Strategy for Success

Marketing research shows that, until people see or experience information at least three times, they often fail to pay any attention. This is why you often receive multiple e-mail messages or mailings for the same seminar. They are generally delivered over a space of time and in some cases are not exactly the same pieces, other than the title and pertinent information. After seeing something several times, you likely will scan through or read it, especially as time to commit comes nearer.

The following are some typical means for getting the word out about your workshop(s). Your choice of marketing strategies will depend on whether you are an internal or external trainer as well as whether you are offering public workshops to a wide variety of people.

e-Mail to a Targeted List

Specialized companies sell lists of people who have attended training events on specific topics or bought such products in the past. This is known as a "qualified" mailing list. An online search for "e-mailing lists" can produce sources for this information. If you are an internal trainer or marketing within a specific client organizations, work with their information services or human resources staff to determine how to get messages to potential attendees and their supervisors.

Mail to Potential Attendees

The tried-and-true form of marketing throughout the United States, mail still has value, especially if you are targeting masses of potential attendees. A benefit of using the mail is that, in addition to the intended recipient seeing the piece, those handling it also view the information and may take action to enroll or follow up. This is why brochures you receive through the mail come without envelopes and the time, date, location, and contact information are clearly visible outside. Like e-mail distribution lists, you can obtain qualified mailing lists by searching the Internet for companies that provide such information.

Telephone Contact

A personal touch is often more effective than an impersonal e-mail or mailing to a group of people. If you have specific people you feel would benefit from your workshop, arrange to personally call them or have someone else do so in order to share information about the workshop, answer questions, and ask for a commitment to attend. After people have registered, arrange a follow-up call the day before the workshop to remind registrants about the coming event and to answer any questions that they have.

Website Listing

A more passive means of getting information to a potential audience is to place complete workshop and registration information on your website. People searching the Internet might come across the site and follow up to register. You can also create an interactive blog on the site that allows people to write comments or ask questions that might lead to potential registrants.

Articles

People love free stuff. You could post articles on your website on topics related to your workshop. There are also public websites for such purposes, for example, www.selfgrowth.com and www.ezinearticles.com, on which you can post free articles for people to read or download. You can include contact information related to the workshop at the end of your articles. In many cases, these articles are picked up by organizational e-zine (electronic newsletters) editors and passed around the world. This becomes free advertising.

E-zines

If you write your own electronic newsletter, include information about your upcoming workshop(s) for your readers in each issue. Offer discounts for registration by a specific date or specials for subscribers.

Flyers or Posters

Depending on the topic and your target audience, consider creating colorful graphic flyers or posters to promote your workshop. If you are an internal practitioner or are conducting a workshop within an organization, post flyers in break rooms and on bulletin boards throughout the building. Send copies to all employees in your target audience (if appropriate and allowed) and their supervisors.

Strategy for Success

Do as seasoned marketing people do and be creative with your promotions. For example, create a workshop flyer that you print on colorful paper. Call it the Bathroom Gazette or some other fancy name, add graphics, and post copies inside the doors of toilet stalls throughout your building. You have a captive audience!

Partnerships

In today's economy, think outside the box to cut costs and increase revenue. One option might be for you to form a partnership with another organization in your area to promote and deliver the workshop. Examples of potential partners include businesses in your industrial park or building, non-competing businesses, chambers of commerce, Rotary and Kiwanis clubs, professional organizations, and community colleges. Such arrangements provide the value of sharing costs, building business and personal relationships, gaining access to other potential attendees, sharing the marketing effort, and gaining additional resources to handle the logistics of coordinating a workshop. Encourage these groups to link to your website or put information about the event on their websites and in their newsletters.

Speaking Engagements

Many local business and religious groups regularly seek experts to speak to their members, customers, and leaders. You can become better known as a resource and people pass your name around by volunteering to speak. Some possible speaking venues include Rotary clubs, chambers of commerce, professional associations, religious groups, scouts, and parent/teacher associations.

Make sure that you provide information to your audiences about upcoming workshop(s) and ALWAYS pass out business cards and brief handouts that have your contact information at the bottom. You might even put a small textbox with information about your workshop at the bottom.

Encourage these groups to link to your website or put information about the event on the group's website and in their newsletter.

Registration

Following the creation of your marketing material and other efforts to attract your audience, the next point at which potential learners encounter you and your organization is through your registration process. This is a pivotal time for the success of your event. You need to have knowledgeable, courteous, and customer-focused people involved in this effort, and your system needs to be easy to navigate and efficient.

Online attendee registration software can help. Many organizations offer such systems on the Internet. Search for such tools using phrases like "seminar registration software."

Strategy for Success

Movement and color attract attention, so consider purchasing an inexpensive electronic sign that can be placed in the cafeteria or break room where potential attendees will see it. You can also attract viewers by adding cute cartoon graphics into most of these messages. Keep your messages short when using these signs, as most people will not stand and watch them scroll for long. Typically, the name of the workshop, time, date, and contact information are sufficient. If possible, put a display of flyers next to the machine so that they can grab a registration form at that moment. Depending on the location, you might also have a drop box where they could sign up on the spot and drop their forms in for you to follow up by contacting them.

Important Factors to Consider

Obviously, you want your workshop to be a success. To be successful you need to remember a number of things as you plan and design your workshop. By properly preparing and striving to ensure that your content and delivery result in meeting the needs and expectations of your learners and their sponsors, you will increase the likelihood of their satisfaction and of meeting stated objectives. You will also help ensure that you deliver a quality, professional learning event.

Obtain Copyright Permission

Many resources available on the Internet and in print can contribute positively to your learning outcome. No matter what your topic, there is likely a wealth of information available to you to reinforce concepts and add value to what you provide to your learners. The authors of most of these resources are happy to share their knowledge. In many instances they will allow you to reproduce small segments of their publications without charge.

One important factor in deciding whether to reproduce or use material created by others, such as music, articles, videos, or software, is to ensure that you have written permission to do so. Most copyright owners will allow you to use their material for educational purposes as long as you give them a citation or acknowledgement as long as you are not reproducing and selling it. Why wouldn't they? You are in effect promoting and endorsing their product, which may ultimately result in more sales or business for them. Always obtain permission from the copyright holder before displaying or passing out copies of any material created by another person or organization. Failure to do so can lead to legal liability for you and your organization.

You can often get permission to use articles, book excerpts, or training materials directly from the author of those materials. If the author has assigned rights to others, such as a publisher, you will have to contact the magazine or publication or the copyright editor for the publishing house. For electronic rights on such products as music, movies, electronic training materials, or software, you may have to check with the production company to determine who owns the rights.

You can normally find information on copyright in the front of magazines and publications, inside the front of a book, or on the case insert for music, videos, DVDs, and software. For music, you may be able to obtain permission from Broadcast Music Incorporated (BMI) or the American Society of Composers, Authors and Publishers (ASCAP) (see the Resources section). It may take a bit of research to locate a copyright owner. However, if the materials are important enough to add value to your session, and you want to use them, it will be worth the trouble.

Make Everything Meaningful

You have already read that training time is precious. The challenge is to get learners to appreciate that what you are delivering meets their needs, matches their personal learning goals, and is relevant in the workplace. As adults and professionals in a given field, they likely already have a basic knowledge of the content. So you must create links or shortcuts between what they know and what you have planned. For example, if you are facilitating a workshop for a group of experienced supervisors, they have likely already been exposed to the basics of coaching, counseling, communicating, motivating, and providing performance feedback to employees. If these are topic areas covered in your session, you will need to think of ways to show learners how to more systematically and logically use the knowledge and skills they already possess to improve their on-the-job performance.

An easy way to help them see the importance of the topic is to present it in the form of a model. You could then give learners a chance to work in small groups to determine ways of applying the knowledge in their work environments. Through this technique, they can take what you give and customize it to their individual needs and receive feedback from their peers on how it might be improved. In this way, when they walk out of the room, they have real-world knowledge, skills, and strategies that can be applied immediately. This always adds value to any learning experience and enhances return on investment. It can also enhance your session evaluation results.

Focus on Specifics

In order to be helpful to participants, provide targeted information rather than throwing out a lot of ideas in hope that some will help. Most attendees will not have the time nor desire to sit through a session in which you provide irrelevant information. For example, if you were teaching a class on creative writing skills and were talking about how to look up information in a dictionary, it would be unnecessary to cover every term in the book. Instead, you should teach them how to find a specific item in the text. Similarly, if you were showing learners how to use Microsoft Word® to create a document and save it, it would be unnecessary to show them how to attach a saved document to an outgoing e-mail message. Even though the latter could be nice to know, learners do not need to know it during your session. By including unnecessary material, you would be likely to confuse and distract learners from your primary goal.

Use the old K.I.S.S. principle (**Keep It Short and Sweet**) when creating and delivering your workshop material. Focus only on what learners need to know in order to achieve stated learning objectives.

Help Learners Make Connections

In Chapter 4 you will read about how the human brain best processes, stores, and accesses information. Adult learners appreciate information that they can add to what they already know. This cuts down on their learning curve and increases the learning experience. The "ah ha" moments or realizations and visual applications come more quickly when learners can relate to something they already have stored in memory.

To help to maximize learning, provide information in small, digestible chunks (chunking) or small bits of material with which learners are somewhat familiar. This reduces the likelihood that you will overwhelm them with volumes of new information. In taking such an approach, you increase the likelihood that they will quickly understand and assimilate what you offer. Anything else can cause overload and shut learning down.

Creating an Effective Workshop

For the purposes of this book, we will assume that following a training needs analysis you determined that there are performance gaps, that training needs do exist, and that you are going to proceed with a training workshop. With your learner needs in mind, you are now ready to begin a workshop design that will address performance gaps, focus on meaningful content, and flow well. From start to finish, you should apply the theories behind sound adult learning that you read about in Chapter 1. You should also consider ways to tap into the brain-research-related to enhancing learning that you will read about in Chapter 4.

Identify Learning Objectives

Most training professionals are familiar with the work of Dr. Robert F. Mager, one of the gurus on writing performance-based learning objectives. In his 1962 ground-breaking book, *Preparing Objectives for Programmed Instruction*, Mager outlined what has become a standard for writing learning objectives. He stressed that, in order to determine whether a learning event truly met the intended goals, there must be specific, measurable objectives. These have come to be known as "behavioral" or "performance" objectives.

Based on what you find the learner needs to be, identify three to five (depending on the length of your workshop) specific learning outcomes that you want. Write learning objectives in a format that focuses on behavioral change. Simply state what learners will be able to know or do differently because of their learning experience. Remember that your goal is to help them close their performance gap(s).

In his book, Mager described the following three key components necessary for successful objectives, and ultimately to achieve learning outcomes.

Behavior

Performance that learners should be able to exhibit following a training session is called behavior. Mager stressed that behavior should be specific and observable. Table 3.1 contains a listing of action verbs to assist you in making behavioral statements. Some examples of behavioral-based statements follow:

♦ Pass the state certification examination

♦ Build a tool shed

♦ Apply strategies for improved cash handling procedures

Conditions

State the circumstances or criteria under which the behavior is to be completed or performed, along with whatever tools or assistance is to be provided to help the learners

Table 3.1. Action Verbs for Learning Objectives

acquire	act	activate	adjust	advise
affect	aid	align	allocate	analyze
apply	appraise	arrange	assemble	assess
assign	assist	attach	attack	avoid
balance	become	begin	bend	block
bond	brace	break	break down	bridge
bring	build	burst	calculate	calibrate
capture	catch	categorize	change	check
choose	cite	classify	clean	collate
collect	combine	compare	compile	complete
compose	compute	conclude	conduct	connect
construct	contrast	control	coordinate	copy
correct	create	cut	deal	debate
decide	defend	define	demonstrate	describe
design	determine	develop	devise	diagnose
diagram	differentiate	discern	disconnect	discriminate
discuss	distinguish	do	draft	dramatize
draw	duplicate	edit	eliminate	employ
enter	erect	establish	estimate	evaluate
examine	experiment	explain	express	extend
fight	figure	file	find	fix
follow	form	formulate	furnish	gather
gauge	generate	get	give	grasp
group	guard	guide	handle	have
hold	hook	identify	illustrate	improve
index	indicate	inform	initiate	inject
input	inspect	install	instruct	interpret
inventory	investigate	issue	itemize	join
judge	jump	justify	keep	know
label	lead	lean	leap	leave

(continued)

Table 3.1. (*Continued*)

lift	list	listen	load	locate
lock	look	lower	maintain	make
manage	match	master	maximize	measure
meet	merge	minimize	mix	moderate
modify	monitor	move	name	negotiate
notify	number	observe	obtain	operate
omit	order	organize	outline	perform
plan	position	post	practice	praise
predict	prepare	present	prevent	print
process	procure	produce	program	project
propose	provide	purchase	put	qualify
quantify	question	quote	rank	rate
reach	read	recall	recapitulate	recapture
receive	recite	recollect	recommend	recognize
record	reduce	regulate	reject	relate
remove	repair	repeat	replace	report
represent	reproduce	request	resolve	restate
review	rotate	run	scan	schedule
score	screen	secure	see	segregate
select	sell	send	separate	set
set up	share	shed	shoot	shorten
show	signal	sign on	simulate	sketch
solve	sort	specify	speed	spend
spread	state	store	stretch	strike
submit	summarize	supervise	support	survey
tabulate	take	teach	tell	test
think	tighten	train	translate	transport
turn	underline	use	utilize	value
verify	volunteer	weave	win	wind
work	wrap	write		

accomplish a task. Examples of condition statements include:

♦ When applying information provided in class

♦ After thoroughly preparing the foundation

♦ When using materials received in training

Standards

State the measure or level of performance that is desirable in terms of measurable standards, including any acceptable range of answers or options that are allowable as correct. Examples of standards include the following:

♦ With no more than two incorrect answers

♦ Exactly as shown in blueprints

♦ That will eliminate all change-counting errors

Below are some examples of learning objectives combing the three elements:

♦ At the end of this workshop, learners will be able to pass the state certification examination, with no more than two incorrect answers, when applying information provided in class.

♦ At the end of this workshop, learners will be able to build a tool shed exactly as shown in blueprints after thoroughly preparing a foundation.

♦ At the end of this workshop, and when using materials provided in training, learners will be able to apply strategies for improved cash handling procedures that will eliminate all change-counting errors.

Note that it makes no difference in which order you structure the three elements of an objective.

Examples of Behavioral Objectives

When creating learning objectives for your workshop, it is important to write them from the perspective of what learners will know or be able to do differently following training. A big mistake is to write objectives from your perspective as a trainer and simply to state what the session covers. The following are examples of both formats.

Example 1. Learner-Centered Objective: At the end of this workshop, and when using the materials provided, learners will be able to write a learning objective, including the elements of behavior, condition, and standard, with 100 percent accuracy.

Example 2. Instructor-Centered Objective: During this workshop, we will examine the three elements of a learning objective (behavior, condition and standard).

Note that the first example includes specific behaviors and measures for determining success. The second example is simply a statement of what the instructor will address with no consideration for how the learners will benefit from or use the information.

Sequence Workshop Content

Once you have put together enough background information on your group and have identified some of their needs, you are ready to start thinking about what will be covered in your workshop. The key is to provide enough content without overwhelming your learners. Since training time is limited, stay focused on what they really need to know and not what is nice to know. For example, you may have a broad knowledge about the background on a particular topic related to the workshop content. Even so, do not go off-track or go off on tangents sharing interesting bits of trivia or stories. This can dilute content and, depending on the generational group and modality preferences of your learners, can bore them. This will potentially result in their being disinterested, missing key points later, and poor ratings on your evaluation at the end of the session.

Researchers have discovered that, because we use our whole brains in processing information and solving problems, information provided in strictly linear fashion may not always be the best approach for content delivery. This is why techniques like mind mapping and other visual representations (see Chapter 7) make so much sense. This concept was made popular by world-renowned educational consultant and author Tony Buzan.

More traditional approaches to content delivery include:

Sequential Order. When covering content relevant to policies, processes, or procedures, this format probably makes sense. Using this approach, you start with the most important items and then introduce subordinate or less important items one at a time, along with supporting concepts or information. For example, if you were teaching how to jump-start a car with a dead battery, you might start by discussing safety tips to prevent a battery explosion, progress through the physical steps of how to position the vehicles, connect and disconnect the batteries, and other important steps once the car with the dead battery has started.

Simple to Complex. Use this approach if you have new employees in the session or mostly learners to whom the information you will cover is new. Examples of the latter might include employees who have never used a product, service, or process that you are talking about. In training such groups, you may want to start from relatively low-level or simple information and then slowly add more as they gain confidence. Your goal is to teach and not overwhelm them with your knowledge or with large volumes of information.

Building-Block Approach. When you have determined through your needs analysis that learners have attended other training programs on the topic or have previous knowledge related to your topic, you can add additional knowledge during your session. Remember that adults have previous knowledge and experiences that you can build on to recognize what they know and involve them. Use this attribute to help ensure a more positive learning outcome.

Categorization. In many instances, the elements of your content can be lumped together in categories and presented in a condensed format to save time. For example, you could use a heading like "Interpersonal Skills" to include and address subtopics of verbal, non-verbal, and listening skills. Of course, how you use this will depend on the complexity of the topics that you plan to cover.

The Instructional Systems Design (ISD) Process

The basis for instructional system design started during World War II when the U.S. military had to create and deliver training programs for thousands of people in a short period of time. To accomplish this, they pulled from research on human behavior and the theory of operant conditioning developed by psychologist B. F. Skinner. Skinner proposed that, to help eliminate common obstacles to learning and thereby enhance the learning opportunities for all learners, one should:

1. *Use small steps when teaching new concepts or ideas, rather than dumping large quantities of information on learners.* This strategy is known as "chunking" today and ties to research by people like psychologist George A. Miller. In 1956, Miller wrote that most people can store seven items (digits, words, or letters), plus or minus two, in their short-term memories. To find examples of how concept is applied in daily life, you need only look around. Examples include:

   - U.S. Postal ZIP—five numbers, plus four numbers

   - Canadian Postal Code—two groups of letters and numbers

   - License plate numbers—typically no more than seven numbers and letters

   - Famous literary characters—*Snow White and the Seven Dwarfs*

   - Television characters—Typically no more than seven main characters (e.g., "Sex and the City" (four), "Gilligan's Island" (seven), "Scrubs" (seven), and "The Simpsons" (Five).

   - U.S. Social Security numbers—three sets of numbers (000-00-0000).

1. You can apply the chunking concept in your workshop design by choosing no more that seven key concepts supported by fewer than seven (plus or minus two) subtopics.

2. *Repeat directions as many times as possible in order to make sure learners understand what they need to do.* Since you will have auditory, visual, and kinesthetic learners, it is a good idea to use various formats and media. For example, you can post the directions on a flip-chart page or slide, verbally communicate them, and give handouts to each learner or group. If you are using an activity that is complex and takes a bit of time to complete, you might stop learners at various points, ask how they are doing, respond to any questions, and repeat the instructions or redirect them.

3. *Work from most simple to more complex tasks.* You can enhance learning by using a basic "building block" approach in which you allow learners to become familiar with basic concepts or more easily master one before adding additional complex steps. Once people master a few less complicated points, they often gain self-confidence to approach more complicated issues or tasks.

4. *Give immediate feedback on performance.* This is one area many facilitators neglect. Rather than waiting until considerable time has passed to provide feedback, it is usually better to build in time to let learners know how they are doing and what they need to do differently. Failure to do this can allow people to go off task during a role play or problem-solving, or team-building events and may create confusion and frustration.

5. *Give positive reinforcement.* Even if participants are not completely successful at a task, let them know in what areas they have succeeded, praise them, and redirect them toward the desired learning objective. Just as children appreciate feedback and praise, so do most adults. In fact, adults expect that they will be rewarded for good behavior or performance. Reinforcement can be something as simple as having everyone give a round of applause for successful performance, or it can be with tangible rewards such as candy, stickers, prizes, or other items tied to the workshop theme or topic.

Building from Skinner's research, learning objectives should be examined from a behavioral standpoint and training should focus on positive reinforcement rather than punishment. He believed that, if tasks were broken down into smaller, more manageable subtasks, learners were more likely to be successful. Through repetition and ongoing feedback, all learners could master information and topics, according to Skinner.

The ADDIE model (Analysis, Design, Develop, Implement, and Evaluate) is often used when learning the ISD process. In each step, trainers must address specific areas. When trainers fail to apply each step appropriately, learners can be negatively affected and the learning process can break down.

Analysis

This phase is one of the most important but is often neglected. Failing to adequately assess learner needs can result in a program that does not accomplish what you promised that it would.

Depending on whether you are an internal or external consultant, you may have to approach the analysis process differently. In an ideal world, you would have all the time you need. You would also have access to all the information you want to examine in order to make sure that a learning event is needed and to ensure that appropriate learning objectives are set. In the real world, many stakeholders (managers, supervisors, or customers) do not want to spend the time, effort, or money required to conduct an adequate analysis. Often this is because they feel that they are experienced enough and "know" what their employees need to know. These people typically dictate what you will provide in the learning event. This often results in your discovering from learners that it is actually the managers or supervisors who require training. The latter point is why it is so crucial to conduct a thorough analysis before proceeding to design. The underlying root cause of poor performance by employees might be managers, policies, procedures, or other organizational elements.

Whether an internal or external trainer, you should examine as much organizational data as is available and gather information from as many sources as possible in order to make an educated determination about the cause of performance gaps (the difference between desired and actual employee performance). Typical data to look at includes:

♦ Performance reports such as sales, production, customer satisfaction, and errors

♦ Employee appraisals

♦ Exit interviews

♦ Organizational mission and vision statements

♦ Job descriptions

♦ Strategic plans

♦ Policies

Once you have reviewed the data from all sources, turn your attention to gathering information from individuals by using the following techniques:

♦ One-on-one interviews with as many employees, supervisors, managers, and customers as feasible and possible

♦ On-the-job observations of performance

♦ Focus groups (eight to ten people maximum) made up of a cross-section of the employee population

♦ Questionnaires or surveys

If you are an external provider, you may not have an opportunity to assess individual and organizational information. The best you can hope to do is get input from attendees as they register or following registration. You can do this by calling those who register or by sending out a questionnaire. Once you have collected enough information to verify participant needs, you can design or revise your program content as needed. If there is no way to gather information in advance, do a quick in-class analysis after participants arrive. You can use an activity in which learners respond to questions posted on the flip chart, a questionnaire placed with their materials, or a quick show of hands in response to questions that you ask during your opening remarks. If you have to use the last option, you must be capable and willing to make quick adjustments in material content and activities as you go along in order to address as many learner needs as possible.

Design

Look at the design phase in the ADDIE process as the step in which you envision the learning objectives, everything that you will need to conduct the workshop, content for the program, and all the details surrounding the environment. In this phase, you are simply planning or listing what you will need to be successful. Making a checklist is very helpful at this point (see Exhibit 3.1). You do not actually create anything until the Development phase of the process.

A crucial part of this phase is to create realistic learning objectives that truly address the needs of your learners, based on the information gathered in the analysis phase. These are what your performance will be evaluated on in the final phase as you test whether you were successful in helping learners attain new knowledge, skills, or attitudes.

Here you will also determine what you need to conduct the event and to share your knowledge. Some common elements to include in a workshop design are listed below.

Common Elements to Consider in Workshop Design

♦ Budget

♦ Size and makeup of your learner group

♦ Learning objectives

♦ Sources for everything that you will need

♦ Maximum number of participants

Exhibit 3.1. Training Pre-Planning Checklist

Program: _____

Date: _____

Action Taken

Facilities

_____	Person to call for help and phone number
_____	Emergency alarm procedure
_____	Location of copy machine
_____	Smoking/eating/drinking/cell phone policy verified
_____	Restroom location
_____	Phone location
_____	Stairs/elevators location
_____	Parking accommodations
_____	Accessible to disabled
_____	Snack/refreshment location
_____	Signs for direction to class

Room

_____	ADA compliance assessment (e.g., doors 32 inches wide, tabletops 30 to 54 inches high)
_____	Check light controls and set level
_____	Check temperature and set level
_____	Disconnect phone in room (if permissible)
_____	Chairs/tables (number and arrangement)

(continued)

Exhibit 3.1. (*Continued*)

Room

_____   Extension cord (at least twenty-five feet with multiple three-pronged outlets)

_____   Electrical cords taped down

_____   Location of electrical outlets

_____   Three-prong to two-prong plug adapter

_____   Pencil sharpener (if needed)

_____   Coat rack (if applicable)

_____   Lectern (if desired)

_____   Water pitcher and glasses on tables

_____   Blinds drawn to avoid distractions

Housing

_____   Block of rooms obtained

_____   Directions to facility

Marketing

_____   Promotional flyers/brochures designed by (date)

_____   Materials printed by (date)

_____   Materials sent to potential registrants by (date)

_____   E-mail follow-up to potential registrants by (date)

Registration/Administration

_____   Set up registrant database by (date)

_____   Send confirmation, agenda, and directions by (date) to all registrants

_____   Create roster

_____   Agenda (if needed)

_____   Note pads

_____   Pencils/pens

_____   Nametags

_____   Create certificates of completion by day of session

_____   Produce handout materials (see lesson plan)

_____   Create slides/transparencies (see lesson plan)

_____   Create flip charts, posters, graphs, and charts
(see lesson plan for list)

_____   Produce evaluation forms by date of session

_____   Obtain all equipment needed (see lesson plan for list)

_____   Obtain additional instructor materials (see lesson
plan for list)

Overhead Projector

_____   Operational

_____   Spare bulb (test bulb in projector)

_____   Focused and positioned

_____   Glass, lens, and mirror cleaned

_____   Focus adjusted

_____   First transparency in place

Computer/Projection Unit

_____   Operational

_____   Slide presentation installed on PC and a diskette
backup copy present

(continued)

Exhibit 3.1. *(Continued)*

Computer/Projection Unit

_____   Compatible with projection system

_____   Connector cables work

_____   Lens cleaned

_____   PowerPoint or other program presentation tested

_____   Remote available and working

_____   Laser pointer (if using)

Video/VCR/DVD Player

_____   Operational

_____   Location/visibility checked

_____   Sound level adjusted

_____   Video/DVD cued up to title frame or opening scenario

_____   Monitor screen clean (if using)

_____   Projection screen set up (if using)

_____   Heads cleaned (if using a VCR)

Music

_____   CDs/cassettes present (see lesson plan for actual items needed)

_____   Cued to music start

_____   Volume adjusted

_____   Power source

_____   Extension cord (if needed)

Screen

_____   Location/adjusted to prevent keystoning (tilted at 90 degrees from top)

_____   Size

Flip Chart

_____ Location (light shining onto paper rather than from behind easel)

_____ Visibility checked

_____ Paper supply

_____ Pages tabbed

_____ Assorted markers (black, dark blue, dark green, red, and checked for dry ink)

_____ Rubber band across top

_____ Masking tape (1-inch width)

_____ Pointer (dowel rod, Squawkin' Chicken, cardboard arrow)

Microphone

_____ Lavaliere

_____ Extra cord length for movement

_____ Sound level checked

_____ Back-up mike

Board

_____ Dry Erase markers/chalk

_____ Eraser

_____ Clean

_____ Whiteboard cleaner (if appropriate)

_____ Rags/towel

Refreshments

_____ Regular coffee

_____ Decaffeinated

(continued)

Exhibit 3.1. (*Continued*)

Refreshments

_____   Tea/hot water

_____   Juice

_____   Soft drinks

_____   Ice

_____   Water

_____   Sugar/cream

_____   Spoons

_____   Napkins

_____   Cups/glasses

_____   Other (e.g., food items)

Final Mini-Rehearsal/Dry Run

_____   Opening

_____   Sequence (individual component) check

_____   Closing

♦ Facilities (size, location, configuration, breakout rooms required, access to electricity, parking, accessibility, catering)

♦ Trainer(s) needed (number and level of experience and expertise)

♦ Equipment (LCD projector, screen, overhead projector, slides, transparencies, flip charts with pads, VCR and monitor, microphone, etc.)

◆ Instructor support materials (lesson plan, tape, colored markers, timers, props, noisemakers, rewards/incentives, etc.)

◆ Furniture and room layout

◆ Participant materials (handouts, evaluation forms, books, pencils, name tents, nametags, markers, or other materials)

◆ Miscellaneous considerations (marketing and registration, registration fees, attendee work schedules, and others)

Develop

Once you have completed your design of the workshop, you must begin the task of gathering all your "stuff" together to make the program a success. You can best ensure this if you use the lists presented in the discussion of the Design phase earlier.

It is important to consider the theories you have read about, how the brain best processes information, and learning modalities when creating lesson plans, activities, and support materials. The key is to remember who will be in your audience and to then create materials that will assist them grasp, retain, and use the concepts you present after the session has ended. Some typical items to take care of during the development phase can be found in the list below.

Typical Tasks for Develop Phase

◆ Procure facilities (reserve or rent) that are accessible to all learners.

- ♦ Schedule session catering services (refreshments and meals).

- ♦ Arrange transportation and rooms for learners, if necessary.

- ♦ Schedule equipment identified during the design phase.

- ♦ Obtain instructor(s).

- ♦ Write the instructor's lesson plan.

- ♦ Request or obtain required furnishings and arrange classroom as designed.

- ♦ Purchase or obtain instructor's support materials.

- ♦ Create learner materials.

- ♦ Send out program flyers, e-mail notifications, and other marketing pieces.

- ♦ Arrange for registration assistance.

- ♦ Obtain miscellaneous items needed. Some examples include extension cords and an instructor table.

Implement/Deliver

In this phase, the proverbial "rubber meets the road." During the implement/deliver phase, you will use all your knowledge and skills as a facilitator to put everything that you designed and created into action. Remember that YOU are not important; your learners are. Everything that you do, say, and use should be focused on helping learners master the session content and concepts and on their being able to apply them in the real-world. You should be continually monitoring verbal and non-verbal feedback to ensure that they are appropriately receiving your message.

Prior to contact with your learners, ensure that you have adequately prepared yourself, your materials, and the environment for success.

Evaluate

The final phase of the ADDIE model is crucial to your success. Unfortunately, many trainers omit or tacitly handle it. The reality is that, if you do not receive and review feedback on every aspect of the program, there is no way to gauge its success. You will also not have adequate information you need to revise and improve your program and content. This could affect your ability to attract future attendees and garner management or client support for your services.

Four Levels of Evaluation

Many trainers use several types of evaluation to ensure that they are adequately meeting the needs of their learners and the organization(s) sponsoring the event. One of the most popular training evaluation models in use is the four levels of evaluation developed by Donald Kirkpatrick. The four levels of Kirkpatrick's model measure the following.

Reaction of Learners

At this level of evaluation, you seek to determine to what degree your learners liked what was offered. For example, did they like the facilitator, learning environment, materials, food and refreshments, and other elements of the learning event. Often this type of feedback is collected on a single sheet hurriedly passed out at the end of a learning event.

Because of the way this evaluation form is normally handled, learners typically place little importance on it and fail to take the time to give valid feedback before leaving the room. As a result, little useful information is obtained because learners just circle numbers on scales provided and do not bother to give any qualitative written comments. If a trainer does an adequate job facilitating and the environment meets minimum needs, most scores are positive. This is why such forms are often called "smile sheets." This results in the trainer having a "warm feeling," but not really knowing anything about how learners really felt or what they learned.

Strategy for Success

To avoid missing the opportunity to gather valuable feedback on your end-of-session evaluation forms, it is usually better to pass the forms out at the beginning of the session. In your opening remarks, encourage learners to write comments throughout the event and pass them in at the end of the session. You can further enhance your opportunity for substantive feedback by building in time for learners to write down thoughts following interim review activities throughout the workshop. This allows them to capture ideas and comments while they are fresh in their minds.

Learning

At this level of evaluation, you are trying to determine the degree to which knowledge or capability increased. The easiest way to identify gains is to test learners against what they knew at the beginning of the program via a comprehensive written or oral test or a demonstration of skills following training. Either will help you identify their level of awareness and their grasp of concepts taught.

Strategy for Success

Have learners take a pre-test on which they respond to questions based on key concepts to be presented in the workshop. At the end of the session, have them answer the exact same questions on a post-test and compare their responses. In theory, if they were able to answer more questions correctly at the end of the session, then learning and retention took place.

Behavior

Training is intended to cause change in KSAs. To figure out whether you were successful here is to monitor and evaluate whether learners are actually applying what they learned in your workshop. At this third level of evaluation, you attempt to gauge the extent to which learner behavior and skills improved and whether they are actually using what they learned in the training. This is where evaluation becomes more difficult, but not impossible.

As an internal trainer or consultant, you may be able to work with human resources and management to follow up with trainees periodically through evaluation questionnaires, focus groups, on-the-job observation, and other techniques to determine how (or whether or not) they are applying what was learned. On the other hand, if you are offering public workshops or are not part of an organization for which you delivered training, getting access to learners may be impossible.

Another problem at this level of evaluation is that other factors, such as policies, procedures, and supervisors, can either aid or inhibit learners who are trying to apply what they learned. If they have a proactive environment that encourages and supports individual growth, they are likely going to be able to apply what was learned, get feedback on their performance, and modify their behavior accordingly. However, if learners do not receive regular, ongoing positive feedback they may not attempt—or will stop using—what they learned. Also, if unexpected events, such as being trained to use new hardware or software applications but not getting access to it for months, preclude learners from immediately using the new knowledge and skills, they are likely to forget or abandon what was learned.

Results

Level 4 of Kirkpatrick's model is time-consuming and expensive to evaluate. For this reason, most organizations never try to use it. In this phase, you are trying to determine the bottom line or return on investment (ROI) from the training event. You are looking at how the trainees' performance affects the business or work environment, either positively or negatively, and to what degree. Most importantly, you are trying to determine whether the investment was worth it in terms of time, effort, and money.

Develop a Comprehensive Lesson Plan

Once you have identified learner needs and defined content for your workshop, a key tool for success is a lesson plan (see Exhibit 3.2). This document lays out everything

Exhibit 3.2. Sample Lesson Plan Format

Title: Lesson Plan Format

Date Prepared: April 28, 1997

Revision Date: March 16, 2009

Prepared by: Bob Lucas

Length: Ninety minutes

Target Audience: Trainers and educators

Maximum Audience Size: Fifty

Instructors Required: One primary

Learner Materials: Participant Workbooks

Pre-Work Assignment: None

Instructor Materials/Training Aids

    Laptop

    LCD projector and screen

    PowerPoint slides

    One flip-chart easel w/pad

    Assorted flip-chart markers

    Masking tape

    Train whistle or other noisemaker

    Incentive prizes

    8-inch Magic Vase

    Hoberman Sphere

(continued)

EXHIBIT 3.2. (*Continued*)

Instructor References

Lucas, R.W. *The Creative Training Idea Book: Inspired Tips & Techniques for Engaging and Effective Learning.* New York: AMACOM, 2004.

Lucas, R.W. *People Strategies for Trainers: 176 Tips and Techniques for Dealing with Difficult Classroom Situations.* New York: AMACOM, 2006.

Lucas, R.W. *Creative Learning: Activities and Games That REALLY Engage People.* San Francisco, CA: Pfeiffer, 2007.

Instructor Notes

Prior to Participants Arriving:

◆ Check equipment to ensure proper functioning;

◆ Put participant materials on tables;

◆ Adjust lighting/heat/air;

◆ Turn on music, if using;

◆ Put masking tape and markers on flip chart easels, if using;

◆ Post quote charts on walls;

◆ Be ready to greet learners as they enter.

Program Title

   I.   INTRODUCTION (_____ Minutes)(Slide Number _____)

      A. Gain Attention: Include a short statement or information to capture attention and lead into the program topic. This may be statistical information, a joke, a short story or experience, or other vehicle to stimulate interest.

      B. Motivate: A brief statement of why they should be in the class or what they will learn. Outline the "Added Value And Results For ME" (AVAR FM)

C. Learning Objectives: At the end of this session, and when using materials provided in the session, participants will be able to:

1.

2.

3.

4.

D. Administrivia: Explain the following.

1. Electronic devices off/on vibrate.

2. No smoking.

3. Breaks/schedules.

4. Refreshments.

5. Materials.

   a. Workbooks

   b. Handouts

6. Leader (time-keeper, group leader, and spokesperson)/scribe (note-taker) system, if used.

7. Reward system, if used.

TRANSITION: Now that we know what we're going to cover and some of the "game rules," let's get started by examining the first key concept, which is. . . .

ACTIVITY: Small Group Activity (Insert title here) (_____ minutes)

Overview the objectives and process of the activity to follow in an easy to read bulleted format. Also, list any materials needed.

Materials

♦ Flip chart and markers

♦ Masking tape

(continued)

EXHIBIT 3.2. (*Continued*)

Process

♦ Pass out. . . .

♦ Form small groups of an equal number of participants.

♦ Explain. . . .

Debrief

♦ Ask learners. . . .

♦ Explain. . . .

    II.   BODY (_____ minutes)

        A. Key Concept 1(_____ minutes)
           (Workbook)(Slide Number_____)

           1.

           2.

             a.

             b.

             c.

ACTIVITY: (_____ minutes)(Slide Number_____)

           3.

             a.

             b.

TRANSITION: With. . . .in mind, let's go to the next level, which is. . . .

        B. . . . (_____ minutes)(Workbook)(Slide Number_____)

           1.

             a.

(1)

(2)

   b.

2.

   a.

   b.

   c.

TRANSITION: In addition to . . . there are. . . . Let's examine a few of them.

   C. . . . . (_____ minutes)(Workbook)(Slide Number _____)

   1.

   2.

    a.

    b.

    c.

   3.

    a.

    b.

Interim Review: Insert short review activities at various points throughout your presentation. You can do this by having participants (as individuals, pairs, triads, or the entire group) review material presented thus far.

You can do this review by writing key concepts on paper or a flip chart, by discussing, or whatever you think of.

At the end of the review activity, have participants take out their program evaluations and write specific comments about what they have and have not liked thus far. This helps ensure that you will receive some valuable feedback at the end of the session. They should not focus on only comments and rating scale (for example 1 to 7) at this point. They can circle or check numbers at the end of the session.

(continued)

EXHIBIT 3.2. (*Continued*)

TRANSITION: The next thing that will help you . . . is. . . . Let's take at look at how that works.

       D. . . . . (_____ minutes)(Workbook)(Slide Number

          1.

          2.

TRANSITION: The final tip to help you better . . . is. . . . Let's explore that a bit.

       E. . . . . (_____ minutes)(Workbook)(Slide Number_____)

          1.

             a.

             b.

          2.

             a.

             b.

             c.

   III. CONCLUSION (1 to10 minutes, depending on length of the overall program)

♦ A. Review of Key Concepts

    To accomplish this, refer back to learning objectives from the beginning and discussing how you addressed each with various pieces of information provided.

  B. Summary

    A brief statement reminding learners of the value of material covered and how they can apply it. These ties back into your motivation statement at the beginning of the session.

C. Opportunity for Questions

> If you have done a good job with interim reviews along the way, there will not be many (or any) questions.

Remember to have evaluations completed and turned in.

If you are giving certificates and/or incentive prizes, use them now.

you plan to do and is indispensable (see the Checklist for Lesson Plan Development below). As I tell my graduate students in training and development courses, and learners in train-the-trainer workshops, "If you stand in front of a group without some type of structured plan, they are not going to get the full benefit of your knowledge." This is because, unless you document all the crucial details and information that will be addressed in your program, you are likely to forget something, get out of sequence, forget to use a training aid, lose track of time, or simply not deliver the content to the best of your ability.

A detailed outline also provides a script in case someone else has to conduct the workshop in your absence. A word-by-word description and explanation of points and activities should be included. If a lesson plan is written correctly, anyone with knowledge of your session topic should be able to pick it up, review it, and conduct your workshop.

Lesson plans have saved me when an emergency arose. For example, I was once setting up my training room for a five-day supervisory training program when the rear seam of my trousers completely split out. Learners were due to arrive within an hour and I was twenty-two minutes from my house. I left a note and a copy of my slides and lesson plan on my supervisor's desk, saying, "An emergency came up. I'll be back as quickly as possible. Please get the session started." My boss had seen me conduct the work-shop, but had not been actively involved before that day. I returned twenty minutes after my supervisor had started the session as she was conducting the opening icebreaker. We transitioned seamlessly and the class went smoothly. Without a lesson plan outlining what she was to do, this may not have been the case.

Look at a lesson plan as a detailed sketch of what you will say and do during your workshop. You should include minute details and leave nothing to memory or chance.

Once you have created your word-for-word outline, have thoroughly rehearsed, and are confident with what is to happen, you can develop a less detailed skeletal or topic line outline with less detail and key concepts and subtop-ics listed, along with timing, equipment, and material references.

Before you begin writing your lesson plan, create a check-list like the following to guide your development in order to ensure that your approach is systematic, addresses adult learning needs, and includes key elements that will make the workshop successful. Check off your list before you start to write and then use it after you have finished. A sample of such a checklist is shown below.

A Checklist for Lesson Plan Development

❑ Is there a detailed cover sheet that lists all required learner and trainer materials and equipment?

❑ Does the lesson plan cover key concepts matched to the identified learning objectives?

❑ Does the plan tell me what to cover as well as how to convey the information to learners? For example, is it in a fully scripted format?

❑ Is there a planned opening activity that quickly gets learners engaged in the learning process?

❑ Have I divided the lesson plan into three distinct sections (Introduction, Body, and Conclusion)?

❑ Are key concepts identified and supported by subtopics throughout the lesson plan?

❑ Does each concept flow effectively and build on previous ones?

❑ Are there distinct transitions to help the trainer move from one key concept to the next?

❑ Is adequate time built in to cover each topic without cramming in too much material?

❑ Are activities built in throughout the lesson to hold interest, keep learners actively engaged, and support what they learn?

❑ Are stories and examples built in to help learners see direct real-world applications?

❑ Are scripted open-ended questions built into the plan for use throughout the workshop?

❑ Are short, fun interim reviews built in at various points in order to reinforce concepts learned?

❑ Is the ending powerful, with an opportunity for a final review of key concepts and a reinforcement of learning objectives?

There are various formats for writing a lesson plan. You can view one style in Exhibit 3.2. Structure is often a personal preference. The key is to be comprehensive and to include at least the following elements:

Cover Sheet. This page provides essential information about the program design. It also can serve as an instructor's checklist because it lists all the essential equipment and materials needed for learners and for the instructor to use during the session.

Instructor Notes. Write down anything that the you need to do prior to the arrival of learners. Making list of tasks can prevent you from overlooking something, as the period prior to the start of a session is often hectic and stressful. This is especially true when something does not go as planned and last-minute adjustments are needed.

Strategy for Success

As a visual prompt, try color-coding items on your lesson plan so that you can scan through it as you instruct and your attention will be drawn to important information. For example, you might use the following coding system wherever these items appear in your lesson plan:

Yellow = visual aids, such as, slides, posters, or flip charts that will be shown to the group

Green = any handout or other material to be given to learners or to which you will refer at a given point, for example, a participant workbook, handout, or job aid

Pink = any group activity or point at which learners are to become actively involved, such as question-and-answer sessions, small group brainstorming, or activities

Blue = any video or DVD segment to be shown to learners

Lesson Plan Text

Many elements must be included in the lesson plan. A typical lesson plan is divided into an introduction, the body, and a conclusion. It also includes references to supporting materials, timing, verbal transitions, activities, and other pertinent content to address in the session.

The lesson plan is actually a script that you will follow and modify as needed. Because less-experienced trainers need more guidance, be as complete as possible to allow anyone else to use the document. It is always better to have too much detail than not enough.

Use complete sentences and write as though you are speaking to your audience, rather than providing instructions on what you should do. For example, say something like, "One of the things that you will be able to do following this session . . ." as opposed to "Tell learners what they will be able to do following the workshop."

The three primary benefits to using a detailed lesson plan are

1. To provide documentation of your workshop. In the event that you are unable to present the material because of illness, delay in flight, or other unplanned catastrophe, anyone else with a basic knowledge of your topic and facilitation skills should be able to pick up the document, prepare, and instruct from it.

2. To keep you on track. For example, if someone asks a questions or an unplanned discussion occurs during the program, you can respond and then check your lesson plan to see where you left off.

3. To ensure that each learner group will receive exactly the same content and experience similar activities and events. This standardization is particularly important when training group members of the same organization at different sessions.

Time Required

As the old adage goes, "Timing is everything." Give careful thought to the amount of time it will take to present key concepts. Be realistic and do not try to cram too much into your lesson plan. It is better to deliver several key concepts in a quality manner than to try to cover excessive amounts of information and seem rushed and still not adequately covering needed material. This latter approach will most likely leave learners frustrated and result in poor evaluation markings for you and your workshop. Use the chunking approach of introducing a key element, then giving small amounts of supporting detail.

As you outline your session in your lesson plan, list the total time it will take for the entire section. You can see examples of this in Exhibit 3.2 beside Introduction, Body, and Conclusion headers. Next, divide that block of time into smaller pieces, noting them next to the key concepts and activities. See the Key Concepts and Activities headers in Exhibit 3.2.

Training Aids and Materials Needed

To ensure that you have all the items that you need as you discuss a key topic area, list these materials and equipment next to the topic or subtopic header in your lesson plan. This will act as a checkpoint to remind you when and where to use a specific item or material. You can see this layout in Exhibit 3.2. Remember that your lesson plan is your detailed guide to what you will do or say throughout the event.

Transitions

Verbal bridges between key points are extremely helpful in focusing learner attention when you move from one area to another: (1) they call attention to the fact that you are closing out one portion and moving to another; (2) they help tie the material just covered to the new content you are starting and help to form a verbal link between the two sections, and (3) transitions make you look more polished, as you will not have uncomfortable gaps between key topics as you glance at your lesson plan or gather your thoughts.

Strategy for Success

When rehearsing your session content, make sure that you familiarize yourself with the transitions so that they appear natural. The verbal interrupters "uh," "um," "like" and "you know" that many people use when speaking to a group are not valid transitions.

Here is an example of a transition phrase:

Now that we have discussed transition phrases, we are now going to look at a listing of possible introductory phrases that you can use to develop some of these "verbal bridges."

Introductory Phrases for Use in Transitions

A key element of . . . is. . . .

Another thing. . . .

(continued)

And that brings up. . . .

As a further consideration. . . .

After you have . . . you should. . . .

After you have . . . the next step is. . . .

After you inspect the . . . (ensure that, examine, look at, look over, scrutinize, scan, pursue, study, devote your attention to, inspect, see that, test) the. . . .

Another idea/option is. . . .

As an alternative to. . . .

Based on. . . .

Before you. . .you should. . . .

Closely associated with the . . . is the . . . known as. . . .

Collectively. . . .

Conversely. . . .

Consequently. . . .

Considering the importance of . . . let's talk about. . . .

Even more than the . . . is the. . . .

Following the . . . you should. . . .

Having done this, let's. . . .

In addition to . . . we find. . . .

In conjunction with. . . .

Joining the . . . is the. . . .

Keeping in mind the . . . let's go to. . . .

Last in the series (process, steps, phases). . . .

Let us now turn our attention to. . . .

Let us now consider. . . .

Let's now take a look at. . . .

Let's take a look at. . . .

More important than . . . is. . . . Let's examine that now.

Next. . . .

Next, we find. . . .

Next, we have. . . .

Now. . . .

Now that we have the . . ., let's take a look at. . . .

Now we find. . . .

Now let's talk about the. . . .

Now that we are familiar with the . . . we can talk about. . . .

Now that we've covered the . . . are there any questions?

Now let us see (observe, note, look at, review, view, notice, make, take note of, give or pay attention to, give thought to, explain). . . .

Now let us turn our attention to. . . .

Not only do you have to . . ., but even more importantly, you must. . . .

On the other hand. . . .

Once you have done . . . the next phase/step is. . . .

One thing that often helps. . . .

Related to . . . is. . . . Let's see how that. . . .

Since. . . .

(continued)

Since we know . . . let's move to. . . .

Since we know . . . let's look at. . . .

Secondly. . . .

Should you have a need to . . . you can. . . . Let's discuss that now.

The next phase of the process is. . . .

The second (third, fourth, etc) method/step/phase is to. . . .

The second method/step/phase is the most important; that is the step known as the. . . .

The following step. . . .

The direct reverse of this is. . . . Let's examine. . . .

There are many ways to . . . but the only one we are going to discuss is. . . .

There are several ways to. . . .

There are many means of . . ., but the best way is. . . .

Very few elements (techniques, processes, procedures, techniques, strategies) are as important as . . .

With . . . in mind, let's now take a look at. . . .

While . . . is important, it is only one. . . . Let's look at. . . .

Activities

As you will read later in this book, activities are powerful tools for helping you to make key points, supplement concepts, and actively engage your learners.

Remember to be specific when describing activities in your lesson plan. Do not assume that someone else reading will know to say or do something at the right time. Give systematic instructions, describe materials and time needed, and explain how to debrief learners following the activity. Like the lesson plan itself, an activity description should contain an introduction (objectives and setup), body (what to do), and conclusion (relate key points back to content or concepts of the workshop and the workplace).

Repetition (Redundancy)

A key component of a successful learning event is repetition. As you develop your lesson plan content and support materials, ensure that key concepts are repeated. In addition to talking about major points, address them in your written materials (handouts, workbooks, posters, and other visual aids) and include interim reviews through which learners review information periodically.

You can also incorporate repetition by connecting information you provide to what learners already know. Build in activities that allow learners to reflect on similar personal events related to what they learn in class and then discuss their experiences with others. Also, you can periodically ask learners to share examples of how they might apply what they learn to their current workplace or how what they learned might have been beneficial in a past situation.

At the end of your lesson plan, include detailed instructions for conducting a thorough review of key concepts. Remember that the more times they see, hear, taste, touch, or feel something, the more likely they are to gain, retain, recognize and recall, and use it later.

Personalizing What You Have Learned

- What are the most important things that you read in this chapter? Why?

- What are some ways that you can immediately apply concepts covered in this chapter?

- What additional resources or topics do you want to research based on what you read?

Focusing on Your Learners

Using Brain-Based Research to Enhance Learning

fter reading this chapter, and when applying what you learn, you will be able to:

1. Explain the relationship between research about the brain and learning.

2. Describe several factors that affect learning.

3. Identify ways to incorporate color effectively into your learning environments.

4. Control the impact of sound and noise in the learning environment.

5. Maximize the benefits of nutrition on learning.

"What we have to learn to do, we learn by doing."

Aristotle

The Brain and Learning

The brain is the most complex portion of the human body and there is a great deal that scientists do not yet know about brain functioning. On the other hand, in the past several decades, they have created volumes of information on how the brain gains and assimilates information. The 1990s was designated the "decade of the brain" by President George W. Bush. Researchers collected an extensive amount of data on how the brain learns during that period. There was an explosion of new knowledge about ways in which humans learn and grow and how the brain functions in order to manage everyday activities.

All of us learn similarly, yet in different ways, based on our unique brains. Through studies and the use of technology such as positron emission tomography (PET) scans, computer tomography (CT) scan (sometimes called a CAT scan), and magnetic resonance imaging (MRI), scientists were able to peer into the brain as it received and analyzed stimuli. In doing so, they were able to view as it addressed the information that was being received. The result was a virtual mapping of the brain that showed where many specialized functions occur. Because of the information from many researchers, we now better understand how and where learning occurs in the brain, and we can develop strategies to strengthen learning activities.

This is not to say that all the hype by some proponents of brain-based learning is accurate. Like any other concept or theory, brain-based learning has limitations and information should always be verified—and in some cases challenged. Still, enough research has been done to indicate the validity of many of the findings of researchers about how the brain learns best.

Implications of Brain-Based Learning

So why should you care about this when designing your training workshops? Basically, because they allow you to enhance your learning environment, prepare yourself and learners more effectively for your learning events, and create a workshop that will not only meet, but exceed, your learners' needs and expectations every time. By applying some basic concepts of brain-based learning, you can help stimulate learners while making your workshops more fun to present. Just imagine being able to play with toys, do magic, show popular video segments, listen to a variety of music, enjoy a smorgasbord of color, draw caricatures, and be paid for it! More importantly, through use of such tools and techniques, you can better engage and interest your learners and increase the opportunity for a more powerful learning outcome.

For years teachers have used games, toys, music, and other stimulating strategies in teaching kindergarteners and elementary school children. Children have fun and play with their friends without even knowing that they are taking in and honing skills that they will use for the rest of their lives. Skills like teaming, interpersonal communication, problem solving, decision making, time and resource management, and much more are being learned right on the floor or playground, with a lot of screaming, laughing, playing, and FUN! So what changes later? Why do adults often expect a learning environment that is staid and rigid, where someone lectures to them and where they have to take notes and figure out the answers to the questions they are asked? This is due to conditioning. At some point, someone started sitting students in rows of desks and talking at them for endless hours, then tested them on their "knowledge." This is the model (pedagogy) that many people coming to your workshops will possess. It is up to you to shake up their paradigm by creating an environment that is brain-friendly and learner-centric—one that will cause learners to sit up, pay attention, and become actively involved in their own learning while taking ownership and responsibility for their learning outcomes.

Strategy for Success

As a trainer, I love to watch the reactions of people walking into my classrooms, where they encounter colorful balloons on the wall, music playing in the background, colored handouts neatly lined up on their tables along with toys and other fun props, while I greet them with a smile at the door and introduce myself. I typically am asked, "Am I in the right room for . . .?" Without having to tell them anything, I am able to pique their interest and engage them immediately. When I ask their reactions to the environment in my opening remarks, I typically hear things like, "This is going to be fun" and "This is different." Their expectations are raised and they are likely to be more receptive to information that I provide.

You can create similar experiences for your learners by gaining more knowledge about brain-based strategies (see the Resources list for books, websites, and creative learning materials) and creating environments in which learners have the opportunity to become engaged in their learning while having fun.

Factors Affecting Learning

Many factors affect the degree to which your learners are able to successfully grasp and retain information and skills that you share with them in training. If you search the Internet, you will find thousands of sources on various elements of learning and the other topics covered in this book. To be successful as a trainer, you must continually update your knowledge of these topics and learn to apply what researchers continue to discover.

Learner Gender

Having an effective environment is not enough to guarantee a successful learning outcome. To be effective as a trainer, you have to recognize the differences between male and female brains and the effect of their uniqueness on learning. You must then plan for these differences in your session design.

Various researchers have shown the following about the difference between males and females and the way that they acquire knowledge and skills:

♦ The typical brain size of men and women differs.

♦ The various areas of the brain that influence and control such things as language, mathematical ability, and spatial skill develop at different points for males and females.

♦ Additionally, areas that influence emotional development and social skills mature at different ages for boys and girls.

The increase or decrease of estrogen in girls or testosterone in boys during daily cycles and at different periods in their lives can affect the ability to process information. These differences affect a variety of learning functions and actions. For example, some researchers have found that some women seek more emotional, unspoken context and detail or background information during communication. Many men typically focus on content specifics, substantiating data, and a more direct approach. Your challenge as a trainer is to balance the information exchange in your learning session to meet the needs of both groups.

Age of Learners

With age come experience and knowledge. Remember that your workshop attendees will likely bring with them the potential for enhanced learning if you create and deliver an effective and dynamic session.

One myth that scientists continue to dispel is that older people cannot learn easily. In reality, we know that, while the brains of some older people process information differently and they may take a bit longer or require different approaches to learn, they are certainly capable and can continue to grow mentally and absorb new information.

The most successful learning for adults over the age of fifty comes from the use of brain-compatible learning strategies described later in this book. When older learners are exposed to such techniques, they are often able to blend previous experiences and memories with what is being taught. Learning experiences related to values, sensations, motivation, and emotions are typically catalysts for discussion, problem solving, visualizing, designing, writing, planning, and other higher-level cognitive processes.

Creating a Brain-Based Learning Environment

A brain-based learning environment differs from the standard classroom in many ways (see Table 4.1). The biggest

Table 4.1. Comparison of Brain-Based and Standard Learning Environments

Brain-Based Environment	Standard Environment
Trainee differences not recognized or addressed	Each trainee is assessed and needs are addressed
Stimulating background music upon entry	Silence
Colorful handouts neatly arranged on tables	White handouts tossed haphazardly on tables
Colorful posters and images displayed	Blank walls
Natural or full spectrum lighting	Incandescent or fluorescent lighting
Upbeat, open, outgoing trainer(s)	Sedate, formal, focused trainer(s)
Plenty of constructive feedback	Minimal feedback
Engaging activities	Lecture-based
Multiple intelligences addressed	Multiple intelligences ignored
All learning modalities addressed	Little focus on learning modalities
Tables arranged for group involvement	Tables in traditional classroom layout
Refreshments and hydration offered	No refreshments or hydration offered
Vegetation present	No plants or vegetation
Multiple training aids used	PowerPoint only used
Interactivity expected	Interactivity discouraged
Problem solving and challenge common	Answers and information provided
Props, toys, and rewards used	No props, toys, or rewards used

difference is that learners really are at the center of the program and room design in a brain-based environment. Since your participants are you sole reason for being there in the first place, it is crucial that everything be truly learner-centric, ensuring that they get the maximum learning possible.

Room/Facility

The facility and room you choose for your event are important factors in the successful outcome of your workshop. When selecting a training venue, it is crucial to ensure that it will support the planned activities, learning objectives, and the needs of your learners. In many instances, you may have no option but to use the training room that your organization or client provides. However, if you do have a say in the matter, consider looking for a site away from your learners' work environment. This will cut down on tardiness and interruptions, since learners will not be running back to their offices to check e-mail and voice messages or have someone call them out to handle "emergencies" throughout the day.

In choosing a room, look for the following characteristics:

Space for Your Group and Planned Activities. There should be additional space in the rear of the room for breakout activities unless you have the luxury of separate breakout rooms. In addition, there should be space to set up tables for refreshments and display any products that you plan to show or sell.

You want a room that will suit your needs based on the number of attendees and the activities that you have planned. A room too small will be cramped and could make some people feel a bit claustrophobic while limiting what activities you can use. A room too large with excess chairs and space might send a non-verbal message that everyone planned did not show up and they might wonder, "What is wrong with this presenter or program?" or "What do others know that I don't?" It is better not to have to avoid potential negatives before your workshop by planning space accordingly.

Strategy for Success

One of the biggest mistakes is to use a break room with plastic chairs or cramped conference room with a heavy immoveable table. These types of facilities have little space for movement or to place equipment or hang things on the walls. They are designed for short-term, specific functions, and training is not one of them. If possible, try to avoid these venues for anything more than short briefing sessions (one hour or less).

Accessibility for All Learners. Accessibility is crucial for learners who have disabilities such as sight, hearing, or mobility impairments. In the United States and many other countries, there are laws such as the Americans with Disabilities Act of 1990 that require such access. Violators of these laws set themselves and their organization up for a liability suit.

When you are selecting a location, consider doorways that are wide enough to allow access for wheelchairs, space between tables to allow for mobility, and the location of chairs or tables so that people with sight and hearing impairments can select a location near the front of the room. Also consider the availability of disabled parking and restroom facilities, elevators, and entrance accessibility. By law, newer buildings in the United States must provide most of this, but older historic ones may be exempt and could create challenges for your learners with special needs. In some countries, the laws may not be as generous with accommodations and accessibility.

Lighting and Temperature Controls. Unfortunately, room controls are typically located in the rear of the room, next to the entrance. Try to have the controls for lighting and thermostats near the front of the room. The optimal position is near you so that you can control them and where learners are less likely to change settings throughout the day to suit their personal preferences.

Ample Power Outlets and Internet Connections. Try to have these located throughout the room to allow flexibility and movement. Otherwise, your activities and delivery points may be restricted. As a backup, plan to have at least a twenty-five-foot extension cord with multiple sockets available in case you need one.

Adequate Lighting. Research is ongoing related to the impact of artificial lighting on learners. Some studies show that cool-white fluorescent bulbs, which many classrooms have, cause a variety of problems. Some of the issues associated with extended exposure to pink and cool-white fluorescent lights include hyperactivity, bodily stress, attention deficit, anxiety, and other distress, which can all lead to poor academic performance and difficulty in focusing. Dr. Jacob Liberman offers information and discussion on this issue in his popular book *Light: Medicine of the Future.*

Daylight is the standard for color quality in indoor lighting. It has a color rendering index (CRI) of 100. Experts use this index as a standard to measure the effectiveness of artificial lighting illumination levels. Remember that, while natural daylight gives off a continuous spectrum of all light wavelengths in blue, red, and green that appear as a bright white, fluorescent lamps give off a discontinuous spectrum or a flickering light that has inconsistent peaks of color. This is why you should allow as much natural lighting as possible to reach your learners through windows or skylights.

When selecting your training venue, look for a room that has plenty of windows with coverings so that you can control the amount of light that enters. If possible, do not depend solely on artificial lighting. At the least, try to find a facility that has full-spectrum artificial lighting that simulates the effects of lighting from the sun.

Probably the least effective lighting is found in hotel ball-rooms. They are designed to look pretty, but were not created as learning venues. If you must train in such locations, plan for multiple breaks to afford learners an opportunity to go outside into the sun to revitalize and stimulate their brains.

A final consideration related to light is that, while you want to control outside distractions, you may not want to close blinds completely. This will allow some natural light to enter during the day in order to supplement artificial lighting in the room. The key is to ensure that there are no shadows cast or glares created. These can be distracting and can cause eye strain for your learners.

Room Temperature. Monitor the room temperature to ensure that the room is not too hot or cold. Keep in mind that you are likely active and moving around, so learners may feel colder than you do.

According to various research studies, the optimal temperature for a learning environment ranges between 68 and 72 degrees Fahrenheit (20 to 22 degrees Celsius). However, since people have different levels of tolerance, it is a good idea to suggest that learners dress in layers or bring coats or sweaters to your program. This allows them to address personal comfort needs.

As mentioned earlier, use a training site where you have control of temperature settings whenever possible. This is important because being in a room that is either too hot or cold can dramatically affect learner concentration and ultimately negatively affect learning. If you must decide between having the room warmer or cooler, choose cooler. This is especially important following a meal when people normally become sluggish. If the room is warmer and you have no control, make sure that there are plenty of breaks and activities as well as liquid refreshments for participants.

Vegetation. Since green, non-flowering plants are a filter for carbon dioxide and introduce fresh oxygen into the air, it makes sense to place them throughout the room. Scientists have found that plants are a simple and effective way to offset some of the pollution that exists in offices and training rooms. In research for the National Aeronautics and Space Administration (NASA), Dr. B.C. Wolverton conducted studies using plants to remove pollutants in controlled, closed environments. He and others found that many common house plants remove contaminants from the air. By placing plants within an individual's breathing zone (approximately 6 to 8 cubic feet surrounding the person), air quality improves. Wolverton recommends placing two to eight small or two large plants every 900 square feet (nine square meters).

Smells and Odors That Stimulate. For years, researchers have been exploring the impact of smells on learning and memory. In studies, the odors of pine, peppermint, osmanthus (a small green, flowering shrub native to Asia), violet leaf, floral, and orange citrus have been found to impact the brain and positively impact learning and recall.

When thinking about smells, keep in mind that some people have allergies. You may want to avoid fresh flowering plants and the plug-in sprayers that are available on the market. Instead, use more subtle approaches with fragrances. For example, use the Mr. Sketch® flip-chart markers, which have difference aromas, instead of some of the more odor-producing varieties that are on the market. Additionally, carefully consider anything that you plan to use in your activities. Spray adhesives and other such products could be an issue for some people with respiratory problem. If you are going to use Artist's Adhesive as a sticky substance on your flip charts, spray it outside the classroom in the fresh air and bring the page(s) in to mount on your wall rather than spraying them in the training room. Even if learners have not yet arrived, the odor might linger and cause problems for some people.

Dry Erase® markers are a common odor in many classrooms. Consider using the non-odor producing varieties on the market. They cost a bit more, but are a good investment.

Strategy for Success

A simple way to introduce smells into your learning environment without overwhelming or causing problems for people who have breathing disorders such as asthma is to put bowls of peppermint candy on tables and have fresh orange slices for breakfast and snacks. Learners get the benefits of small snacks and the stimulating aromas that help stimulate brain neurons.

Safety Mechanisms. Your have a responsibility to ensure learner safety. When selecting a training facility, find the emergency exits, where fire extinguishers are located, evacuation procedures, and what is expected of you during an emergency or power outage. There have been many instances over the years where trainers and educators were unprepared to deal with dangerous situations. Examples of this include the rash of shootings that have occurred at schools and universities. Part of your role is to plan for all potential situations and have a contingency plan. It is unlikely that learners have thought of the possibility of an emergency, so you must do it for them.

Strategy for Success

When conducting a workshop on-site for your organization or client, learn about emergency exits and equipment, their locations, and how to handle evacuations. Speak to a human resources representative responsible for this function or contact the building safety/risk manager.

If you are at a hotel or other venue, speak to the front desk manager about safety procedures. For example, if you are on an upper floor and have attendees in wheelchairs, find out how to move these learners safely to the ground floor and out of the building. All one needs to do is recall the chilling stories of disabled employees being carried down stairs by rescue workers and peers during the 9/11 attacks in New York City to realize the importance of this issue. You need a plan before something occurs.

Furniture

According to an old training adage, "The brain can absorb only as much as the rear can endure." If you are conducting a workshop that is going to last more than one hour, try to ensure that seating is comfortable and that there are arms on the chairs. Otherwise, learners will be distracted by discomfort. Never use metal folding card-table-type chairs for an event that will last more than an hour. If possible, do not use them at all or learners will be focused on their discomfort rather than listening to what is going on. Ideally, use padded, adjustable seating with arms to allow learners to adjust for their own comfort and provide plenty of chances for movement and breaks.

Two key elements of learner-centered environments are moveable furniture and portable technologies. This means avoiding rooms with heavy, dark wooden tables that cannot be repositioned. Also, evaluate rooms carefully in which technology, such as VCRs, computers, and LCD projectors, are mounted on walls and ceilings or can only be used in certain locations due to availability of electrical outlets and Internet connections.

When you are selecting or creating a training venue, make sure that there is enough table space for all learners to comfortably spread out and not be jammed together. If using rectangular tables, try to find ones that are designed to seat the number of people planned. For example, folding tables with brackets underneath can be uncomfortable if you put three people at a table designed for two. Similarly, putting someone at the end of a folding table that has legs and a crossbar can be uncomfortable. When using round tables, it is best use only two-thirds of the table so that everyone faces the front of the room and has a writing surface. This is better than having participants with their backs to you who have to turn around in their seats to view you and visual aids.

Having enough of the right types of tables and chairs is just part of creating an effective room layout. Another aspect is arranging them to support planned activities and to allow interaction between you and your learners and among themselves. (See Figures 4.1 through 4.14 for examples of possible interactive room layouts.)

Figure 4.1. "V" or Chevron Style Seating Without Tables, Using Ceiling-Mounted LCD Projector, and Laptop on Instructor's Table

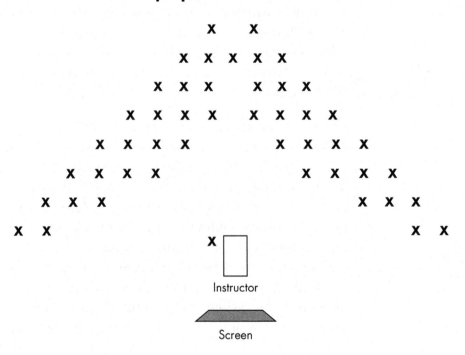

Figure 4.2. U-Shape Style Seating with Tables, Breakout Tables, Four Flip Charts, VCR, Laptop on Instructor's Table, and Ceiling-Mounted LCD Projector

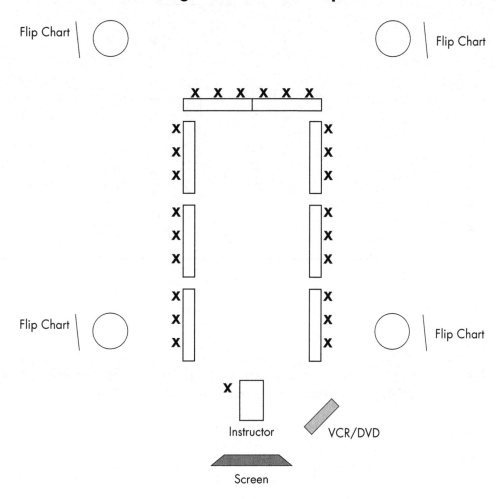

Figure 4.3. Double U-Shape Style Seating with Tables, Using Flip Chart, Laptop on Instructor's Table, and Ceiling-Mounted LCS Projector

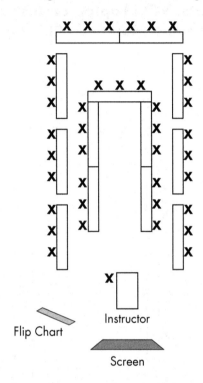

Figure 4.4. Crescent-Style Seating with Tables, Using Flip Chart, VCR, Overhead Projector on Instructor's Table

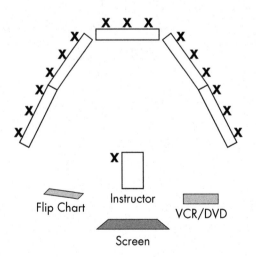

Figure 4.5. Horseshoe-Style Seating with Tables, Using VCR, Flip Chart, Laptop on Instructor's Table, Ceiling-Mounted LCD Projector

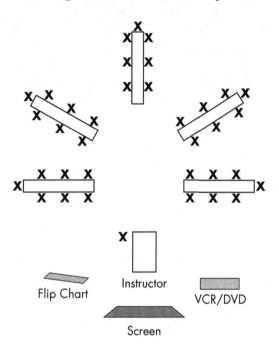

Figure 4.6. Circular-Style Seating with Table

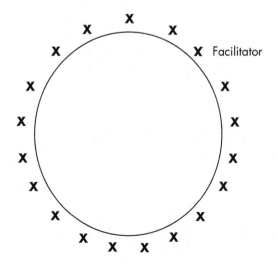

Figure 4.7. Cluster-Style Seating with Tables, Using Flip Chart, VCR, Laptop on Instructor's Table, and Ceiling-Mounted LCD Projector

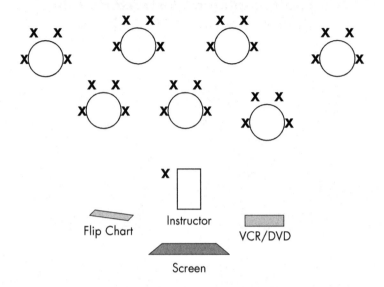

Figure 4.8. Hollow Square and Solid Square Seating with Tables

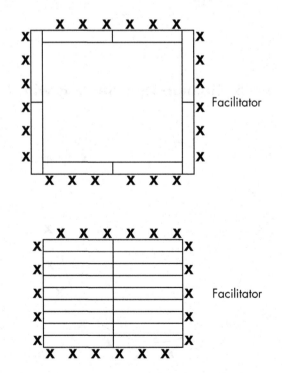

Figure 4.9. Open Square Seating with Tables and Flip Chart

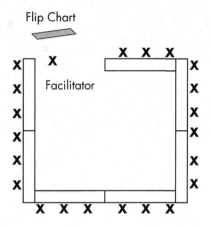

Figure 4.10. Rectangular and Conference-Style Seating with Tables

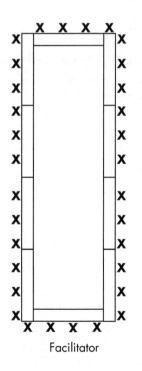

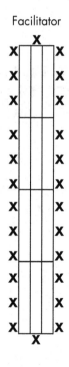

Figure 4.11. Circular-Style Seating

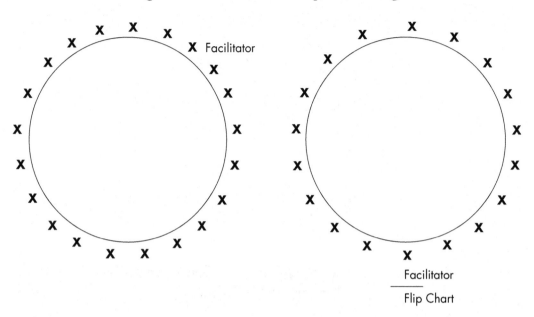

Figure 4.12. Crescent-Style Seating Without Tables with VCR, Flip Chart, Laptop on Instructor's Table, and Ceiling-Mounted LCD Projector

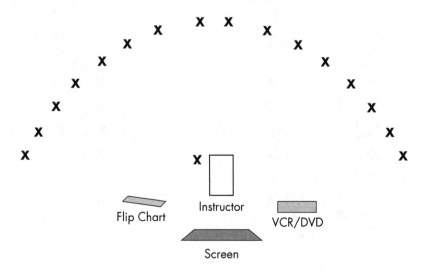

Figure 4.13. Cluster-Style Seating Without Tables for Small Group Activities

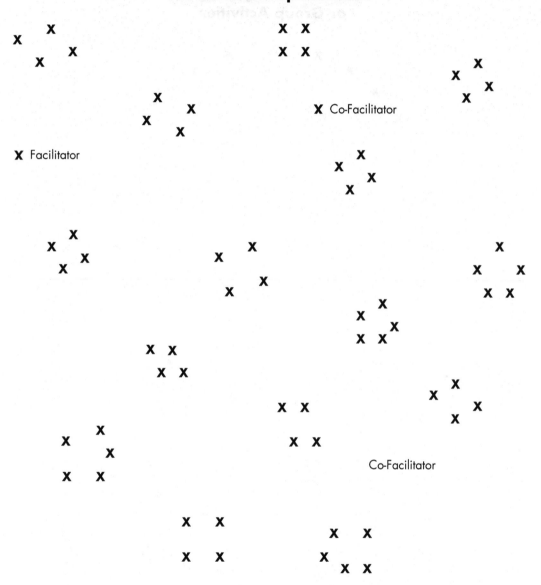

Figure 4.14. Fishbowl-Style Seating Without Tables for Discussion, Role Play, Demonstration, or Group Activities

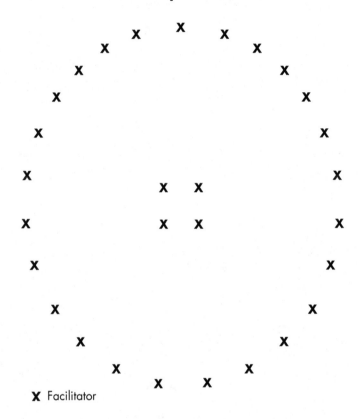

X Facilitator

Tablecloths add an air of professionalism, if they are available. They also help hide participants' personal items and add a bit of privacy for women wearing skirts or dresses. If you have the luxury of having various colors of tablecloths, you can use them to group learners for activities and friendly competition. For example, you could have blue, green, white, red, or black teams based on tablecloth color. This would also provide added color to the room and tie to brain-research regarding the use of color to stimulate the brain.

An additional piece of furniture that is common in a training room is the instructor's table. A six-foot rectangular table will likely provide adequate space for your laptop, projector, lesson plan, and any props and incentive prizes that you plan to use. You can always place another table against the wall for additional handout materials or other items. Smaller tables seem too crowded.

Strategy for Success

Typically, I position the instructor's table vertically (lengthwise) in front of the projection screen instead of horizontally (sideways). This is something I learned from internationally known trainer of trainers, Bob Pike, years ago in a creative training workshop. Using this configuration, I can get deeper into the classroom and closer to my learners, while eliminating the psychological and physical barrier that the horizontal layout creates between them and me.

Equipment

Having the right type of functional support equipment and having it properly placed are crucial factors for ensuring that you effectively communicate your message to learners. When choosing a facility, make sure that the equipment identified in the design phase of the ADDIE process is available and that there is adequate room to position and use it. For example, if you plan to use an LCD projector and PowerPoint® slides, do not forget to request a projection screen. Many locations only have a Dry Erase® board as a screen. This can create a glare when you place the projector directly in front of the board. To avoid this, either use a ceiling-mounted projector or tape several pieces of flip-chart paper together and hang the paper in front of the board to use as a makeshift non-glare projection screen.

Flip Charts. If you have been delivering information to groups for any period of time, you have probably had one of those embarrassing moments. You know, like when you are writing on a flip-chart pad and the easel tumbles over because one of the legs is not locked into position. Another common problem occurs when a tripod frame and the legs slowly start getting shorter because the locking nuts were either not securely tightened or have worn out, allowing the weight of the flip-chart pad to pull the whole frame slowly toward your knees!

To avoid these types of embarrassing moments, make sure that you use sturdy (solid-backed) flip-chart easels. Many organizations buy the cheap three-legged portable easels with retractable legs and two pegs at the top to mount a pad of paper. Unfortunately, the legs get bent over time and will not extend or retract, the pegs often do not fit the hole size of your pads, they wobble when used, and there is no place to put your markers. Not a very professional image.

Another point to consider when using a flip chart is where to position it (see Figure 4.15). If you place the easel so that the light shines directly onto the front of the paper, there will be no shadows. Placing it with lighting behind it can cast shadows and make information difficult to read from a distance.

In addition to considering the location of your flip chart, think about where you will stand when using the

Figure 4.15. Positioning Your Flip Chart

Incorrect Positioning   Correct Positioning

equipment and position it for ease of writing. Typically, right-handed trainers should stand to the left side (as you face the flip chart) and left-handed trainers should stand to the right. If you are one of the fortunate people who can write equally well with either hand, your options are open. Just make sure that you do not block your learners' views as you write. They may be trying to copy or read what you have already written. To avoid this, stand to the side as you write. Unfortunately, some people will not ask you to move, so you have to be very diligent about not blocking their view of the flip chart or other visual aids. These tools do not work if your learners cannot see them.

One mistake that some people who use flip charts make is that they fail to remain facing their audience when speaking. If you must capture information or write, do so, then turn to the audience as quickly as possible to continue your comments. Try to avoid addressing the flip chart by writing and talking simultaneously. This can be perceived as rude and may inhibit the participants from concentrating on your words. Additionally, it makes hearing what you say difficult for people with hearing deficits or those who speak English as a second language. They might miss what you are saying if they depend on reading your lips or your voice projection in order to grasp what you say.

Another important consideration with flip charts is to make sure there is an ample supply of paper and assorted colors of water-based markers. You will also need some painter tape (typically blue) to hang pages on walls. This tape is designed to be used on paint and will not damage painted surfaces, although many non-trainers will argue this point with you and tell you not to hang things on the wall. Be careful about using masking tape, especially if it is old, since the glue on certain varieties may stick to wall paint. For additional suggestions on using flip charts, see *The Big Book of Flip Charts* in the Resources section.

Laptop/Internet Connection. If your training plan calls for the use of a laptop computer and/or an Internet connection, make sure that you check both tools before learners arrive to ensure everything is connected and working. Also set up any PowerPoint slide presentations and have the slideshow started in advance, rather than wasting time moving between programs while learners watch. This helps to demonstrate your professionalism. As a backup in case slides or your computer fails, make transparencies from your slides and have an overhead projector on hand.

Strategy for Success

Considering some of the concepts related to use of color, music, and novelty, I often have a rotating slide presentation called *Reflections for the Senses* (available from www.globalperformancestrategies.com) playing as learners enter the room. I also use them for breaks. Depending on my session topic, I choose from a series of different CDs such as Learning, Customer Service, Communication, and Teamwork. Each CD contains twenty beautiful photographic images, with a quote related to the workshop topic, accompanied by pleasant background music. As participants enter the room, they are greeted with a visual and auditory stimulus that ties to the session topic and fills the silent void that is often present in training rooms.

Overhead Projectors. If you are still using overhead projectors, make sure that you request the dual-bulb type and have a backup spare projector bulb handy. If this is not possible, it is a good idea to have a second unit on hand as a backup.

The Power of Color

Color has the ability to attract and hold attention and to stimulate emotions. Marketing experts have known and capitalized on this knowledge for years. Research reported in an article by David Embry (1984) suggests that color can increase learning from 55 to 78 percent. Virginia Johnson (1992) also points out that adding color can enhance comprehension by 73 percent. Certain colors like pastels can calm, while reds and others can evoke powerful feelings and prompt a call to action. According to research by CCICOLOR Institute for Color Research (www.ccicolor.com/research.html), "people make a subconscious judgment about a person, environment, or product within ninety seconds of initial viewing and that between 62 percent and 90 percent of that analysis is based on color alone." See Table 4.2 for some of the effects that color can have.

You can introduce color into your learning environment in many ways. Many trainers and educators do not consider how color can affect the outcome of their events. They miss opportunities to introduce it effectively into their learning environments.

Some possible areas for color introduction include the following.

Clothing. What you choose to wear can help or hurt your information delivery and the reaction that people have to you. The style of clothing is important, but so is color. As you can see in Table 4.2, color can evoke different types of emotion.

Since color has the ability to attract attention, you may want to consider wearing a splash of conservative color such as light blue, yellow, or pink. These colors can send a message that you are not formal and rigid, as opposed to wearing a starched white shirt or blouse, which can do just the opposite. In addition, if you are standing in front of a whiteboard or white wall, colored clothing can help you contrast with your background and help to stimulate the brains of your learners.

Handouts. A simple way to introduce color into your learning environment is to create handouts in multiple colors. This is an easy way to identify them when you are

Table 4.2. The Emotions of Color

Color	Emotion/Message
Red	Stimulates and evokes excitement, passion, power, energy, anger, intensity. Also can indicate "stop," negativity, financial trouble, or shortage.
Yellow	Indicates caution, warmth, mellowness, positive meaning, optimism, and cheerfulness. It can also stimulate thinking and visioning.
Dark Blue	Depending on shade, can relax, soothe, indicate maturity, and evoke trust, tranquility, or peace.
Light Blue	Cool, youthful, or masculine image can be projected.
Purple	Projects assertiveness or boldness, youthfulness and contemporary image. Often used as a sign of royalty, richness, spirituality, or power.
Orange	Can indicate high energy or enthusiasm. Emotional and sometimes stimulates positive thinking. Organic image can result.
Brown	An earth tone that creates a feeling of security, wholesomeness, strength, support, and a lack of pretentiousness.
Green	Can remind of nature, productivity, positive image, moving forward or "go," comforting, growth, or financial success or prosperity. Also can give a feeling of balance.
Gold/Silver	Illustrates prestige, status, wealth, elegance, or conservative image.
Pink	Projects a youthful, feminine, or warm image.
White	Typically used to illustrate purity, cleanliness, honesty, wholesomeness, enhance colors used, and provide visual relaxation.
Black	Represents a lack of color. Creates sense of independence, completeness, and solidarity. Often used to indicate financial success, death, seriousness, or heaviness of situation.

Source: R.W. Lucas, *The Big Book of Flip Charts*. New York: McGraw-Hill, 1999, pp. 40–41.

ready to pass them out and it is a way to group people for small group activities.

Strategy for Success

I often print my participant workbook cover sheets in a variety of colors. I first decide how many copies I will need, then I print the handout covers equally in different pastel colors, based on an activity that I have planned. For example, if I have twenty-four participants and want to have four equal groups for an activity, I would use four different colored cover sheets and have six copies of each (4 × 6 = 24). When ready to conduct the activity, I announce that those people with like-colored handout cover sheets should gather at specified places in the room. Thus, I have randomly divided my learners into equal groups and potentially separated cliques of people who know or work with one another and often sit together when they attend a session. I have also subtly introduced color into the environment.

Colored Text on Visual Aids. A relatively simple way to introduce color is to use a variety of color on visual aids such as flip charts, slides, graphs, charts, and transparencies. Typically, you should choose a maximum of three colors per visual aid. For example, one color for title lines and two for alternating lines of text. These colors should contrast and background colors and lines of text should complement one another. You can also use light-colored text on dark backgrounds, and vice versa, to make the text stand out.

Colored Graphics. When creating slides, flip charts, job aids, graphs, charts, posters, and other visual aids for your walls, use colorful photos and clip-art images to enhance the text messages and add visual variety. You can also add colored and themed borders around your flip-chart pages and other aids. For example, if you were doing a workshop on effective telephone skills, you might have a border of connected telephone receivers that circled the outside edge of your handouts, posters, or flip charts.

Colored Props. A very simple way to enhance your learning environment is through the introduction of props such as toys, actual items, or other materials. For example, you could reward learners with colorful small toys or prizes related to your session topic. These might be small smile-face-type plastic figures, pencil sharpen, erasers, coffee mugs, or other similar items for a customer service or interpersonal communication class.

Another way to use props is to place groups of different items on tables and allow learners to select them randomly. Based on what they select, group them with others who chose similar items or colors for activities.

The Effect of Sound and Noise

If your participants cannot effectively hear what you and others say in the room, their learning will be limited. To ensure that they get the most out of the event, check your audiovisual sound levels from various points in the room before learners arrive to ensure that you can be heard everywhere. Rooms such as cafeterias and break rooms typically are not designed for presentations. Because of echoes or other distracting noises, you can negatively affect learning by using such facilities.

Encourage Everyone to Participate Actively and to Speak Up. Learners bring a lot of knowledge and experience with them. However, if others cannot hear their comments and questions throughout the learning event, the value of their knowledge is often lost. In some cases, you will have learners who are sitting farther away or have hearing deficits and will not hear a response from a peer. They may be too embarrassed or simply not want to bother to ask for a repeat of the information. To prevent this from occurring, encourage everyone to speak up or stand up when making a comment or asking a question. Also, make a statement in your introductory remarks that if anyone has difficulty hearing he or she should let you know so that you can adjust the sound or ask others to speak up.

Distractions Can Impact the Quality of Learning Outcomes. It is important to monitor outside noise and control it to the best of your ability. When planning a session or class, try to locate a room that is away from large gatherings, special events like weddings or ceremonies, planned construction, maintenance work, and foot and vehicular traffic. Additionally, check the room in advance to make sure there are no humming fluorescent lights, that the projector is not buzzing or rattling, and that no distracting noise is present. If any of these distractions exist, attempt to resolve them before learners arrive.

Learners Can Add to Distraction. Participants often contribute to noise levels in learning events by using cell phones and other electronic devices and by having side conversations or talking in loud voices during small group activities. This type of noise can actually cue you that learners are bored, preoccupied, or have completed a small group task. In the latter instance, when participants finish discussing an assigned topic, they will typically begin networking, laughing, and doing other things that cause the noise level to escalate. This should be your cue to recapture their attention and move on.

Strategy for Success

I use a variety of noisemakers to attract learner attention in my workshops. When I want to gain their attention, instead of yelling "May I have your attention?" I:

Start pre-recorded music.

Blow a train whistle (wooden whistle that sounds like a train steam engine).

Use some other type of musical instrument, such as a metal gong or jumbo hand clapper.

Sound an Attention Getter (small stopwatch device that has three pre-recorded sounds [Tarzan yell, trumpet sounding, and rooster crowing]).

Such tools help focus attention while adding novelty, sound, and fun, which tie into the brain-based learning concepts that you read about in Chapter 2. All of these are available from Creative Presentation Resources in the Resources section.

The Value of Music

Henry Ward Beecher once said, "Music cleanses the understanding; inspires it, and lifts it into a realm which it would not reach if it were left to itself." Researchers who have studied the impact of music on the brain in musicians have observed that it does change the brain and enhance their mental functions. It also impacts their mental capabilities in areas other than music. For example, a number of studies have found that musically trained adults have better word memory test performance than their counterparts who have not been involved with music throughout their lives. Further, other studies (Society of Neuroscience, 2000) have found that preschoolers who took piano lessons for six months outperformed other children on puzzle-solving tests.

For years, there have been studies on the impact of music on one's ability to process information more effectively. One such debate, on what was coined the "Mozart effect," continues among scholars and researchers. The concept originated from studies that found listening to certain music by classical composer Wolfgang Amadeus Mozart increased a person's cognitive abilities and their spatial-temporal reasoning ability (Jensen, 1996). Some studies point to results of enhanced mental performance by study participants, while others debunk such claims.

Eric Jensen, in his book titled *Brain-Based Learning*, discusses a study by the Center for the Neurology of Learning and Memory at the University of California's Irvine campus. He states, "A study measured the impact of listening to Mozart before taking a standardized test. The participants who listened for ten minutes to Mozart's Sonata for Two Pianos in D Major raised their test scores in spatial and abstract reasoning. On an intelligence test, the gain was nine points after just ten minutes!"

According to Don Campbell (1997), additional studies have found that listening to Mozart and others can calm patients with seizures, aid children with attention deficit disorders, and relax people with stress disorders. While there is controversy over the effectiveness of using such music, it does merit further consideration and exploration.

Disagreement aside, there is strong support for using music in the classroom and workplace. Consider the number of schools and institutions of higher education that apply it, workplaces that pipe in music, airlines that play it while a plane is on the runway, and athletic events that use it at various points. There is a definite mental connection between music, brain functioning, and mood.

Think of songs that you hear on the radio and instantly are able to recall who sings it, when it was released, and what you were doing when you first heard it. Obviously, they had an impact on your brain.

Some studies have found that, when studying and listening to certain types of music, people were able to recall more information when they were able to listen to the same music during a test. This occurs because the brain makes a mental association between the music and information stored in their brains. An Internet search on this topic will provide a variety of websites, articles, and opinions on this concept.

For activities in which learners are going to think, reflect, visualize, or process information, it is best to avoid songs that have lyrics or that people will immediately recognize and start singing along with in their heads. This can lead to distraction. Instead, use instrumental tunes that have no lyrics. In her book, *Soundtracks for Learning*, Chris Brewer (2008) outlines many examples of the these types of music that help to accomplish learning without distraction. All of this ties into brain-based research related to stimulation of brain neurons.

One important factor to consider when using music created by others is that you must honor international and federal copyright law; otherwise you and your organization may be subject to liability. For more information on licensing and using music in your sessions see the Resources section under Music.

There are a number of outcomes possible with music:

Use Music to Spark Emotion. Music sparks an emotional connection and aids memory. It can be a conduit to thoughts, ideas, and information stored in the brain, which is why you may want to consider using it in your learning events.

Music can be used to help tie to training topic themes and connect to key concepts. For example, you could create a CD of songs related to time for a session on time management. Titles on this topic might include "Time Won't Let Me" by The Outsiders, "No Time This Time" by The Police, or "This Time" by Verve. You could also choose upbeat, powerful songs to tie to a session on motivation or leadership, such as "Don't Stop Believing" by Journey, "Gonna Fly Now" (theme from *Rocky*) by DeEtta Little and Nelson Pigford, or "Chariots of Fire" by Vangelis.

Strategy for Success

According to Eric Jensen in *Top Tunes for Teaching*, depending on the tempo of the music that you select, you can increase or decrease the energy level in your sessions. Jensen recommends:

Forty-sixty beats per minute can help relax or calm your learners and can be used in activities like visualization, reflection, or journal writing.

Sixty to seventy beats per minute can help maintain alertness when learners are thinking or working on a project in a workshop on problem solving or creativity.

Seventy to one hundred forty beats a minute can be used to energize your learners, get them "pumped up," and encourage movement, for activities in which dance or physical activity is involved or when you are trying to move them toward completion of a deadline.

Provide Stimulation Before a Session Starts and During Breaks. If you have ever entered a sterile classroom that has no color, nothing on the walls, and is silent and in which people do not know one another and no one greets you, you understand the significance of using music. As participants move into your training venue or leave during breaks, you can use music to fill that empty void that often occurs. Choose upbeat music that gets their hearts pumping and raises their mood, rather than more sedate new age or classical music that will lull them into a state of relaxation.

Another positive aspect of using music is that, when you are ready to start or restart your class, you simply turn off the music that was playing during the break. The silence will grab attention and signal learners that something is about to happen.

Develop a Backdrop for Physical Movement. Lenn Millbower, a writer and former magician and musician, uses music from a CD he composed called *Game Show Themes for Trainers* (see Creative Presentation Resources in the Resources section) as what he calls "traveling music." Whenever he asks someone to come to the stage during a conference presentation, he plays a short snip of one of the tunes to fill the quiet void as the person walks forward. If you notice, they do the same thing on game shows as audience members move forward. In effect, Lenn is tying into people's life experience, since so many have seen such game shows.

By using upbeat music as a background, you can also increase the heart rates of learners as you have them engage in group activities. Think about how children are engaged in games like musical chairs in which they circle chairs until the music stops and them jump into a seat or ring around the rosy while singing or listening to music. The same concept can be incorporated into your training plan.

Strategy for Success

I use a variation of musical chairs as a review activity using a musical pass the pickle prop, which is green with a funny face painted on (see Creative Presentation Resources in the Resources section). Learners form circles of six to eight people and pass a humorous looking rubber pickle that plays music that randomly stops. As each person receives the pickle he or she must shout out a key concept or term learned in the session before passing the pickle along. The person caught holding the pickle when the music stops shouts out a term, then sits down.

I reward the last person in each group with small prizes and have everyone receive a round of applause for their efforts. This all ties to brain-based learning concepts by adding aspects of fun, novelty, color, movement, and music (sounds) to the session.

Build Activities Around Music. You can use recorded music or have learners either create their own songs that parody popular songs or are original and based on popular music in order to engage them. For instance, you could give everyone a kazoo and a slip of paper with the name of random popular songs, such as "Happy Birthday," "All Around the Mulberry Bush," or the national anthem. Choose songs that you think everyone should know based on your group makeup. Based on what the learners find on their papers, they hum those tunes through their kazoos as they search the room for others humming the same song. They then form groups with those people, introduce themselves, and discuss an assigned topic.

The Importance of Nutrition on Learning

"Brain foods," which are rich in specific nutrients and readily available, are essential for proper brain functioning. Researchers continue to explore the nutritional value of various types and groups of food and other beverages. From a learning perspective, this is important because, depending on nutritional content, the brain can be helped or hindered in its attempts to access and process information effectively by the food and beverages the body receives.

If you are responsible for planning refreshments and meals for your learners during a learning event, seriously consider your choices. Some data suggests that providing protein-rich foods, such as soybean products can increase alertness in your learners, while plant-based foods can affect mental stamina. Further, beans, whole grains, fruit, and food that contains iron and foods or drinks with Vitamin C can help increase attention span and improve learning ability. On the contrary, carbohydrate-laden foods can make learners sluggish or sleepy and slow mental functions. Some foods good for learning are listed below.

Nutritional Foods for Learning

Protein Foods (Building Blocks for Learning)

- Cheese

- Eggs

- Fish

- Grains, including bread and pasta (wheat, rice, oats, and cornmeal)

- Lean meats (beef, veal, pork, and lamb)

- Legumes (peas, beans, and other pod vegetables)

- Lentils

- Milk

- Nuts and seeds (peanuts, almonds, cashews, sunflower, flax, and pumpkin)

- Peanut butter

- Poultry (skinless chicken)

- Tofu

- Soy milk

- Yogurt

Iron-Rich Foods (Support Brain Development and Intelligence, Increase Energy and Oxygen to the Brain to Aid Memory)

- Almonds

- Apricots, prunes, and raisins

- Beans, peas, and soybeans

- Beef

- Chicken (especially dark meat)

- Spinach, green beans, and broccoli

- Sunflower seeds

- Turkey

- Venison

Low-Fat Foods (More Nutritious and Appropriate When Eaten in Moderation)

- Lettuce

- Carrots

- Tomatoes

- Strawberries

- Spinach

- Egg whites

- Baked potatoes

- Grapes

- Angel food cake

- Oatmeal cookies

- Breakfast cereals (most non-sugared brands)

- Watermelon

- Air-popped popcorn (without added butter)

- Light tuna (canned in water)

- Green peas

- Wheat bread

- Pancakes

- Beans

- Rice

- Pretzels

- Vegetable soup

- Chicken soup with rice

- Milk, 1 percent, reduced fat, and skim milk

High-Fat Foods (Avoid or Eat in Moderation)

- Chocolate candies

- Trail mix (especially varieties containing chocolate chips)

- Cheese sauce

- Ricotta cheese made with whole or part skim milk

- Chicken pot pie

- Pie (pecan, cherry, chocolate crème, for example)

- Condensed milk (sweetened)

- Homemade white sauce

- Ribs

- Macadamia nuts, pecans, and cashews

- Potato salad

- Au gratin potatoes

- Hash brown potatoes

- Cheesecake

- Spinach soufflé

- Baked beans with franks

Jump-Start Your Session. Providing a morning snack in your workshop can also be very beneficial in providing the nutrients that you learners need to be successful. This is based on the assumption that you make the right foods and beverages available. Because many people skip breakfast, it might have been twelve to fifteen hours since the person ate dinner by the time he or she eats lunch. That means the person has deprived his or her body of precious nutrients for an extended period of time before arriving at your session. Without food, the body's glucose level is drained, so the person's ability to process information is impeded and his or her memory is negatively impacted.

The human body depends on glucose (a form of sugar) for fuel and to power the brain. Since the body does not naturally produce this substance, it depends on a continuing supply through the bloodstream in order to maintain peak performance. The body extracts this substance from starchy and sugared foods such as grains, potatoes, legumes (beans and peas), fruits, and other vegetables, so plan to include such items in your program plan. When deciding what to serve in your workshop, remember that the human brain requires a lot of energy to perform at peak capacity. Because of this, you may want to reconsider those donuts, pastries, and other sugar-intense items at the beginning of the day. For breakfast, try a selection of fruit and fresh juices along with bagels and croissants. Along with the caffeinated coffee and tea, offer decaffeinated types and lots of water as well.

While glucose from fruits, grains, and vegetables helps to fuel the brain, heavy manufactured sugar products or refined carbohydrates can actually deprive your learners' brains of glucose. By providing only the latter type of food, you actually deplete your learners' energy supply and inhibit their ability to concentrate, gain, retain, and recall information effectively.

Keep Your Learners Nourished. For lunch, choose a variety of low-fat, protein-rich foods rather than heavy carbohy-drates. Be careful about offering turkey or mashed potatoes and other carbohydrates for lunch. The reason is that turkey contains an amino acid called L-tryptophan that travels to the brain and is converted to chemical known as serotonin, which relaxes the body and induces sleep, while carbohydrates weigh heavily in the stomach and create sugar, which slows down mental function. This is why after eating a big Thanksgiving dinner, and then heading off to the television to watch the big game, many people doze off.

Provide an Afternoon Boost. The poor nutrition issue is often compounded when people who do not eat breakfast later load up with a heavy carbohydrate-type lunch. This often leads to a mid-afternoon mental slump and a hunger for sugar to replenish an already depleted system. If you provide only cookies and soft drinks for a mid-afternoon snack, you are literally feeding learners products that will further clog their neural passageways and reduce learning capacity. Instead, provide plenty of water and alternatives to sugared products. For your afternoon break, provide lighter, more useful foods such as air-popped popcorn, pretzels, and nuts and fruit trail mix, along with a selection of decaffeinated and sugar-free drinks such as coffee, bottled water, and unsweetened iced tea. You can always provide artificial sweeteners along with sugar for those who prefer it.

Obviously, some of these items are better than others for learners. You cannot dictate their preferences or restrict their lifestyle totally. You can offer more healthy alternatives that aid learning and still provide a selection from which they can choose.

Personalizing What You Have Learned

- What are the most important things that you read in this chapter? Why?

- What are some ways that you can immediately apply concepts covered in this chapter?

- What additional resources or topics do you want to research based on what you read?

CHAPTER 5

Engaging Your Learners

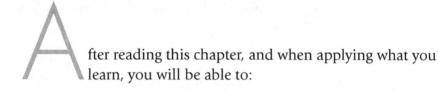fter reading this chapter, and when applying what you learn, you will be able to:

1. Create a workshop structure that allows all learners to excel.

2. Apply learning strategies that build and reinforce rapport with participants.

3. Use training strategies that help gain and maintain learner interest.

4. Select training activities that add fun and excitement while teaching and reinforcing key session concepts.

"Learning is an active process. We learn by doing.
Only knowledge that is used sticks in your mind."

Dale Carnegie

Create a Stimulating Learning Event

Learning occurs in different ways for each person. There is
no one right way of presenting information and sharing
your knowledge. Unfortunately, many trainers and
educators do not realize or capitalize on this fact. Instead,
they provide information in a traditional lecture-based
manner or in their own preferred format in hopes that
everyone will get something out of it. The sad fact is that
in many instances this strategy fails a percentage of
learners in their group.

Rather than taking a narrow delivery approach of using
one or two methods through which you provide
information, consider better ways to address learner
needs. Think about what you have read regarding the
ways in which the brain best processes information. Look
for ways to create a learning environment that continually
challenges and stimulates the brain and that supports the
message that you are delivering.

Many options exist for getting people involved in the
learning process and to have them share ideas and
information. You can use activities, puzzles, games,
question-and-answer (Q&A) segments, interim reviews,
role plays, demonstrations, brainstorming, and many
other events to challenge learners and get them to
participate actively in their learning. You are limited only
by own imagination and any lack of desire to try other
approaches.

Strategy for Success

Technology has added a variety of new tools from which trainers and educators can benefit and enhance their learning environments. Research shows that the brain responds well to elements such as fun, novelty, engagement, motion, color, light, and sound. To capitalize on this data, you can add electronic games to your workshop to capture and hold learner attention while reinforcing key program concepts. Game Show Presenter® and Classroom Jeopardy® (see Creative Presentation Resources in the Resources section) are both excellent vehicles for sharing and reviewing information in a learning environment. With such software, you can create your own categories based on key session topics, then develop questions to which learners respond individually or in teams. The book, *I'll Take Learning for 500*, provides great ideas for incorporating game shows into workshops.

Choose the Right Workshop Structure

It is no surprise that allotted time for training is in short supply for most workers today. Due to the assignment of multiple job responsibilities and other time-consuming tasks, compounded by downsizing, rightsizing, and all the other "sizings" being done in organizations to save money, many employees find little time or funding for self-improvement and professional development. All this is supposedly done in the name of gaining efficiency and serving customers better, while many workers continue to struggle to meet demands as they do more with fewer resources. Because of all these obstacles, you should carefully consider how you will structure your workshop and look for ways to maximize transfer of training while reducing time required for an event.

In some instances, several shorter learning sessions might make more sense than a single longer one. For example, rather than offering an eight-hour workshop, you may want to divide the content into shorter segments.

Of course, one key determining factor is who will be attending. For example, are all learners from one organization in a single location or are learners from multiple organizations and locations? The latter will result in more coordination effort and cost due to travel time and expenses. It may also limit your format options if you are conducting training in a classroom. Additionally, if you are using an off-site facility rather than an organizational training room, you will have to factor in availability and costs related to renting such a venue. These are all considerations in the design/planning phase of the ADDIE model.

Built Rapport with Learners

One point to remember when designing activities and planning your delivery strategy is that some learners may be uncomfortable being a focal point in your workshop. This could create challenges if you call on them to role play or ask them to share ideas and information, be a small group leader, or read material to others. Their reluctance may be due to their cultural backgrounds. For example, some Hispanic, Asian, and Middle Eastern cultures teach children to respect their teacher and those who are older or from a higher social class and not to question or challenge them. It might also be due to personality style or because the person is more introverted. Because of learner comfort levels, you may have to rethink activities, session format, and overall structure of the content and delivery.

Another factor to consider is that learners generally need to build a comfort level with you and their peers before they participate in certain activities or become actively involved. Based on personality style and the degree of trust that learners have for you and trainers in general, it may be difficult for some to feel at ease early in a workshop. Because of this, it is a probably a bad idea to schedule a role play or learner presentation early in a workshop if people do not know one another well. To help increase the comfort level among learners, many trainers and educators use icebreaker activities early in their sessions so that participants can start to get to know one another. They also use various verbal and non-verbal strategies, such as greeting learners, using their names, smiling, shaking their hands, and other interpersonal techniques to build early rapport and relax learners.

Strategy for Success

Tell participants in your opening remarks that it is okay for them to "opt out" of a volunteer role, such as small group leader or note-taker, or when asked their opinion. To limit the number of times that they may choose not to participate, explain the importance of their input and ideas and encourage their involvement.

In order to encourage sharing of ideas by everyone, build in a variety of activity formats so that learners have a chance to participate at their levels of comfort. For example, build in large group Q&A and activities, but also use small group activities in which four to six learners work together on a task. The latter allows a more intimate setting, and many learners who are uncomfortable in large group settings will open up in the smaller ones.

Another option to obtain input from all learners is to have them write down ideas or questions on paper or 3-by-5 cards and either pass them in anonymously or put them into a pile. Each sheet or card can then be selected and read for discussion or comment by the entire group. This allows shy people and those who are reluctant to challenge the instructor an opportunity to voice their questions, ideas, or concerns.

Gaining and Maintaining Interest

A time-tested technique for making sure that your learning events will be a success involves getting your learners "pumped" and eager to listen and learn. It is not enough to have solid content. For learners to focus on what you have to say, you will have to plan and design strategies that will help them get involved.

You can engage learners through the way that you deliver information and "work the room." By that, I mean use your body, voice, movement, and other training skills to come into contact and interact with learners throughout the workshop. All of these are learned skills. They require you to work continually to upgrade your knowledge related to effective training techniques and the latest in brain-based research on how people learn best. For example, by continually repositioning yourself throughout a workshop, you can visually attract learners. You can also manage learner behavior by closing the distance between you and them when they are distracted, engage in side conversations, or "zone out" and start daydreaming. A "U-shaped, crescent, or horseshoe table configuration such as those found in Chapter 4 (Figures 4.2 through 4.5) allow for better classroom management. With such arrangements, you can move in close to learners as you casually discuss a topic, stop in front of, or even sit on the edge of a table as you communicate with the class or with a specific learner. Smile, make eye contact, and continue to talk as you send a non-verbal message to a learner that he or she is distracting others or that he or she needs to refocus attention.

The following are some additional approaches for helping to engage learners and help motivate them to learn:

Use Learner Names. You may have heard the expression, "The sweetest sound to anyone's ear is his or her own name." Most people are social beings and enjoy being accepted and around others. If you have a small group (twenty-five or fewer), try to get to know all people's names quickly and use them throughout the workshop. This technique helps cement their names in your memory and personalizes your content delivery. It also serves to form a friendly learning environment, which can encourage participation and less antagonistic behavior. Use name tags and have name tents onto which learners write their first and last names on the front and back of the cards so that people anywhere in the room can see who they are and use their names when addressing them. If you do not have formal "A" shaped cardboard tent cards, take pieces of white 8-by-10 writing or copier paper, fold the sheets into three equal sections so that they form a triangle, then tape the openings together with adhesive tape or a staple from your trainer's toolkit. Learners can then write their names on two sides and the paper stands up.

Strategy for Success

A simple technique that I have used for years to help remember the names in small groups is to create a seating arrangement chart (see Figure 5.1) that I keep on my instructor's table next to my lesson plan and other materials. I put each learner's name on it based on his or her location in the room and refer to the sheet throughout the workshop. By using names, I personalize my information delivery and continually refocus attention when I call on or refer to someone.

Figure 5.1. Sample Seating Chart

Mike Johnson	Areatha Sherry	Michelle Dupre	Al Simons

John Smith   Renee Morris

Miguel Peres   Tony Bishop

Sue Spencer   Begum Tolgay

Bob Hyatt   Shavon Ellis

Doug Myers   Cindy Foy

Alicia Howard   Bill Waters

Carol Wilson   Ingrid Johanson

Aimee Jones   Darrell King

Involve Learners Immediately and Regularly. By getting learners actively engaged in the learning process early in the workshop and doing so periodically after that, you set up an expectation that you will not be the only person talking throughout the event. It also encourages the sharing of ideas, information, and solutions from everyone in the room. This creates a more fruitful learning event in which you and your learners gain from one another. Use activities, questions, and other techniques that you have read about so far to accomplish this goal of engagement.

To help ensure that you are making your workshop interactive and that you are adequately focusing on the needs of a diverse group of learners ask yourself the following questions:

◆ Did you identify learner preferences (modalities) for each group of participants?

◆ Is your learning environment stimulating to a variety of learning modalities?

◆ Do you continually mix up your delivery techniques to address auditory, visual, and kinesthetic learners?

◆ Are you providing something for as many of the different intelligences as possible?

◆ Are you incorporating a variety of interactive, learner-centric activities and delivery methodologies in your workshop?

◆ Are you engaging learners regularly throughout your learning events?

◆ Are you challenging learners to think about what they learn and how they can immediately apply the information in the real world?

◆ Do you provide opportunities for learners to work together, share ideas, and practice skills learned and then receive feedback on their performance?

◆ Do you provide professionally designed handouts, job aids, and other takeaway materials for use as reference materials by learners?

Tell Stories or Anecdotes. Most learners love instructors who share meaningful ideas, tips, information, and humorous stories in a casual, conversational manner, rather than standing behind a lectern and reading from prepared notes or projected slides. Make your delivery style personal and friendly. Strive to deliver information as if you are having a conversation with a friend; just do not forget to tie the story to a session topic.

You can prompt yourself to share a specific tale of something that you have experienced by putting a note in your lesson plan that reminds you to tell the story. Write it out in enough detail that someone else using your lesson plan can also use the story or anecdote or can substitute a similar of one of their own.

Show a Sense of Humor. When people are having fun, they typically focus better and enjoy themselves more. Additionally, time passes more quickly and does not drag along as it does during pure lectures or other instructor-dominated formats. To tap the humor factor, use jokes, humorous stories, and other forms of frivolity to captivate your learners and reinforce key points. Just ensure that you use humor in a non-offensive manner and that whatever you choose relates to content and does not waste time while it entertains.

Strategy for Success

While it is true that not everyone is funny or able to tell jokes effectively, you can still introduce humor into your workshops. You can do this by using clip art or caricatures of yourself on posters, slides, and handouts. You can also save jokes and cartoons related to your session content and use them where appropriate.

Many commercial companies create humorous business movies that tie to many workplace topics. For example, there are Muppet Meeting Openers clips that can be used as session openers, closers, energizers, or to introduce a topic for discussion in a humorous manner. Additionally, you can use many clips from well-known movies to inject a bit of humor into a workshop and make or reinforce a key point at the same time. Examples of this approach include the use of a classic clip by Abbott and Costello called "Who's on First" in a session on interpersonal communication, customer service, or team building. The clip shows how two people can be having a conversation about the same topic yet entirely focused on different outcomes. Another humorous episode can be found in the first *Rush Hour* movie with Chris Rock and Jackie Chan. In that segment, Rock (a New York police detective) assumes that Chan (a Chinese detective) does not speak English when they first meet. As the movie progresses, this assumption leads to some hilarious dialog and the revelation that Chan speaks English well, but that Rock had simply assumed and not asked. This is also a great clip for interpersonal communication, team building, customer service, and similar workshops.

As with all copyrighted material, get written permission to incorporate movie clips into your program.

Exhibit Enthusiasm. It is hard to expect that your learners will become excited about your session content and format if you are not. Smile, have fun, and make your content delivery interesting for you and your learners. By periodically adding new approaches, activities, props, music, and other stimulating items to your workshop format, you can update content and help enhance your own desire to deliver the workshop. This is important for helping to keep you from getting "stale" or lackadaisical if you deliver the same material regularly.

One important thing that some trainers and educators forget is that their job is to deliver the most effective, stimulating learning event possible. If you do not enjoy being a trainer or do not like your topic, let someone else conduct the training. Anything less is unfair to you and your learners and will ultimately damage your reputation and limit your future professional opportunities.

Strategy for Success

One simple way to maintain your enthusiasm for session content that you deliver frequently is to substitute the activities that you use.

Many trainers use the same boring activity all the time when doing a repetitive training session. For example, as an icebreaker, they have learners turn to the person to their right or left, introduce themselves, get to know one another, then share three new things that they learned about their "new friend" to the rest of the group. This activity can help people relax and allow them to get to know a bit about each other; however, it has been around for about a gazillion years and many people have experienced it in training sessions before. There are thousands of alternative activities that can do the same thing. Look on the Internet or in books to find other activities if you do not have alternates.

By having a variety of strategies and activities from which you can pull, you can use a different one each time you present a session. This causes you have to stop and think as well as rehearse. The mental challenge this creates can help stimulate your brain, make you think, and keep the session fresh for you. If you are enjoying the session yourself; chances are learners will be also.

Mix Up Your Techniques. Experience and technology have conditioned the average human brain today. The result is often lost focus during training. For that reason, you will have to be prepared to change the pace of events regularly.

Think about how fast scenes change on television shows and in movies. How often do commercials run and for how long? These events have helped train humans to expect quick change on a regular basis. As a result, normally after about fifteen minutes or so, you need to switch to a different delivery format in your session. For example, if you were lecturing, break learners into a small group for an activity after about fifteen or twenty minutes. Following that, do quick, fun physical activities such as brain gym or a content review, then go back to an instructor-led discussion. Repeat this pattern throughout the workshop, using different techniques.

Encourage Friendly Competition. One way to spark interest among learners is to provide a bit of fun through lighthearted competition. Make such activities a festive and fun event. You can even create a theme around your competition by using party decorations and music similar to the Jeopardy theme or the music CD *Game Show Themes for Trainers* (see Creative Presentation Resources in the Resources section).

Competition can be accomplished by providing puzzles, questionnaires, or other tasks that learners must complete within a given timeframe or under specific guidelines. The first person or group that knows the correct responses or accomplishes the assignment might be rewarded with candy, small toys, or prizes related to the session topic. For example, in a workshop on time management, you might give small bendable toys in the shape of monkeys and tie that to the concept of "keeping the monkey off your back" through good time usage. In a session on non-verbal communication, you could give smile-face toys or incentives such as squeezable foam balls, stickers, key chains, or other such items. Such competition reminds people of games they played as children. Group or team activities serve to encourage completion of the task because most people feel peer pressure to participate and contribute in order to help their teammates win.

Since there should never be any losers in a learning environment, always ensure that you provide a "major" or bigger perceived value prize to the winner or winning team and then give smaller tokens to all other learners. Everyone should receive a round of applause for contributions and efforts.

Strategy for Success

To encourage learners to return from breaks and lunch on time, tell them before they leave that there will be a puzzle, quiz, or whatever you are using on their chair when they return. The first person to complete it will win a prize. This often encourages people to arrive back early to work on the activity.

A variation of this technique is to assign teams before learners leave for break and announce that the first team completing the activity correctly wins a prize. This encourages peer pressure since some team members will monitor time and push others back to the room on time.

Select the Best Training Methods to Aid Learning

Many factors determine what techniques you should use in order to get your key concepts across to learners and maximize their learning. The options for activities and training techniques are overwhelming for many trainers and educators. New strategies are being developed on a regular basis. The key is to create a learning event that will be effective, efficient, and deliver the highest degree of learning and assimilation. Like any other aspect of training, you want to use a solid combination of proven strategies without trying to do too much. Remember that it is not about the "show" but rather about how well learners master the intended KSAs and their immediate ability to apply what they learn. Some questions to stimulate your think ing when choosing assessment methods are listed below.

+ Does the method reinforce the session KSAs?

+ What learning objective(s) does the strategy or technique support?

+ What key concepts are learned through the method?

+ Does this activity address all three learning modalities?

+ Do learners possess enough knowledge or ability to participate effectively in the activity?

+ What are the time requirements?

+ What is the available budget to buy equipment, props, materials, or other needed items for the activity?

+ What are the equipment and facility requirements?

+ Does the trainer possess the experience and expertise to conduct the activity?

+ Will the activity potentially cause any type confusion or embarrassment for learners?

+ Does the activity fit with the rest of the session in terms of time required and format?

Strategies to Engage Learners

When designing the workshop, one of your goals is to get everyone involved at various points throughout the learning event and keep them engaged. By encouraging each learner to become an active participant, you enhance everyone's opportunity to maximize learning and leave the event with new KSAs. Engagement also aids other learners because they gain from the knowledge, ideas, and insights of their peers. Through engagement, you ultimately make your own job as facilitator easier because the number of learner "ah ha" moments when someone recognizes a key point or ties in to something they already know increases.

Time-Proven Active Techniques

There are many ways that you can encourage your learners to become active participants in the learning process. The following are some time-tested means.

Brain Gym. Through a series of movement activities, you can help relax learners and aid their learning and retention while introducing a bit of fun and novelty into your workshop. Dr. Paul Dennison developed the concept of Brain Gym® in the late 1980s as part of an effort to determine how movements affect the ability of the brain to learn various academic skills. One focus of a Brain Gym is that it promotes the ability to learn and retain information at a whole-brain level. When learners are relaxed, they more easily access their sensory systems for seeing and listening and are more comfortable expressing their feelings. You can find more information on this technique at www.braingym.com.

Brainstorming. Since learners typically bring knowledge and many experiences with them, they have a plethora of ideas and information that can aid others and enhance the learning experience for all. Make sure that you include opportunities for a small group activity in which learners identify issues related to the workshop topic and discuss possible solutions that they can carry back to their workplace following the session. This adds real value to the learning experience and allows learners and their sponsors or supervisors to feel that the time and money invested in attending was well worth it.

Strategy for Success

The goal of a brainstorming session is to generate as many ideas as possible, no matter how outrageous, within a specified period.

Before starting a session, develop or have learners develop a set of guidelines for the brainstorming activity. These "rules" will often help keep the activity moving along and will encourage productive generation of ideas. Some typical guidelines include:

No criticism of ideas allowed.

Quantity, not quality, is encouraged.

Anything goes; all ideas are valid.

"Piggy-backing" of ideas is fine.

No discussion of ideas during brainstorming.

Everyone participates.

No observers.

One person speaks at a time.

Use inclusive language (consider diversity).

Following the brainstorming, learners can discuss, group, modify, combine, or do whatever is appropriate with the list generated during their session.

Case Studies. Learners and their supervisors or sponsors really appreciate efficient use of training time and programs that result in practical ideas for immediate implementation. To ensure that you provide such experiences, have learners work to identify issues and possible solutions to real-world workplace issues through case studies. These are powerful vehicles for learning and can allow learners to apply what they learn in your workshop in the workplace immediately. These activities usually are based on a real workplace issue and are often used in sessions related to topics like problem solving or decision making with supervisory through executive staff members.

Depending on available time, you can often spread the lessons learned over a longer period by giving learners a small portion of the case study at a time. For example, following a lecture on a key workshop concept, you might give background information about the case and a key element of the issue or problem for learners to discuss in small groups. Have groups also discuss possible causes or solutions. Following their discussion, debrief that portion of the study to ask for their input or recommended solutions. Next, provide another key concept of the workshop and pass out an additional information sheet that adds a bit more depth to the case study situation or adds a new twist to what they read earlier, for example, something they were not aware of that is having an impact on the case. Continue this approach throughout the workshop until you disclose the entire case and possible solutions are determined.

A case study allows learners to think about similar issues that they are experiencing in their own workplace, obtain input from others, and come up with potential solutions that they can go back to apply right away.

Demonstrations. Demonstrations are good for attracting learner attention and showing the correct steps of a process or reinforcing what you have told them. The technique can engage multiple learner senses and can help ensure learning and understanding while emphasizing important points or concepts. Demonstrations sometimes involve analogies, and you typically conduct them. In some instances, learners may assist with your demonstration. As you will read later, demonstrations are key elements in the behavior modeling process.

Strategy for Success

When conducting a demonstration, it is important for you to remember that, although you have a lot of knowledge about your subject, your learners may not. Do not assume anything when demonstrating a product, process, or technique. Take your time, use a logical progression, and show each step. Periodically pause and get learner feedback or ask for questions to ensure that they are following what you are saying. Also avoid language such as, "This is easy," "Anybody can do this," or "You should not have any trouble with . . . " Such language stifles questions out of fear of looking stupid when learners do not understand. In addition, when learners cannot grasp a point, they lose confidence by thinking there must be something wrong with them if others find the process easy.

Artwork or Drawing. You can create an activity around art in a variety of ways. This gets learners engaged and thinking about a workshop related topic or theme. It also ties to Gardner's visual/spatial intelligence and brain-based research that has found that art aids in various mental processing areas and supports the need of a portion of your learners to have material presented visually.

Some ideas for including art are

♦ Forming teams and having learners create a team logo or crest.

♦ Creating an image that ties major concepts or ideas identified in the session or in a small group activity together.

♦ Drawing an image of how they envision an ideal implementation of some concept that they learned.

♦ Putting together an image of how they see themselves using information, skills, or ideas identified in the workshop.

Dyads or Triads. A small group setting is ideal when you have learners who might be reluctant to participate in front of larger numbers of people. You can also use this approach as a way to facilitate networking and to help learners get to know others in the room. To accomplish the latter, have learners find different partners for each dyad (two people) or triad (three people) activity throughout the workshop.

Training topics such as interpersonal communication, customer service, team building, and behavioral styles are just some that lend themselves to the use of dyad (pairs) and triad (three learners) activities. During such events, learners can work with others to identify issues or solutions to problems, discuss an assigned topic, or practice a skill. An example is sending, receiving, and interpreting non-verbal feedback with a partner or within a group.

You can also use dyads and triads to share personal experiences, to present thoughts about something covered in the workshop, or to generate strategies for completion of an assigned task.

Games. Games are terrific tools for sharing and reinforcing key concepts in your workshop. They also tie directly to brain research from the standpoint of injecting novelty, fun, movement, and repetition into the learning environment. Games can provide a valuable vehicle for helping learners recall and apply what they have learned. For example, you could use a variation of the game Monopoly in a workshop on life skills to reinforce areas such as the use of resource management related to money and property, problem solving, financial management, decision making, and strategic planning.

Most people learn to enjoy games at a very young age and often have fond memories related to playing them with friends and family members throughout their lives. Many adults regularly play cards, board games, or sports. You can tap into this love of gaming in your training programs with a little effort and creative thinking. There are numerous commercial games that can be adapted to various workplace topics and issues in order to teach cash handling, resource management, communication skills, teamwork, strategic thinking, problem solving and decision making, and other life skills. Some of these games include Clue, Monopoly, Risk, Payday, Pick-Up Sticks, and Life. You can modify a game by creating your own game cards and adapting the rules and game boards in order to teach or reinforce specific topics in your workshop. You can also buy component game parts and design your own games. Many sources of information exist on how to accomplish this (see The Thiagi Group in the Resources section or conduct an Internet search for Training Games).

Like any other aspect of your workshop, you should choose games based on their ability to reinforce learning objectives and not just because learners enjoy them. Some guidelines are presented below to help guide you about incorporating games into your session.

Guidelines for Choosing Games

♦ Make sure that the game selected or created ties directly to your session learning objectives in order to maximize learning outcomes. You do not want learners and their supervisors to perceive the game to be a waste of time in the interest of simply having fun.

♦ Ensure that you are thoroughly familiar with the game and rules.

♦ Decide how you will connect various elements of the game to session content and objectives.

♦ Determine needed facilities, equipment, and materials for the game and have them prepared in advance.

♦ Select a game that involves all learners, rather than having observers who might become bored, hold side conversations, or get involved in other tasks such as text messaging or reading work-related materials. Such activity could distract them and other learners, thus decreasing the effectiveness of the game.

♦ Test the game and its rules before using it in the classroom. Failure to do so could lead to your embarrassment, learner confusion, and wasted time. By playing the game with others beforehand, you can spot and correct potential problem areas. As you would with every other aspect of training—practice, practice, practice!

Journal Writing. A number of brain research studies have found that memories are strengthened through emotional connections to an event (e.g., time, environmental factors like music, odors and color, and reinforcing activities or reviews). To tap into this connection, periodically have learners write their feelings, reactions, or thoughts about what they just experienced in a journal. For example, following a role play or small group team-building activity, have them document how they felt about the process and what they learned and how they will apply the learning in their own environment(s).

Nominal Group Process Activity. The purpose of the nominal group process is to generate ideas individually without undue influence from others, present the ideas, then discuss and vote on them as a group.

This type of activity is very useful for generating and rating ideas in the order of what learners perceive as important or more critical. You must ensure that you state the question or problem clearly and succinctly to achieve meaningful results.

To conduct a nominal group activity:

♦ Prepare two flip-chart pages, one with the Principles of Nominal Group Technique (see the list below) and one with a workshop topic questions, issue, or problem to be discussed written out.

♦ Assemble learners into groups of eight to ten.

♦ Show the pre-drawn flip-chart page with a question, issue, or problem written on it.

♦ Have learners silently and individually think of as many solutions or answers as possible and write these on a piece of paper.

♦ After five to ten minutes, stop them.

♦ Go around the room and elicit one idea at a time from each person as you write them on the flip chart.

♦ Repeat this process until you have written all learner ideas on the flip chart.

- Post completed flip-chart sheets with learner input on the wall.

- Discuss each idea to ensure that everyone understands them.

- Next, have each person go to the lists and write a "1" by his or her first choice of a solution or idea, "2" by the next preferred choice, and so on through "5." Note: As an alternative, you can also give each person five different colored dot stickers and assign a value to each color. For example, yellow is their first choice, blue is their second, and so forth.

- Once everyone has voted, write the items that received the most number 1 choices on another piece of flip-chart paper.

- Have further discussion on the value and drawbacks of each of the top five choices.

- At the end of discussion, again have learners vote, except this time choose only two or three items, depending on the time available.

- Rewrite the top choice from this second round on a new flip chart.

- Discuss how to implement the idea, additional concerns, advantages, disadvantages, or whatever is appropriate, based on the topic of your workshop and desired learning outcome(s).

- Capture ideas and comments on a flip-chart page for use later or to forward copies to learners or members of management, as appropriate. An alternative is to have a learner volunteer to capture all the notes and give it to you following the activity.

Principles of the Nominal Group Technique

♦ Individual ideas become those of the group.

♦ Helps avoid superficial discussion or rushing to a decision.

♦ Encourages channeling of ideas.

♦ Helps focus decision making.

♦ Reduces redundancy of ideas or discussion.

♦ Allows all ideas to surface.

♦ Each person has a vote in the final decision.

♦ Group ownership of final idea(s) increases because everyone was involved.

Practical Application or Experiential Learning. Have learners actually perform a task or put knowledge and skills to immediate use. This practice can reinforce what they learned and allows you to provide immediate feedback using a behavioral modeling approach. The steps of this process are presented below.

Steps in Behavioral Modeling

1. **Explain** what the learner is to perform.

2. **Demonstrate** how to perform the task.

3. **Elicit** questions that learners have about what they saw and then provide answers to their questions.

4. **Have learners perform** the task as you demonstrated it for them.

5. **Elicit feedback** on learner performance by asking:

- What do you think you did well in completing the task?

- What do you think you need to improve upon?

- What would you do differently in the future in performing the task?

6. **Provide positive feedback** on learner performance in the following manner:

   - Explain what you saw the person do well. Even if he or she only did the task partially right, praise that portion of the behavior so that the person feels good about what he or she accomplished and do not lose self-confidence.

   - Explain what you saw that needs improvement.

7. **Elicit questions** that learners still have about the process or the feedback received.

8. **Repeat Steps 1 through 7** for any portion of the task that still needs to be improved.

Puzzles. Most learners have an emotional attachment to puzzles because they remember doing word search, crossword, hangman, picture and other types when they were children. You can tap into these memories and childhood fun by creating custom puzzles (see Creative Presentation Resources in the Resources section for software or search the Internet) that contain clues and words related to any session content. You can use your puzzles as interim and final review or energizer activities throughout your workshop in order to reinforce key words or concepts and to add a bit of fun and novelty into the program.

Question-and-Answer (Q&A). You should build in opportunities for instructor-led questioning throughout your workshop. Q&A is a quick means to engage learners, gauge their understanding of content that you delivered, and reinforce learning of key concepts through repetition. This occurs because during Q&A they hear, think about, and repeat what they have learned.

You can also use a reverse Q&A process in which learners work in small groups to generate questions they have related to session content, its application, or how to overcome obstacles when attempting to implement what is learned. These questions can be read to the entire group and anyone (including the instructor) can provide input or answer.

Role Play. A popular technique used for decades by trainers and educators is role play. In a role play, learners assume fictional roles and portray what they believe someone in that role in real life would do. Such activities can either be highly effective or a waste of time, depending on how they are conducted. To ensure that you get maximum benefit from role plays that you might use, consider the following process.

Form dyads or triads and assign roles for each learner. For example, you might have two people assuming opposite roles such as a salesperson and a customer, a supervisor and an employee, or teacher and a student or parent. In some instances, you may want to assign three people to a group so that you have an observer to take notes and provide feedback to the role players. This is sometimes necessary when you have an uneven number of people in a workshop and want to ensure engagement by everyone. An alternative to using an extra learner as an observer is to pair the additional learner with an instructor. Of course, in doing so, you limit the instructor's ability to walk around and monitor role plays in action. Try to avoid using the trainer as a role player if possible, since giving feedback is important during role plays. During the activity, the trainer(s) can listen in, interject comments, or refocus dyads who get off task or are unsure of their roles.

To make sure that your role plays are successful, spend time beforehand going over instructions, desired outcomes, and defining roles. Stress time limits and the do's and don'ts for players. Also answer any questions that learners have.

Strategy for Success

Once the role play begins, walk around and listen in to ensure that players are using their time effectively and accurately portraying their roles. When you hear a lot of laughing and the noise level in the room goes up, players are typically finished or off task.

Following the role play, debrief the event to ensure that learning occurred and the appropriate perceptions surfaced. Ask questions of each player in the following order:

1. The primary player.

2. The role player's partner.

3. Observer(s).

Ask the following questions of each person.

What did you do well? or What did the primary role player do well?

What did you not do well? or What did the primary role player not do so well?

What would you do differently next time or if you find yourself in a similar workplace situation? or What could the primary role player do differently next time in a similar situation?

Following comments by all learners, provide any feedback or comments that you have about what you saw, or the situation in general.

Storytelling. Have learners work individually or in small groups to create a story using the concepts identified in the workshop or something they have learned. Have them base their stories on a classic story format such as a fairy tale (once upon a time), fable (the moral is…) or other familiar tale, but ensure that it relates to topics that they have experienced in the workshop and in the real world.

Visualizations (Visioning). Have learners close their eyes and reflect on something they have learned in your workshop or imagine using the concepts or information that you covered in some environment. To use this technique, play new age or instrumental type music in the background and ask learners to close their eyes. Encourage them to think of an environment in which they are going to use concepts or processes they have learned in the workshop. Ask them a series of questions to prompt their thinking and allow a minute or so for them to think about the question before asking another one. For example, you might ask:

♦ What does the environment in which you will be applying what was learned look like?

♦ What materials or components will you need to implement the concepts or processes learned successfully?

♦ What does the environment feel or sound like?

♦ What obstacles might inhibit successful implementation?

After a few minutes, turn off the music and have them open their eyes and write down what they saw. By doing so, learners reinforce their mental image and again have to review the concepts, process, and its use in their minds. This cross-referencing helps strengthen memory and learners will be more likely to recall and use what they learned.

Worksheets. Provide learners with worksheets that can be used to transfer key ideas or concepts learned into an action plan at any point in the workshop or be used when they return to work or another environment. For example, in a class on effective résumé writing, give learners several worksheets of résumé formats that they can use as guides when creating their own employment résumé (see Exhibit 5.1. Sample Chronological Résumé Worksheet).

Exhibit 5.1. Sample Chronological Résumé Worksheet

First and Last Name:

Street Address: City, State, ZIP:

Telephone Number and E-mail Address:

Professional Summary and Objective

This section contains your "sales pitch" to potential employers and outlines the type of position that you desire. It also helps them determine whether you are a fit with their job needs.

Use three to five grammatically strong sentences to tout your capabilities and any unique experience. Emphasize results and focus on both hard (computer, equipment operation, or writing ability) or soft (customer service, sales, or negotiation) skills. Make sure that you relate your skills and experience to the position for which you are seeking.

Experience

Most Recent Job Title, Organization, City and State: _____

_____

(Month, Year to Month, Year): _____

Provide a brief overview of your responsibilities. If the organization is not well-known, also include a brief description of it and the industry under which it falls.

♦ Do not lose your focus on the fact that the purpose of a résumé is to get an interview. Do not attempt to tell everything you have accomplished.

♦ List your job experience from newest to oldest position and follow the same bulleted format for each.

Previous Job Title, Organization, City and State: _____

_____

(Month, Year to Month, Year): _____

♦ Use short and succinct summaries, using clear and concise descriptions.

♦ Use bullet points to summarize your most outstanding accomplishments, using quantifiable data (percentages, sales, savings, budget managed).

♦ Stress leadership roles and focus on results that you achieved, not just your job responsibilities.

Previous Job Title, Organization, City and State: _____

_____

(Month, Year to Month, Year): _____

♦ Older positions require smaller amounts of information,

♦ List older positions primarily to show workplace history.

♦ Explain gaps in employment in the interview.

(continued)

Exhibit 5.1. (*Continued*)

Education/Credentials

Start with your highest level of accomplishment (degree or certification) and work down. Show degree (JD, MBA, BS, AS), along with the university or college name.

♦ Graduation date is optional but often included if the degree is recent.

♦ GPA is not necessary; however, if above 3.5 or honors (magna cum laude or Dean's List, you may want to include it.

♦ List any leadership roles or special recognitions received from the university/college if you have limited workplace experience to show initiative, involvement, and accomplishment.

Skills/Qualifications

♦ This section is optional, but you can use it to show specialized skills related to the job for which you are applying.

♦ Highlight anything that makes you stand out from other applicants (software development capability, instructor status, journeyman certification).

Memberships/Affiliations

♦ Use this section to demonstrate involvement in professional organizations or volunteer efforts.

♦ Stress leadership roles (committee chairperson, president, volunteer coordinator, conference director) to highlight accomplishments.

♦ Recent graduates can use this section to show that they are striving establish themselves quickly in their profession.

Personalizing What You Have Learned

- What are the most important things that you read in this chapter? Why?

- What are some ways that you can immediately apply concepts covered in this chapter?

- What additional resources or topics do you want to research based on what you read?

PART

Getting Ready to Train

Looking Like a Consummate Training Professional

After reading this chapter, and when applying what you learn, you will be able to:

1. Prepare yourself and learners for a positive learning event.

2. Project a more professional personal appearance to learners.

3. Apply training, presentation, and facilitation skills that create positive learning outcomes.

"The best thing you can do is get good at being you."
Dennis the Menace

Preparing for a Positive Outcome

Preparation is the key to success in virtually everything you do. Training is no different. If you fail to prepare; your program is likely doomed to failure. It does not matter how smart you are or how much you know about a topic, if you do not take the time to design an effective interactive program based on actual learner needs, your efforts are wasted.

Many subject-matter experts who thought they knew their material well have tried to "wing it" or speak extemporaneously in a classroom. What they failed to realize is that being an expert on a topic and being able to train others on that topic involve different skill sets. Without a sound knowledge of adult learning, skill at presenting information in a group or a one-on-one setting, the use of established learning objectives and a lesson plan, and preparation and use of professional support materials, their messages lost their impact. Within minutes of opening their mouths, their audiences knew the horrible truth—the trainer had not taken the time to prepare adequately. Such an approach reflects poorly on the facilitator and negatively impacts learners and their organization.

From the time that you open your mouth during the introduction until the time you end the workshop, learners will go though a typical attention curve (see Figure 6.1) unless you effectively communicate and engage them. At the beginning, attendees will often be

Figure 6.1. Learner Attention Curve

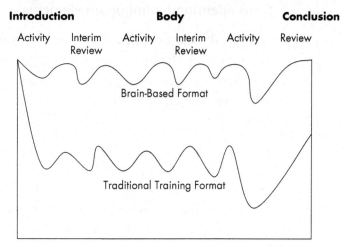

excited about learning. There will then be high and low points in their attention spans throughout the remainder of the program. During these periods, they will likely drift in and out of attention and think of other things. They will mentally check back in during activities and reviews, and periodically throughout the session, to see whether there is anything of interest before drifting away again. Toward the end of the workshop, they will start to focus more in hope of catching some key concepts and hearing a solid review of important information that they might have missed.

How do you prevent as many lapses in learner attention as possible when creating and delivering your own workshops? Quite simply—prior planning. By designing and delivering workshops that address the various modalities and the needs of your learners and regularly engaging them, you can increase their interest, participation, and level of learning. As part of your design, build in ample activities and interim reviews to draw attention back to the session content and to help focus attention on important elements.

To be truly successful as a trainer, you must continually think outside the box related to design, development, and delivery. You must possess a variety of skills and attributes to help you create a memorable learning experience.

Your ultimate success is delivering a dynamic workshop in which learners are excited, participative, and walk away with valuable KSAs. That success will depend to some degree on characteristics that you possess. One of the most important factors is experience as a trainer. Other important characteristics are listed below.

Attributes of a Professional Trainer

♦ Dedication to your profession and topic

♦ Sound knowledge of adult learning principles and how to apply them

♦ Responsible attitude related to ensuring a successful learning outcome

♦ Desire to work with learners

♦ Effective interpersonal communication skills such as listening, non-verbal and verbal communication, and feedback

♦ Ability to draw learners into discussion through thought-provoking questions

♦ Sense of humor

♦ Approachable personality

◆ Presence in front of a group of learners

◆ Creativity and adaptability

◆ Ability to respond quickly to learners and events

Projecting a Professional Image

You obviously play a central role in the success or failure of your workshop. It is up to you to think of everything that is needed, content to be covered, and format to follow. Learners will show up assuming that you have done all this. If you do not accomplish these tasks effectively, you and the workshop will fail and attendees will lose an opportunity to gain important KSAs.

Be Prepared

The easiest way to lose the respect of a group of learners is to appear unprepared. Until you show up and open your mouth, learners likely view you as a professional. When you step in front of the group, you have to show that you are worthy of that respect.

Through proper planning and execution of planned activities, having necessary supplies (see the toolkit list below), equipment, materials, and other essential items, you say non-verbally, "I am ready to help you learn." Do not take anything for granted. Create a detailed plan as described in Chapter 3, practice until you are thoroughly familiar with content, and check and double-check everything before learners arrive. By doing these things, you ensure a more positive learning event for everyone.

Professional trainers and educators have learned from experience to bring along common administrative supplies and training aids in case they need them. Classroom veterans typically carry a "trainer's toolbox" that contains at least the items listed below. You can put your own items in a flat resealable storage container. These keep everything in one handy location and are easy to pack when traveling. Some of the materials often needed are listed below.

Trainer's Toolkit

- Adhesive tape
- Assorted colors of Dry Erase markers (preferably the odorless type)
- Assorted colors of water-based flip-chart markers
- Blank 3-by-5 cards (for activities or notes)
- Blank name tags
- Blank name tents
- Blank writing tablets
- Binder (bulldog) clips
- Noisemakers of various types
- Painters/masking tape
- Paper clips of various sizes
- Pens/pencils
- Push pins or thumbtacks
- Stapler and staples

- ◆ Scissors

- ◆ Rubber bands

- ◆ Ruler

- ◆ Stopwatch

- ◆ Transparent adhesive tape

Dress Professionally

The way that you dress can have an affect on learner's acceptance of you. Deciding what to wear in your workshop can sometimes be difficult. A good strategy is to choose clothing that is equal to or "one step above" the type that you anticipate learners will wear. For example, if attendees are executives who will wear suits or skirt and jacket combinations, you should dress similarly. Keep in mind that a conservative clothing style of good quality and color is normally a good choice, as opposed to selecting items that will be out of place with your group. Just make sure that whatever you wear is clean, well-pressed and maintained, and looks professional.

"Business casual" is common in organizations today, yet that phrase has so many different meanings to people that you may be unsure what it means. If you are presenting to a group within an organization, the simplest way to determine what to wear is to contact the HR or training representative or a sponsor and ask how employees typically come dressed for work. Then take your clothing style to the next level. For example, if you are a man and male employees normally wear business slacks and button-down dress shirts, add a tie and sport coat. You can remove these once you start if it seems appropriate. If you are a woman and female employees normally wear skirts and a nice blouses, you might wear a professional-looking suit or dress and jacket. If employees wear jeans or really informal clothing, you may want to wear a nicely pressed pair of khaki slacks and professional looking shirt/blouse and possibly a light jacket or sport coat, which can be removed. No matter your gender, if you are speaking to a professional conference group, it is best to wear a conservative dark-colored business suit, since you are likely to have all manner of dress represented in the audience. A suit normally portrays an image of success, professionalism, and expertise.

Remember that you can always "dress down" once in class by inviting learners to get comfortable and remove their jackets and ties so that they can relax and focus better. As you make your introductory session remarks, take off your jacket too.

Part of your clothing consideration should be the color of what you wear. For executive-type functions such as senior management strategic planning meetings, go with a more traditional and conservative black or navy blue suit, matched with muted-color conservative accessories. When conducting a workshop to lower-level attendees or in a non-business setting, you can likely get away with more business casual clothing. The key is to fit in with your group. That means recognizing different styles of dress that are appropriate for the session content and geographic area in which you are delivering the training. For example, an expensive suit might not be appropriate for a group of high school students or for teaching a class on computer software. Likewise, cowboy boots would not likely go well at a training event on Wall Street.

Strategy for Success

Consider wearing pastel colors such as light blue, yellow, or pink shirts or blouses instead of white ones for your learning events. A white shirt can make you look too formal or even washed out, especially if you are standing in front of a whiteboard.

Since color attracts attention, people are more likely to focus on you. Pastel colors also have a "softer" impact and make most people look more approachable.

Demonstrate a Positive Attitude and Enthusiasm

You expect and appreciate a positive attitude from your learners, and they should do the same with you. A positive attitude and enthusiasm come from loving what you do and enjoying the topic(s) that you teach. If this is not true about you, then perhaps you should seek another profession. You affect the learning and, in some situations, the lives of your learners. Your failure to come prepared to a workshop or to come with less than a "can do" attitude is unprofessional and deceitful. We all have down days when things do not go the way we would hope or plan. However, when you step in front of a group, your issues are unimportant and should not detract from your mission. Do the best possible job that you can and try to instill a feeling of excitement and anticipation in your learners that lasts throughout the workshop. Do this by using all the tools and strategies that you read about in this chapter and in the rest of the book.

Strategy for Success

Sometimes the little things we do as trainers can send a negative message and taint a learning event. Avoid focusing on negatives when around your learners. For example, statements like the following do nothing to create a positive atmosphere and build learner enthusiasm:

"I asked for an LCD projector for this session, but the sponsor did not want to spend the money."

"We were going to have a really cool video on _____, but the DVD did not show up."

"If we had more time, I could show you several strategies that would really help you on the job."

"I would have included some time-tested tips for improvement in your workbooks, but I did not have time to research them."

Statements such as these say, "I did not care enough to do more or prepare" or "Management does not really support this workshop." Neither says much about your professionalism or the concern that the organization has about employee training. If you cannot do something or you do not have time to build in other material, keep it to yourself. If you never share these things with learners, they will likely never know about it and you will avoid perpetuating negativity.

Be Confident, Not Cocky

In the past, you may have experienced trainers, presenters, educators, or others in a learning environment who demonstrated a powerful "me" attitude. Their sentences often start with "I" and they do a LOT of the talking throughout a learning event. In the end, you know quite a bit about the trainer and what he or she believes, but not as much as you would like about the session topic. The point is that most learners really do not care about you, your accomplishments, your political, religious, and personal views, or your opinions on a variety of non-workshop related topics. What they DO care about is what you know and can share with them related to the session topic. They also want to know how you can help them improve personally and professionally, advance in their professions, and make more money. Stick to the task at hand. Real-world examples are often helpful in clarifying key points and appreciated by learners. Stories about your own experiences and issues that have nothing to do with the topic and waste time are not.

The key difference between a trainer who has confidence and one who is cocky or consumed with him- or herself is that the confident trainer walks the talk and can back it up without doing a lot of self-aggrandizing. The cocky trainer is too focused on him- or herself to care whether learners gain anything from the workshop.

Confident trainers prepare, plan, rehearse, and have plenty of backup material in case of problems. When it comes time to deliver workshop content, the confident trainer will arrive early, feel comfortable about what will follow, greet learners in a personable fashion, and immediately begin to build rapport with them. Throughout the event, this trainer will perform professionally and without arrogance, will listen to and appropriately answer learner questions, and will end the session on a high note and on time.

Admit When You Make a Mistake

Learners do not expect you to be perfect, but they do expect you to be truthful and have integrity. Both of these impact trust, which you will read about in Chapter 8. As a trainer, you are under continual scrutiny in the classroom. Whatever you do and say can affect the ultimate outcome of your workshop. If someone in the room can show that something you present is wrong, based on his or her knowledge or expertise, it can tarnish your effectiveness.

For that reason, if you make a mistake or realize that you are wrong about something, quickly acknowledge it and recover.

Depending on the severity of a mistake, you can sometimes use humor to get past it. For example, if a learner points out a spelling error that you made when writing something on a flip chart, or you realize it yourself, you could light-heartedly say something like, "I'm sorry. It's these cheap markers I am using, they don't have spell-check on them," and then correct the error and move on. When more serious errors occur, such as giving misinformation, apologize, admit that you made an error, correct the information, if possible, and then move on without dwelling on the issue. Your learners are likely to respect you for taking ownership of the error, as long as you do not make an ongoing series of such mistakes. Multiple mistakes can destroy your credibility. You can avoid this problem by doing your "homework," thoroughly research-ing your topic, and preparing in advance to deliver it.

Strategy for Success

Here are two solutions for dealing with spelling errors on handouts and visual aids at the beginning of your session:

Inform learners that they might find a few spelling errors throughout the day since you are human.

Humorously state, "I have planted a few spelling errors throughout the workshop materials so that you will have something to look for during the session. If you find one, I will give you a prize." The latter approach has the dual value of engaging learners and providing rewards for per-formance throughout the day. It also shows that you have a sense of humor and can make you appear more approachable. Just to make sure that learners do find a couple errors, you might intentionally misspell a word or two when writing on the board or flip chart.

Strategy for Success

You can creatively combine your stopwatch and noisemaker needs into one item to save space in your Trainer Toolkit by using a TAG *Attention Getter*. This is a stopwatch that also has three recorded sounds—a Tarzan yell, racing trumpets, and crowing rooster (see Creative Presentation Resources in the Resources section). You can also record a short fourth sound of your choice.

Training, Presentation, and Facilitation Skills

Trainers use a variety of skills to share knowledge and ideas with learners. They often apply skills used by other professionals to get their message across. While the people who fulfill the roles of trainers, presenters, and facilitators typically share common characteristics, each has a slightly different focus and purpose.

Trainers are often subject-matter experts who have expertise in educating and training adults and are effective in delivering workshops on various workplace topics. They understand the importance of the ADDIE model and have studied many areas of human development and workplace issues like behavioral and management styles, interpersonal communication, motivation, diversity, and teamwork. They also incorporate much of this knowledge into their program designs. They are familiar with the use of various types of learning technology and how to create an environment in which learners are comfortable and can best gain from their learning experience. All of these are just some of the knowledge and skills areas that you must master to be ready to create and deliver your own effective training workshop.

Professional trainers also read books and articles about their profession and workplace topics, they explore information on the Internet, and they network and hone their knowledge and skills through attendance at meetings and conferences sponsored by professional organizations. They also demonstrate their knowledge by gaining professional recognition and certifications such as Certified Professional in Learning and Performance (CPLP) through ASTD, Certified Toastmaster (CTM) through Toastmasters International, and Certified Speaking Professional (CSP) through the National Speakers Association (NSA).

Some excellent resource organizations include The American Society for Training and Development (ASTD), International Alliance for Learning (IAL), International Society for Performance and Instruction (ISPI), National Speakers Association (NSA), and Toastmasters International (see contact information in the Resources section under Websites).

Presenters generally prepare and deliver a finite bit of information to a targeted audience and then move on to another audience where they present virtually the exact same speech to a different audience. Their purpose is often to inspire, inform, motivate, or cause people to reflect on a topic. In doing so, they sometimes use audiovisual aids and occasionally engage members of their audience in question-and-answer sessions. The best of this group often attain the CTM and CSP designations.

Facilitators focus on objectively helping groups of people plan, work through issues, identify and solve problems, come to consensus on an issue, and understand their common goals and objectives. In doing so they use many of the skills demonstrated by trainers and presenters, such as questioning, use of audiovisual aids, and leading discussions. They often network through the same groups mentioned earlier and attain the Certified Professional Facilitator (CPF) designation through the International Association of Facilitators (IAF).

The challenge for successful trainers is to be aware of and master the skills of all three of these professions, along with those common to educators.

Communication Skills

Two of the most powerful tools that you have at your disposal are your voice and body. The way that you speak and communicate non-verbally with your learners can determine the level of success that you achieve in transferring knowledge and teaching skills. If you have poor speaking and non-verbal skills and use ineffective strategies in communicating ideas to others, you are likely to have dissatisfied learners and receive negative session evaluation feedback. You will also likely lose management support and registrations for future sessions. To avoid all of these potential pitfalls, make sure that you take the time to prepare yourself to give the best possible workshop or presentation possible.

One important point is that your messages should always be congruent. This means that your verbal and non-verbal messages should match. For example, if you said, "I'd like you to remember four things . . . " while holding up three fingers, confusion is likely to result and learners might be distracted. Research shows that when verbal and non-verbal cues are used together, the non-verbal normally overshadows the verbal message because more people are visual rather than auditory or kinesthetic learners.

Another thing to remember is that certain words have the power to draw learners to you. Identify and use such language regularly throughout your workshop. When working with learners, use language that reinforces and encourages learners and that helps build trust. The following are some words and phrases that can aid relationship building in your workshop(s).

Words That Strengthen Relationships with Learners

Please	You are right.
Thank you.	May I . . .?
I can/will. . . .	Have you considered . . .?
I'm sorry	I apologize for. . . .
I was wrong/incorrect.	I understand/appreciate your perspective.
Would you mind if . . .?	What do you think?

The following are some other strategies for strengthening your relationships with learners and making your learning events stand out in the mind of attendees.

Polish Your Speaking Skills

Successful trainers can do many things to make themselves memorable. In addition to being subject-matter experts, they also put forth the effort to refine their ability to convey messages verbally in a way that holds interest and in some cases spellbinds listeners. Trainers often attend professional development programs that teach effective interpersonal communication skills and allow them the opportunity to give practice presentations and receive feedback on their performance from their peers and instructors. They then fine-tune their delivery skills to a point at which they have the ability to share concepts and ideas while drawing learners into the learning process.

Another simple practice to hone your communication skills is to listen to and watch other professionals who have reached the pinnacle of success in communicating to groups. Some inspirational speakers include Zig Ziglar, President John F. Kennedy, Dr. Martin Luther King, Jr., Robert F. Kennedy, Prime Minister Margaret Thatcher, First Lady Laura Bush, President Barack Obama, President Bill Clinton, and Tony Alessandra. The speaking style of each of these people is distinctive. For example, President Kennedy spoke at an average of 180 words per minute, while Dr. King's "I Have a Dream" speech started at around 90 words per minute and ended at around 150. To help you regulate your rate, think about how fast you are speaking and consciously speed up or slow down for dramatic effect. Additionally, use pauses occasionally after statements and questions. This allows you and your learners to think and gives you time for a deep breath. Also couple your verbal message with distinctive non-verbal cues, facial expressions, and gestures. This means that your message is congruent and that you delivery formats complement one another.

You can also watch nationally known news broadcasters to see how they communicate. Pay close attention to their articulation or pronunciation of words, use of verbal pauses, semantics (word usage), and avoidance of verbal fillers such as uh, you know, and ummm. Monitor how they are often able to use small nuances such as eye contact, body position, gestures, and movement to supplement their verbal messages. Listen to the manner in which they punctuate key words or ideas with a raised voice or change in inflection or tone. All of these tools are powerful in getting people to understand and react to what you say. Such techniques can be summed up in the old adage, "It is not what you say, but how you say it that matters."

Be conscious of the way your voice sounds when you are in front of a group of learners. Many trainers fail to generate enthusiasm because they sound like they are not excited or committed to what they are saying. If this happens, your learners may quickly become bored and lose focus during your workshop.

A number of aspects of the voice can influence how well you come across to learners. By recording yourself as you present to a group, you can often spot some potential problem areas. Consider the following:

The average rate of speech for most adults in the United States is about 125 to 150 words per minute. People from larger metropolitan cities and urban areas often speak a bit faster than those from small, more rural areas. This can be attributed to the difference in the pace of life in each area. Your challenge is to speak fast enough to be interesting, but slow enough to be understood.

Control the volume of your voice to add maximum value and attract learner attention. By periodically raising and lowering your volume you can attract and hold the interest of your learners. In fact, the loudest message that you can send with your voice is silence. If you have learners who become distracted or if you want to regain attention, simply stop talking and stand still. Eventually, learners will realize that you have become quiet and will look toward you to see what is going on. You can them resume your presentation.

Monitor the inflection in your voice as you speak, since people can be attracted or turned off by the way your voice sounds. By changing the inflection on certain words, you can add vocal emphasis to your message. For example, when you are excited or happy about something, your voice pitch is typically higher than normal. In the same way, when you ask a question, your inflection often goes up and that puts a vocal question mark at the end of the sentence.

To help improve your delivery style, take a look at the common verbal distracters used by many trainers when they deliver information to learners and work toward eliminating any similar habits that you have when speaking. As you strive for improvement in your verbal delivery skills, think about habits or distracting things that you have seen others use and work to avoid such communication gaffs yourself. See the list of common communication mistakes below.

Strategy for Success

Practice changing your inflection by saying the following statements, emphasizing only the italicized word in each one. Record your voice as you speak and notice the difference in inflection. Note how it can change your message meaning simply by emphasizing a single word in a sentence.

I cannot believe you did that.

I *cannot* believe you did that.

I cannot *believe* you did that.

I cannot believe *you* did that.

I cannot believe you *did* that.

I cannot believe you did *that*.

Verbal Communication Breakdowns

♦ Repeatedly using distracting verbal fillers such "um," "uh," "like," "uh," or "you know."

♦ Speaking in a monotone that lacks enthusiasm or energy and excitement. You have to show conviction and sound like you care about what you are saying. If you do not, why should your learners?

♦ Talking too quickly or too slowly.

♦ Speaking to loudly or softly. Either way, you can cause learners to miss information, become distracted, or tune out.

♦ Using terminology, jargon, and language that learners do not understand. Keep it simple! Learners do not know everything that you know in most cases. Acronyms like NAFTA (North American Free Trade Agreement) and contractions such as I'd or you'll can cause confusion, especially to speakers of English as a second language. If you are going to introduce an acronym or technical term, write it so that everyone can see the spelling, then define it before moving on.

♦ Failing to enunciate words. If you do not clearly pronounce each word, you can distract learners or cause communication breakdowns. Slurred words such as "wouldja," "didja," or "hafta" can all cause difficulty in comprehension. This can be a real problem if you have learners with hearing impairments or who normally speak another language.

♦ Use Exhibit 6.1 to rate yourself on communication basics.

Exhibit 6.1. Communication Self-Assessment

Periodically make an audio or video recording of your training sessions. Listen to or watch the performance and rate yourself objectively on the following areas:

	Low				*High*
Overall presentation	1	2	3	4	5
Volume level	1	2	3	4	5
Rate of speech	1	2	3	4	5
Diction (word clarity)	1	2	3	4	5
Fillers used	1	2	3	4	5

Suggestions for improvement: _____

_____

Practice Non-Verbal Communication Skills

An easy way to determine how you come across is to use a video camera and tape yourself and then review your performance, making note of areas for improvement. One thing to look for is any gesture(s) that you use frequently. To identify these, play the tape on fast forward without words and just watch. You will quickly see repetitive gestures that you need to address.

Another way to improve your non-verbal communication is to pay attention to how professional trainers and speakers dress and their clothing and accoutrements such as jewelry and accessories, body posture, facial gestures, hand movements, and facial expressions as they speak. This will give some indication of the way you should dress when in front of an audience. In particular, pay attention to how they use gestures to gain and hold attention or to emphasize key verbal messages.

Some presenters gesture a lot. Less-experienced trainers often do not have the confidence to gesture effectively. They appear uncomfortable using their hands to gesture in front of groups. In some instances, they clasp their hands behind their backs or interlock them at waist level or hold them at chest level in a modified praying position. Other trainers cross their arms or rest their elbow on a lectern as they attempt to appear relaxed and casual. Still others put their hands in their pockets and jingle change, place their hands on their hips, or simply let their hands hang limply by their sides.

A good stance to assume is facing your learners with elbows bent and hands at about waist level. From that position you can easily gesture left, right, or with both arms to emphasize a point or attract attention. For example, if you asking the question "What do you think?" you might spread your arms hands out, palms up, toward learners, indicating that you are giving them the floor. You are both verbally and non-verbally eliciting a response. When asking for feedback or encouraging input, you might say something like, "Please share your thoughts with me on _____" while gesturing with open arms toward your learners then sweeping them inward toward your chest in a gathering motion to indicate that you are inviting their input.

Gestures generally are used to emphasize or highlight something you say the way that training aids supplement verbal messages. When used properly, the hands can add punch or impact to your vocal delivery.

Movements should appear natural and spontaneous. Do not wring your hands, keep fingers interlaced or clasped, crack your knuckles, pick your fingernails, play with rings, or repeat other nervous hand gestures. Use gesturing correctly to clarify or emphasize.

In your quest to improve your non-verbal delivery skills, think about habits of other presenters that irritate or distract you and make a concerted effort to avoid similar behavior.

The following are some examples of distracting behavior:

Non-Verbal Communication Distracters

♦ Fidgeting or playing with your hair, a pen, pointer, or marker, or a ring or other jewelry

♦ Having to push your glasses up on your nose continually

♦ Pacing aimlessly from one point to another across the front of the room or stage

♦ Gazing regularly at the ceiling or floor as you talk

♦ Talking to the projection screen, flip chart, or writing surface instead of facing learners

♦ Using laser pointer dots that bounce around as you attempt to indicate items on a projection screen or writing surface

♦ Jingling change or other noisy items in your pockets

♦ Keeping hands on hands on hips, in pockets, behind the back or folded across the chest Turning your back on learners as you write or read from a projection screen

♦ Shifting body weight back and forth or rocking from one foot to the other

♦ Failing to make eye contact with all learners at various points during a workshop

♦ Holding and reading verbatim from notes

Hone Your Questioning Skills

Questions often result in getting exactly what you ask for. That can be a real problem if you do not word the question appropriately. In such instances, you can get useless information that can lead to frustration and the need for additional questions. It also can make you look less than professional.

The key to asking good questions is to do it very often. Practice the skill in your personal life until it becomes second-nature in the training room. A humorous example of how inappropriate questions can lead to communication breakdown occurred in my home a couple of years back between my ninety-two-year-old mother and me. She lives in our home and is a real sweetheart, very active, and likes to help around the house. Apparently, mom wanted to be helpful and get dinner started one night, since I was working on a book and my wife was not yet home from work. As I worked on a book manuscript on my computer, mom came in and asked, "Would you like me to cook baked potatoes for dinner?" (a closed-ended question). I stated that would be fine, thanked her, and went back to work. A few seconds later I noticed she was still standing in the doorway and I asked what she needed. She responded, "How many potatoes do you want?" (another closed-ended question). I was behind on a book deadline and was not fully listening to mom and I was also a bit irritated at the second interruption. I replied, "One is fine," then went back to typing. I again realized that mom was still standing in the doorway and, as I looked up, she looked confused as she said, "Well, what are MJ (my wife) and I going to eat (a third closed-ended question)?" I sort of laughed and said, "I don't know, mom, I only want one potato. If you two want potatoes, then feel free to fix them."

It occurred to me later that my mom and I had the type of communication breakdown that often occurs when trainers ask their learners the wrong types of questions. They do not get the information needed or expected, more questions are required, time is wasted, and frustration often results. My mom wanted to know how many potatoes to fix for dinner, but she did not ask that. I responded only to the closed-ended questions she asked and, as a result, we were both frustrated and wasted unnecessary time.

Use questions often in your workshops, as they are an excellent way to give you a break from speaking and can engage learners. If you use questions effectively, you can often determine learner interest and their willingness to participate, gauge understanding of a topic you just covered, and elicit ideas, issues, concerns, or solutions.

Two typical question types include:

♦ *Open-Ended.* These types of question start with "Who," "What," "When," "How," "Why," or "To what degree" and are designed to offer your learners an opportunity to become engaged in a dialogue, offer opinions, responses, ideas or questions. Use such questions to help determine what learners have grasped about a concept that you just presented. For example:

- "Who would be your best resource when working on _____ and how might you get them to help you?"

- "What is the best way to apply what I just shared with you?"

- "When you use this technique, what are some potential outcomes?

♦ *Closed-Ended.* When questions begin with an active verb such as did, could, should, would, or might, they are closed-ended and normally result in a one-syllable, short-answer response such as "one," "yes" or "no," or "okay."

In a learning environment, these types of questions are good for verifying or validating something already said but they do not usually result in extended dialogue or discussion. For example, you might use a closed-ended question to make sure that you remember or heard something correctly by asking something like, "Levon, if I heard you correctly, you would like me to further explain step one. Is that correct?" If you wanted to obtain further input from Levon in this example, you could use an open-ended question like "Levon, what other information did you need about step one of the process that I just shared?"

Practice Positive Communication

Trainers sometimes cause inadvertent communication breakdowns because of the words that they use. You can avoid this with a little forethought. Think of alternatives for language that might be offensive. For example, look at the following language and some alternative ways of saying the same thing with less potential negative result. Instead of:

♦ "Tell" use the word "share," since it subtly conveys collaboration or partnership, rather than a directive approach.

♦ "But" use the word "however," because "but" tends to negate anything positive that you have said before it.

♦ "You are wrong" use something like "While that may be true in some instances, in what other way might _____?" The latter acknowledges the learner's previous contribution while encouraging him or her to think about other alternatives.

♦ "I never said" use "What I meant to say was _____," which allows you to take responsibility for the comment and provide the information a second time without challenging the learner or his or her perception of what you said.

♦ "Listen to me" use a statement like "If I may, I'd like to share with you _____."

♦ "Problem" use words like "issue," "situation," or "challenge," because "problem" by its very nature conjures up negative images of things gone wrong.

♦ "Do you understand?" use "How do you see yourself using/applying what I just shared?" The latter encourages interaction and dialogue while eliciting ways in which something might be used by the learners. If they cannot respond effectively to the question, then they likely do not understand.

♦ "Why?" use "What is the reason for _____?" because the first question sounds harsh and will likely remind learners of a time when they were teenagers and did not get the responses they wanted when they asked that question of their parents or caregivers. The result is that the "why" question is often connected to negative personal memories.

♦ "This is easy" use "Let me show you a less complicated way." You do not want to use language that may intimidate or make your learners feel like there is something wrong with them if they do not grasp a concept or skill immediately. Remember that learners may not possess your level of knowledge, experience, and education. They may also lack confidence in their abilities initially. Your role as a trainer and coach is to instill a level of confidence in them through your approach to sharing knowledge and skills.

Listen Intently to Learners

Many people use their hearing to gather information. Unfortunately, there is a difference between hearing (passive physical process) and listening (active mental process) and most people have never received any formal training on how to listen effectively. Even if you have received training on how to be a better listener, you may want to do a quick self-assessment using Exhibit 6.2.

To get information correctly from your learners, you must use your own sense of hearing effectively by practicing active listening. Failure to do so can lead to an impression that you are not professional or that you are not concerned about your learners. It can also waste time since you might respond inappropriately to questions or

Exhibit 6.2. Listening Awareness Self-Assessment

How well do you listen? Take a moment to respond truthfully to the following statements by placing a check mark in the appropriate column (Always, Often, or Never). Once you finish, total the check marks. Any area in which you do not rate yourself in the "A" column is an area for improvement.

A O N

☐ ☐ ☐ 1. I focus all my attention on the speaker when conversing.

☐ ☐ ☐ 2. I consciously look for issues or action items during conversations.

☐ ☐ ☐ 3. I avoid planning my next remarks until after I have heard the entire message.

☐ ☐ ☐ 4. I approach conversations with interest and a desire to listen.

☐ ☐ ☐ 5. I avoid letting my emotions get in the way of my listening.

☐ ☐ ☐ 6. I avoid daydreaming as I listen.

☐ ☐ ☐ 7. I try to put myself in the speaker's place and empathize with what he or she is saying.

☐ ☐ ☐ 8. I avoid assumptions about what someone will say in order to not jump ahead in the conversation.

☐ ☐ ☐ 9. I feed back, in my own words, what I heard the speaker say in order to verify my understanding of the message.

☐ ☐ ☐ 10. I check my understanding of a speaker's meaning by asking for clarification of words or comments I do not understand.

☐ ☐ ☐ 11. I use a variety of techniques to stay focused while someone speaks.

☐ ☐ ☐ 12. I make eye contact or look at the person as he or she speaks.

(continued)

Exhibit 6.2. (*Continued*)

A	O	N	
❑	❑	❑	13. I consciously think about how someone might respond to what I say.
❑	❑	❑	14. I allow the speaker to present his or her ideas, even when I am emotional about the topic.
❑	❑	❑	15. I do not let other things distract me as I listen.
❑	❑	❑	16. I listen objectively and do not judge the speaker.
❑	❑	❑	17. I take notes as I listen, when appropriate.
❑	❑	❑	18. I listen for ideas and concepts and not just details or facts.
❑	❑	❑	19. I select a location that aids effective listening and limits distractions before beginning an important conversation.
❑	❑	❑	20. I observe and evaluate the speaker's physical posture and gestures as he or she speaks.

---

provide information that learners did not ask for or request. The following are some strategies to help ensure that you are effectively listening to learners throughout your workshop(s).

Strategies for Effective Listening

♦ *Stop Talking!!* You cannot listen effectively and talk at the same time. Besides, talking while someone else does is rude and can negatively affect the trainer-learner relationship.

♦ *Be Patient.* Not everyone communicates at the same rate of speech or in the same manner as you. Take the time to let a learner finish speaking before you start talking. This is often especially important when speaking with someone who speaks English as a second language or has a hearing impairment.

♦ *Avoid Biases.* Do not let your preconceived opinions about a learner or group distract you from the message a person is delivering. There may be value for you and others in the room in what a learner is saying. If you do not listen, you could miss an opportunity.

♦ *Ask Appropriate Questions.* Ask probing, open-ended questions in order to gather pertinent information and prevent misunderstandings.

♦ *Paraphrase What You Hear.* Repeat what you believe you heard the learner say in your own words. This helps to ensure you heard the intended message.

♦ *Use Phrases That Indicate You Are Following the Message.* For example, phrases such as "I see," "Uh huh," "Really?" or "Interesting" can let the speaker know that your are listening to him or her. Just do not overdo this or sound rehearsed.

♦ *Send Positive Non-Verbal Cues.* Facing the learner, making eye contact, and smiling can send a message that you are willing to listen.

♦ *Avoid Getting Defensive.* If you disagree with a point made by a learner, remain objective. Use facts or examples to counter or substantiate your own views, if appropriate. Also, be willing to hear learners' views or concerns. In some cases, you might even ask the entire class what they think about something that was just said. This takes the pressure off both of you and eliminates a situation where it is you against them.

Increase Multicultural Communication Awareness

The world is now connected as never before. In a less than a day you might be standing on foreign soil ready to deliver your workshop material to a group of people who may or may not speak your language well. Or you may find your learning audience to be widely diverse, with many cultures and ethnic groups represented.

To prepare for this inevitability, you should read or take courses about other countries, learning about their people, customs, languages, and cultures. The more you know about other societies, the less likely you are to say or do something that will confuse, anger, upset, or embarrass one of your learners.

Since there are too many possibilities to cover in this chapter, I have provided a number of book titles in the Resources section on the topic of cross-cultural communication. Having such books on your bookshelf and reading and referring to them often will help you to be successful as a global trainer.

Depending on your training situation, you may need to consider hiring a translator. If you do so, make sure the person is a professional translator and not just someone who speaks multiple languages. This will help ensure that your words are correctly interpreted. Some technical terms cannot be translated, and a professional will recognize that fact and be able to communicate the concept more effectively. See the guidelines below for communicating with those from a different culture.

Guidelines for Communicating in a Multicultural Environment

♦ Give learners an opportunity and adequate time to voice their thoughts without interrupting them.

♦ Due to embarrassment about their language skills or fear of making a mistake, some learners may be hesitant to share information or volunteer. Additionally, it takes a few moments for some non-native speakers to receive your message, translate it in their minds, and then convert their responses to English before speaking. Set a friendly environment (as described elsewhere in this book) in order to help everyone feel comfortable and want to participate.

♦ While the average speaking rate of about 125 to 150 words per minute may be comfortable for you, to someone who speaks another primary language, this can seemed rushed. Speak slowly and clearly, without insulting learners by overly exaggerating your pace.

♦ Recognize that, while you may be frustrated, so are the learners when they have difficulty communicating their ideas. Take the time to focus on what the person is saying and try to understand the intent of his or her message. Do not interrupt, even when you believe you know what he or she is trying to say. Do not provide words or help people as they speak.

♦ Pause frequently to allow others to comprehend and think about what you just said.

♦ Use a normal tone and volume when speaking with someone from another culture. Many people raise their voices when speaking to someone who does not speak their language. Just because someone has to translate does not mean that he or she is hard of hearing. Do not embarrass yourself or your learner by making such a mistake.

♦ Paraphrase or repeat in your own words what you believe the speaker said, if appropriate. This helps ensure that you understood a question or comment.

♦ Use words with one or two syllables and shorter sentences to help ensure that you do not confuse any of your learners.

♦ Take time to frequently verify that learners understood what you said before moving along. Failure to do so can lead to information overload and frustration, as well as having key points missed.

♦ Avoid using culturally specific examples or analogies. For example, a trainer from North America might incorrectly use any of the following:

- "Win one for the 'Gipper'" (referring to Notre Dame football coach Knute Rockne)

- "I'll need your 'John Hancock' on this form" (referring to a U.S. historical figure)

- "Looks like we scored a home run on that last activity" (refers to American baseball)

- "If plan A fails, we'll drop back and punt" (referring to U.S. football)

Strategy for Success

Some simple guidelines that can assist in making your presentation more powerful and making you look more professional include:

Do not use your lectern as a crutch on which you lean or hold tightly throughout out your presentation. Doing so can make you seem nervous or insecure and puts a physical barrier between you and your learners. If you must use a lectern, place your notes on it, glance at them occasionally as you move from one point in the front of the room to another, but do not stay stationary behind it.

Get up close with your learners by regularly repositioning yourself in the room. Since movement attracts and holds attention, you can engage learners simply by interacting with them.

Use your hands to emphasize key points and to help create mental images. For example, if you are talking about how small someone like a young child is, hold your hand parallel to and closer to the ground and bend a bit to indicate short stature. To stress someone being older, such as a teenager or young adult, raise your hand parallel to the ground at a higher level to show that the person has grown taller.

Do not point at someone with your index finger or gesture with your palm up as you twitch your index finger toward yourself for someone to come closer. The first gesture is considered rude in many cultures, while the second is used in some countries to call animals and is offensive. Instead, gesture toward someone with an extended arm and hand with your palm up, fingers and thumb joined together. To have someone move towards you, simply ask them, "Would you please come up and stand next to me?" Do this as you gesture with an extended palm to a point on the floor next to you.

Personalizing What You Have Learned

- What are the most important things that you read in this chapter? Why?

- What are some ways that you can immediately apply concepts covered in this chapter?

- What additional resources or topics do you want to research based on what you read?

CHAPTER 7

Putting Power into Training Aids

fter reading this chapter, and when applying what you learn, you will be able to:

1. Recognize the power of training aids in enhancing learning.

2. Design and use audiovisual aids that stimulate the brain and increase learning.

3. Create static training aids that support your message to learners.

"If a child can't learn the way we teach, maybe we should teach the way they learn."

Ignacio Estra

The Power of Training Aids

Using effective training aids in your session can help reinforce your verbal message, while stimulating the brains of your learners and tapping into different learning modalities. By creating and using effective support materials you can help ensure that you will hold learner interest while helping them gain, retain, recognize, recall, and later use the information to which they are exposed.

Two key things to remember about using training aids is that (1) they are supposed to *supplement* your message, not replace it, and (2) you must keep your learning aids simple. Do not become so distracted by adding glitz and sparkle when creating training materials that you forget their intended purpose, which is to reinforce your primary message.

Trainers and educators traditionally use many types of material to help put their message across to learners. Virtually anything can become a training aid. Many commercially produced products are available. You can also design, build, and use many items that you create yourself to enhance a learning environment. There is no hard-and-fast rule about what classifies as a training aid. If something works, use it.

Audiovisual Aids

Training aids that tap primarily into the auditory and visual learning modalities fall into the audiovisual category. These can be viewed with an electronic projection device or listened to through a playback system such as MP3, laptop computer, or compact disk or cassette player. They can add a more polished and formal appearance to your delivery when designed and used effectively. They can also add valuable input from other professionals who have recorded ideas and information that can supplement your session content.

Computer-Generated Slides

Depending on the computer software used to create your presentation, you have an opportunity to add a variety of enhancements to inject pizzazz into your slides. Examples of popular presentation software include Microsoft® PowerPoint®, Harvard Graphics™, Lotus Freelance™, Adobe Persuasion™, or Novell Presentations™. If done correctly, these tools can help ensure effective message delivery and create a powerful impact.

Slides should include key topics and not have your entire outline written out line-for-line in very small print. Use them as a guide to highlight important points and not as a script from which you will read. The latter approach is boring and unprofessional. It also sends a message that you are unprepared or that you assume your learners cannot read the material themselves. If you need to give detailed information about topics to your learners, do so with handouts that they can read later or can review before you discuss the content in class.

There are a number of ways to include sound, images, and movie clips into your slides. By using such add-ons you can demonstrate concepts and give new information during your presentation. Companies are continually creating new, useful, and dynamic visual aids. Just remember that you should ALWAYS obtain written copyright permission before incorporating it into your session.

To add a bit of visual variety, try using creative graphic fonts for title slides or title lines. For example, use the WordArt feature on the toolbar of Microsoft Word to include colorful pre-designed graphic lettering (see Figure 7.1) in various shapes and sizes. You can also download such graphic fonts from the Internet or buy inexpensive font software CDs at major office supply chains or other stores in your local mall.

If you have one image or object that you want to use in various ways, you can flip it in a different direction, as shown in Figure 7.2. For example, you might have two versions of your own caricature facing one another on either side of the slide at the bottom. To do this in PowerPoint, insert the same image twice into your slide and then click on one of the images with the cursor to highlight or capture it. Next, click "Draw" on the toolbar, then select "Rotate or Flip" from the drop-down menu that appears. Finally, select the direction that you want the image flipped or rotated. The image will change based on the choice you make. You can now click and drag the image to wherever you want it positioned on the slide.

Add a three-dimensional effect in which letters or words appear stretched or coming in from the distance. A number of font software add-on packages allow you to modify text and images. Check with your local office supply or software dealer for suggestions.

Insert charts, tables, or text boxes into slides to help explain key points of the presentation. Remember that by adding creative graphics you appeal to the visual learning modality.

Figure 7.1. Sample WordArt Slide

PRESENTATION PIZZAZZ:

Adding Impact to Learning

A Special Presentation

for

by

BOB LUCAS
President, *Creative Presentation Resources, Inc.*
(an affiliated company of *Global Performance Solutions, Inc.*)

© Copyright 1993, 2001
Creative Presentation Resources, Inc.
P.O. Box 180487
Casselberry, Florida 32718-0487.
(800)308-0399/(407)695-5535.
E-Mail: blucas@presentationresources.net
All Rights reserved.

Figure 7.2. Sample Mirror Images

BRIGHT IDEAS

Use this page to capture any ideas, concepts, thoughts, or tips that you picked up during the program and that you want to review, think about, or share later.

Strategy for Success

There are numerous add on packages that you can use with Microsoft PowerPoint to deliver a more creative visual effect. One such package is VoxProxy® (see Creative Presentation Resources in the Resources section). It has a variety of animated cartoon characters that walk, stand, sit, and talk on the screen. These characters assume a variety of positions and movements based on what you select from the menu. They speak the words that you type into the software. You might use the characters to introduce new topics or to draw attention to a key concept. For example, a character might walk across the screen, face the audience, reach into his pocket to extract a note sheet, and then say something like, "Hello, My name is _____ and I'd like to introduce our next topic, which is _____."

Animated characters tie to brain-based research principles of adding fun, novelty, and humor to your presentation. They also involve sound, color, and movement that help attract and hold attention.

Using Slides Effectively

Before participants arrive, check the operation of your computer and focus your projection unit. Make sure that you position your screen so that all learners can see it.

Many times your presentation will work fine on your home or office computer but will fail at the training site. This might occur because some operating systems and components such as cables, microphones, or speakers are not compatible with others. A common issue with slide presentations is that software programs are incompatible because the version on the training room computer is an older version that the one used to create the file. The result is that technical problems occur. For example, the computer cannot find or open a slide show file or the sound does not work. To help overcome such glitches, ALWAYS plan backup training aids in case of equipment failure. This is crucial if you are training at a remote location or using someone else's equipment. Make copies of your slides onto transparencies and ask that an overhead projector be available in case you cannot use your slide presentation. In the latter case, remind the sponsor to check to ensure that the projector bulbs work and request a dual-bulb unit. This will allow you to shift to a backup bulb without wasting time if one burns out during the workshop.

Place your projection screen where learners can see it from any point in the room. Project your slides to make sure that the font size and color on them can be clearly seen. Go to each area of the room to view the slides so that you know everyone can see.

Because electrical hookups are often a problem and extension cords are often not available, take your own 25-foot extension cord in your trainer's kit.

Dim the lights directly over the projection screen to prevent glare and make sure that there is no sunlight glare.

Follow a standard format for all slides by printing them either vertically (portrait format) or horizontally (landscape format) to make reading easier and avoid distraction. Your learners' brains will get used to one format and can be temporarily confused when you switch unexpectedly. When this occurs, your learners might miss a key point that you cover.

Limit lines of text to eight to ten and words per line to six to eight to avoid a cluttered appearance.

Use at least 1/4-inch sans serif lettering of approximately 26- to 30-point size for text when presenting to groups of one or two hundred. Title lines should be slightly larger

(36- to 40-point) to differentiate and make them stand out from text lines. These sizes assume that your room configuration is simple theater-style seating and your learners' view is unobstructed.

When preparing slides you may want to use all bold upper case fonts for title lines. Similarly, use upper case for the first letter of a word on a new topic line and for proper nouns followed by lower case for the remainder of text lines. This makes reading easier.

Add color to your slides by typing your title line in a different color from the rest of the text. You can use any dark color such as navy blue, black, brown, or forest green to make the title stand out if you have a light background or white, yellow, light green, blue, or other easy-to-read color on a dark background.

Choose two different colors complementary colors such as yellow and white for text lines when using a dark background or navy blue and forest green when using a light background. For each new bullet point or line, alternate the color of the text. For example, point one would be in yellow, point two in white, point three in yellow, and so forth. Avoid the color red for text lines because lettering tends to look blurred and is difficult to read, especially from a distance or for people who have red color blindness.

Ensure that your slide fonts and background colors are complementary. If you are unsure about a combination, either refer to a source such as an artist, a book on color and graphics, or another person with good color perception, or do not use the combination.

Special effects are helpful and can add impact to your slides, unless you use too many. Just because your software contains dozens of options does not mean you have to use them all. When designing slides, select one or two options and carry that theme through the entire presentation. Do not make your media the focal point of your workshop, as it may distract from your message. For example, if you are using PowerPoint choose one or two types of slide transitions like drip, dissolve, or fade and use them on all slides.

Use clip art to tie into the brain-based learning concepts of novelty and fun, but do not use so many images that you distract from the written message. Remember that you are there to share knowledge, not entertain your learners. Add images that complement the written words on your slides in order to help attract and hold attention. To help accomplish this, keep your images small so they do not distract from the slide text.

If you use a commercial video segment, become thoroughly familiar with the content before learners arrive. Have prepared comments to introduce the segment, give participants specific information to watch for in the clip, and review what they saw afterward, if appropriate. People are more likely to focus on the video content if they know that they will be responsible for reporting in front of the group later. You can use this strategy to encourage learners to become actively engaged in the program.

When possible, use a remote control to allow you to move around the room and still operate the slide show. This frees you from having to stand next to the computer to punch a button when you want to advance a slide or to enlist the help of one of your learners to rotate slides.

If you are nervous, DO NOT use a laser pointer to direct learner attention to something on the projection screen. Your hands will be shaking and the nervousness will be obvious and magnified as the red dot dances around the screen.

Using Overhead Transparencies

Slides have replaced transparencies as a medium in many training environments, yet they are still used in many situations. Follow the guidelines for slides that you read above related to color, font, format, graphics, and other layout strategies when designing transparencies. Keep them simple and professional.

Some trainers would tell you that a nice advantage of transparencies over slides is that you can quickly grab one that you already viewed from a stack and project it again when a learner asks a question or the opportunity to refocus attention on its content arises.

Unlike slides, which you have to scroll through or stop and search for, transparencies are readily available. Of course, instructors who are advocates of slides might argue this point. Whichever media you choose to use often comes down to your familiarity with it, availability, budget (LCD projectors are expensive and not always available), and your comfort level in using it. Here are some tips for using transparencies.

Tips for Effectively Using Transparencies

♦   Position your projection screen to prevent a "keystone effect." This occurs when a projected image appears stretched across the screen and is larger across the top of the screen than at the bottom because of the angle at which the projector screen is set up. To prevent this from happening, make sure your screen is straight in front of your projector and that the top portion is forward at a 90-degee angle.

♦ Number your transparencies in case you drop them or they get out of sequence and put corresponding numbers or reference notes in your lesson plan.

♦ To protect your transparencies, place them in specially designed plastic "transparency protectors." Some brands like 3M are three-hole punched and have a strip attached on either side where you can write notes to prompt your thinking as you glance down at the transparency on the overhead projector.

♦ An alternative, but heavier, way to protect your transparencies is to tape a paper cardboard frame to each one. You can then three-hole punch and put them into a binder for ease of transport, storage, and protection. You can also write margin notes around the frame.

♦ Position your transparency correctly on the projector glass. Do a quick check of the screen to ensure that you center the image so that it is readable, then discuss key points on the transparency.

♦ Look at your transparency on the projector in order to gather your thoughts and speak directly to your learners. Do not read from the screen or turn your back on your learners.

♦ Use small, colored plastic pointers in the shape of arrows or fingers to draw attention to a word or line of text on the projector (see Creative Presentation

Resources in the Resources section). You can also cut out arrows or other shapes from construction paper or lightweight cardboard. Avoid using round items like pencils as pointers since they often roll off the projector onto the floor or table and can distract learners.

♦ Be careful about taping a small piece of paper over the lens portion of the projector to cover it as you discuss a topic with the projector still on. The lens magnifies the intensity of the heat coming from the projector light and can catch the paper on fire. To get an idea of the impact, think of the magnifying glass that you used to start fires from a sunbeam as a child! If you are not using the projector to show a transparency, turn it off to increase the bulb life, cut down on noise from the motor fan, reduce heat near you, and avoid the glaring bright projected light that can distract learners. Remember that one of the principles of brain-based learning is that light attracts attention or can distract.

♦ Always ensure that you have a spare bulb or an extra projector on standby in the room.

Strategy for Success

Place a heavy piece of paper over your transparency when you are not referring to it or when you do not want learners reading from the screen. As you address each line of text or key points, move the paper down to disclose only that item. Trainers and educators refer to this as the "revelation technique" because they are revealing one line at a time. This is similar to bringing in one line of text at a time on a computer-generated slide. When ready to discuss the next point, move the paper down again until all points are exposed, then change transparencies.

Digital Visual Projectors

The digital projector is a modern-day update of the old opaque projector that projected images of book and document page onto a screen. In addition to being able to project book pages and documents, these devices now allow you to project images of three-dimensional objects or specimens onto a screen where large groups can view and discuss them. This allows you to demonstrate components, assemble and disassemble objects, and much more. Most models also allow you to transmit the images into your computer or store them on a secure digital (SD) flash memory card or a universal serial bus (USB) flash drive to transport and forward to others.

Audio Recordings

Depending on your session topic, you may be able to incorporate an audio recording. For example, if you were doing a workshop on effective listening skills, you might play someone reading a portion of text as learners listen. Afterward, you could have them individually write down everything that they can remember about what they heard. Next, form teams to compare and discuss what they wrote. You could follow this activity by a period in which learners brainstorm reasons why some people heard things that others did not. You could also summarize all this with the entire group and a lead a discussion on how to improve listening, which could tie all the content pieces together.

Other ways to incorporate this medium would be to use music during a visioning activity, tape-recorded role-play scenarios that learners analyze and discuss, or short, lecture-based segments from well-known authorities. The latter can add credibility to what you have said if the experts validate and support your information.

Videotape/DVD

Consider using training and commercial videos or digital video discs (DVDs) if you want a bit of visual stimulation that can add to many session topics. There are thousands of topics available with prices ranging from $79 to $1,000. As you have read before, just remember to get copyright permission before using. If you purchase the video, that is usually not a problem because purchase grants you individual use. If you have questions about your rights to use something, contact the publisher.

As with all training aids, make sure that you are thoroughly familiar with equipment and that you cue up the video in advance to the beginning of the scene you wish to show. This will prevent wasted time in class and prevent any embarrassment that might occur when you cannot get the video to play, pause, and rewind. Also make sure that you have a screen large enough for everyone to see from any location in the room.

Because most learners have a limited attention span, show only short segments of the video at a time. Fifteen to twenty minutes is a good range. If you want to use an entire video, consider breaking it into sections and showing each segment at a different point to reinforce and relate to key concepts made during your workshop.

Strategy for Success

If you are going to use a segment of a video, make sure that you preview the content in advance. Let learners know what specific concepts to watch for and conduct an effective review at the end to identify key points that tie to your session content. A handy source that provides an overview and suggested uses for a variety of different videos for training is the book *101 Movie Clips That Teach and Train* by Becky Pike Pluth (see Creative Presentation Resources in the Resources section).

Multimedia

There are various interpretations of what multimedia involves. Typically, the term refers to any learning medium such as a website or slide show that includes a combination of several sources for communicating information or concepts. Examples of multimedia include text, pictures, video, and sound.

If you have ever entered a conference hall where multiple screens have projected rotating images and/or video playing with musical background and subtitles that are displaying information across the bottom of the screen, then you have experienced a multimedia presentation. These might be used to offer a chronology of events related to your workshop topic through images, text, and music. Another way you can incorporate multimedia into your workshop is to have learners access websites that offer multiple forms of information as part of their learning experience.

Internet

There is literally any topic that you can imagine on the World Wide Web. It is a great source for information and documentation, as well as a source that learners can access for projects and research. You can tap the Internet in class to project images of websites, products, or information that ties to your session content. You might also have individual learners or groups search for material that they will present to the class in short "teach backs." This type of event can help to stimulate learning and add variety to your delivery, while allowing participants to become more actively engaged in their own learning.

Static Visual Aids

"Static" visual aids are training aids that supplement your spoken message and add a different level of sensory stimulus to your workshop. Use static aids to enhance the learning environment and content that you present. The term comes from the fact that these materials are typically stationary and provide a more prolonged element of support, as opposed to slides and videos that are used and then replaced. Static aids include models, photographs, posters, actual objects, and props.

Flip Charts

These training aids have been around for decades and are still one of the most cost-effective portable products on the market. Unfortunately, many people view them as low-tech and obsolete. This is far from true. With flip charts, you can prepare your pages in advance using multiple colored water-based markers. You can add additional color with graphics, colored borders, stick on figures, or through any number of other creative means.

In the classroom, you can use flip charts for small group note-taking, brainstorming, capturing participant remarks, to make a point visual quickly, or to add pizzazz to the room. For example, you can put colorful quotes, statistics, or session-related graphics and information on the walls.

Some creative trainers and educators use two flip charts in tandem during a session. They either alternate prepared images between the two charts or they have prepared pages on one easel and use the second to capture participant comments or to add more information to a topic during the session. If you decide to try this technique, put a number with a small piece of tape in the upper corner of each easel and then make a notation in your lesson plan to remind you which easel to use at a given point in your session. This can prevent embarrassing confusion. It is also a good idea to have a set of markers on each easel and leave them there, rather than having to walk across the room to get one from the other easel during your program. Like any other strategy you plan to employ, always practice with your easels before you actually step in front of learners. See *The Big Book of Flip Charts* in the Bibliography for more creative ideas on using flip charts.

Designing Creative Flip-Chart Pages

If you are going to create your flip charts before the session begins, give some thought to what you will include on them. Find a large flat writing surface and spend some time writing out key points and adding any illustrations you would like on a writing tablet first. This will save wasting expensive flip-chart pads when you make errors or decide to change something. If the paper is not lined, you should use a straight edge of some sort to ensure that lines of text are evenly spaced and are not at distracting angles.

Visibility is important if you want learners to grasp concepts and refer to your written materials. To help ensure that everyone can see what is on your flip charts from thirty to forty feet (9.144 to 12.192 m) use block type font that has straight lines without fancy curls at the ends. Make sure that lettering is at least one to two inches

(2.54 to 5.08 cm) high. This type and size of lettering will make reading easier for learners.

Use upper-case letters or a larger size for title lines in order to help emphasize the words and help visually define the topic. Combine upper and lower case for text lines to allow for a more natural reading format. Consider the design of books and other publications. They have bold headers followed by text that is in upper and lower case letters. Extensive amounts of text in all capital letters is difficult to read and not normally used.

To avoid a cluttered look and to allow more lines of text to fit onto a sheet of paper, limit the number of words to six to eight per line and the number of lines of text to six to eight (the "six-by-eight rule").

When writing, use horizontal lettering that runs across the page, as opposed to vertical lettering that runs down the page from top to bottom. The exception would be if you are discussing an acronym, such as ADDIE, and wanted to the letters down the left side of the page and a line of text for each letter.

Strategy for Success

Use numbers, symbols and abbreviations to avoid unnecessary words and save space when creating flip charts. For example, instead of:

"One" use the number 1.

"And" use the ampersand symbol (&).

"Manager" use Mngr.

If you are going to use vertical columns of information, use no more than three columns per page so that there is a slight space between columns. Generally, you would only use this format for lists of words, numerical figures, or shorts points, rather than sentences.

Limit yourself to one topic per page and avoid cramming irrelevant information onto the page. It will only confuse your participants.

Avoid using the bottom one-third of the page as some participants in the rear of the room will have difficulty seeing it over the heads of others.

Make sure to use water-based markers for flip charts to prevent ink from seeping through the page onto the next one. Dry Erase markers do not work well and appear lighter on paper, and they dry out quickly. Permanent ink markers can "bleed through" or leave marks and ruin subsequent pages. If you use the wrong type of markers, it can be costly and waste paper. It can also damage flip-chart pages that you spent hours creating. One way to prevent ink seepage is to leave a blank sheets of paper between the ones you create.

When writing text, use the broad edge of your markers to make lines wider and more readable. Use dark colors such as black, dark green, brown, and dark blue to write. As you read earlier for slides, red is good for highlighting key words or phrases and drawing icons but should not be used for text. Pastel and lighter colors are good for borders and art to add color and pizzazz; however, they should be avoided for text because they are difficult to see.

Underline title lines and key words or concepts with bright colors to draw attention to them.

Strategy for Success

Before learners arrive, write little reminders or cues with a pencil in the upper corner of pages on the side of the page where you will be standing. You can refer to these little notes as you are turning to the next page to prompt your comments and lead into the next topic. Your participants will never know you "cheated" since they cannot see what you wrote from a distance!

Electronic Flip Charts

A relatively recent modification to the standard flip-chart easel is an electronic version. This type of flip chart allows you to write information onto a standard writing pad and then capture what you wrote with a hand-held camera scanner and save it into a computer file. You can distribute notes later as handouts on standard laser printer paper or as an electronic information file. This eliminates the need for learners to take extensive notes and allows them to focus on the discussion. It also allows others who cannot come to the workshop to see a snapshot of key issues identified and discussed.

Strategy for Success

Many trainers use clip art, caricatures, and other graphic images to add color to and enhance their written messages on flip charts. They do this by drawing and tracing figures related to their session topic onto their pages in advance or by lightly tracing simple figures onto the pages in pencil so that they can see them but learners cannot. When ready to "draw" an image, they simply use a marker to darker the penciled lines. Learners think their trainer is a budding Rembrandt.

You do not have to have artistic ability to create acceptable artwork. You can use simple icons, dots, stars, arrows, smile faces, circles, or other geometric figures as bullet points down the page next to each written item. You can also draw small items related to your session topic. For example, you can use a small telephone handset as a bullet point in a session on telephone skills or call center customer service, or an ear in a workshop on listening skills. There are many books, videos, and software packages available to help you learn to draw simple images. Practice a few line images or cartoon characters, master them, and use them regularly. Once you are comfortable with those, add a few more to your artistic toolbox.

If you absolutely believe that you cannot draw but want to use images, photocopy an image onto transparency film, project it onto your flip-chart paper with an overhead projector and trace it before your learners arrive. This might be useful on a "Welcome. . ." page that also has the name of the session.

One tip for using images of people or animals is to have them face the text on the page. This is because the human eye is subconsciously drawn in the direction in which the figure is looking. In addition, it makes more sense to have a purpose for the image by having it look at the text.

Using Flip Charts

If you are facilitating a brainstorming session and capturing comments from your participants, make sure to write down their exact words, rather than paraphrasing in your own words. This is so that you do not inadvertently change their intended meaning. Some learners will not challenge or correct you. They will simply say something like, "That's close enough" when you ask them if that is what they meant. A better approach is to ask THEM to shorter their thoughts to put them onto a single line of the flip chart.

When not writing, PUT THE MARKER DOWN!!! Playing with it by clicking the cap on and off as you speak or using as a pointer can be distracting and communicate nervousness.

Use large pointers made of wooden dowel rods with a dark plastic tip that are available at craft, teacher, and home supply stores. You can also use arrows cut out of poster or other heavy colored paper. Other props like a rubber Squawkin' Chicken pointer or a metal expandable pointer with small plastic hand and extended index finger (see Creative Presentation Resources in Resources section) are terrific for drawing attention to a word or a line of text. Such items also add a bit of novelty, color, humor, and fun to your session.

Hang two-inch strips of blue painter's or masking tape along the side or rear of the easel for use in posting completed pages on the wall. Make sure that you position the tape along the frame or legs so that it will not stick to pages as you turn them on the easel.

Consider putting tabs made from strips of masking tape along the edge of pages. Attach one end of the tape to the back side of a prepared flip-chart sheet, then fold it forward and attach it to the front side of the page. This makes it easier to find specific pre-written pages. You can number or label the tabs for easy locating when needed. The tabs also allow you to return quickly to a page if you want to review a key point. An alternative is to use the clear colored stick-on strips produced by 3M. Reference the colors in your lesson plan or notes so that you can easily find desired pages.

Dry Erase Boards

This modern day, less messy update to the traditional classroom chalkboard provides a large viewable writing surface for printing notes or key concepts for discussion or for learners to copy. You can also use them spontaneously to capture participant comments. When using these aids, use the odor-free Dry Erase markers to cut down on smelly fumes. They are bit more expensive, but worth it.

Dry Erase writing surfaces can also provide an alternate projection screen if space or budget is limited. The down side of this is that the high-gloss surface causes a glare from the projector bulb for those seated directly in front of the board.

Strategy for Success

If you ever find yourself in a room without a projector screen or with only a whiteboard to use as a screen, try the following tip. Tape four sheets of blank flip-chart paper to the board as a makeshift projection area. Put the tape on the rear of the paper so that it is not visible and does not impede viewing of your projected images. This will prevent the glare that often results when a projector bulb reflects off the glassy Dry Erase finish.

Magnetic Boards

Many whiteboards are metal, so you can use them to attach visual aids with magnets. If your writing surface is not metal, use a solid-backed flip chart easel without a writing pad.

You can add visual variety to your session by cutting strips of colored poster board and printing key concepts on them. You can also cut out small shapes such as stars, circles, rectangles, or squares, to use as bullet points. You can buy a roll of magnetic strip at an art supply store and glue small pieces of it to the back of your poster board, shapes, photos, drawings, or anything else you want to display. This approach adds a bit of flexibility over flip charts because you can easily move your key concepts and images around, discuss them individually, and remove them once you have discussed a topic. The key is to make the displayed items large enough to be seen and read easily from anywhere in the room.

Felt Boards

Another clever training aid that has been used for decades, but is not seen often in the age of technology, is a felt board. To create one, go to a yardage store and purchase some dark felt material. You can either hang this material from the top edge of a whiteboard or chalkboard or cut out a side of a large cardboard box and staple the cloth smoothly to it. Next, purchase some Velcro and coarse grade sandpaper. Cut the Velcro sandpaper into small strips and tape them to the back of poster board strips, photos, or other items that you wish to display. When ready to display them, just stick them to the felt surface.

Electronic Writing Surfaces

The electronic writing surface (digital whiteboard) is a relatively new product. These creative items combine the simplicity of a whiteboard and flip chart with the technical capabilities of a computer and printer. Information written on the board with an electromagnetic pen is captured through sensors and saved as a document in a computer. You can then print notes or e-mail them to others.

Electronic writing surfaces are terrific timesaving devices because you no longer have to transcribe notes from class for use later. You can also connect the board to a printer, produce copies, and pass them out to learners while in class.

Static Cling Pages

3M and several other companies produce an alternative to the flip-chart pad in the form of thin plastic sheets that typically come on large pads like flip-chart paper does. The sheets will cling to most surfaces via static electricity without the use of tape. This will please many building and hotel catering managers who fear that blue painter's and masking tape will stick to their walls or remove the paint.

Static cling sheets are portable, reusable, and lightweight. You can print your message on them using Dry Erase markers, roll them, and put them in a shipping tube to transport them to your classroom or remote location. If you decide to erase and reuse them, all you need is a Dry Erase eraser or a damp paper towel. If you want to reuse the information that you write, use flip-chart or permanent ink markers to prevent smearing and erasure.

Posters

You can add color and a little extra pizzazz to learning environments with printed posters. Posters are excellent for making or reinforcing a point, since they can be on brightly colored paper. You can also add graphics, graphs, charts, and other components to make this training aid stand out and inform. By creating charts in advance to supplement concepts that you will be covering in the session, you will create a thought-provoking environment before learners walk through the door.

Because posters are portable and can be colorful and graphic, they are effective tools for reinforcing or expanding learning. Posters use pictures, vibrant colors and appropriate text to add new dimensions to the room and tie into the brain-based learning concepts that you read about in earlier chapters.

Depending on your topic, there are a variety of ways to use posters in your sessions. For example, if you are facilitating a workshop for managers or supervisors and want to show trends in attrition, alternative forms of motivation, patterns of change in the workplace, or other such concepts, you could prepare graphs and lists related to these issues and tape them to the walls around the room. During the session, you might call attention to a specific poster by standing next to it and discussing its content. In other workshops, you might hang posters with models or inspirational quotes related to the topic.

A shortcoming of using posters is that, from a distance, learners cannot see or read them well. For that reason, if you plan to refer to posters or if they are an intricate part of the program, purchase multiple copies of the same poster and put them at various points throughout the room.

Another downside of posters is their cost and short lifespan. They are not durable unless protected by the large plastic sleeve protectors that are available for flip-chart pages. These protectors come in multiple sizes and have a clear, write-on matte plastic surface with Velcro on the back edges. The matte finish cuts down on glare from lights and the sun.

Graphic Organizers

You can use timelines, statistical data, the chronological order of some project or event, schedule of events, flowchart, or a series of intervals plotted on lines to show the path of some event or process. To present one or more of these, you may want to include a chart, graph, or diagram on a slide, flip chart, or poster or include it in participant handouts. This will make the idea visual and help people conceptualize better. This is especially helpful for your analytical thinkers and visual learners.

The nice thing about graphic organizers is that you can use many word processing and other computer programs to create the image after you input the numerical data. All you have to do is hit the "Create" button and the computer will do the rest.

A helpful reference on using these mediums is Zelancy's book *Say It with Charts: The Executive's Guide to Visual Communication* (see the Bibliography).

Mind Maps

You can capitalize on how the brain best processes information, using both the logical left side and the creative right side, by creating a visual picture of key concepts for your session. Doing this allows you to use a less formal and more visually appealing approach. To create a basic mind map, put a key concept in the middle of your map and create a branching of key ideas from it. For each key concept, branch off with supporting points or ideas related to it. If you want to tap further into learning brain principles, add small graphic icons related to your key concept topics at the end of each branch to make each concept more visually memorable. You can create a mind map for virtually any purpose. For example, if you were using this book as the basis for a workshop and wanted to show the relationship of key concepts from it, you could easily create a mind map on a single sheet that you could either turn into a slide or convert to a handout. The central idea would be the title of the book (*Training Workshop Essentials*); key concepts would be the chapter titles, and the headers in each chapter would branch from the key concepts. You could then add small graphics to illustrate the chapter concepts (see Figure 7.3).

This type of visual approach supplements your verbal delivery and appeals to your visual learners.

Tent Cards

Many trainers and educators use tent cards as a way to identify learners by having them print their names on them and display them on the tables. Tent cards are also an excellent form of static training aid when you print things like agendas, activity guidelines, questions for discussion, key concepts, rules to follow in the workshop, or inspirational sayings, quotes, or phrases related to session content on them. Use them as training aids during your workshop and then, depending on what you printed, learners can take them back to their workplaces as job aids.

Job Aids

Once learners leave your workshop, they will often have questions or need clarification on material or concepts they receive. For example, someone attending a session on Microsoft Excel® might have trouble remembering the process for creating a spreadsheet. In such instances a job aid that outlines the process step-by-step would be

Figure 7.3. Sample Mind Map

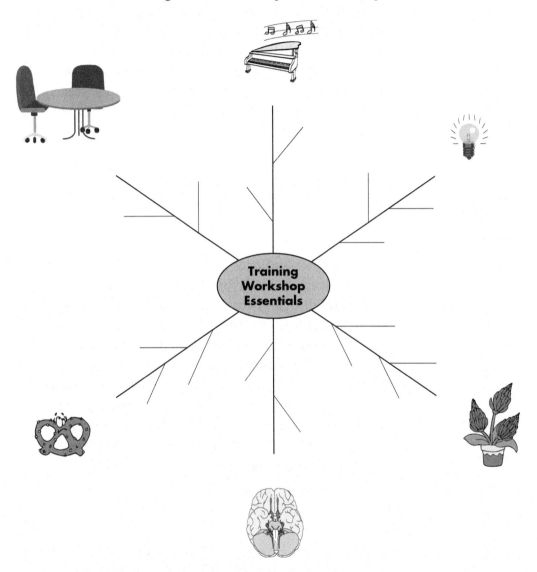

invaluable. Such a product would not only help learners successfully do their jobs, but also would eliminate their need to call you or someone else to assist them. In this instance, the job aid might be a laminated sheet with an outline of how to create a spreadsheet. They could take this aid out at any time to refresh their memories and remind them how to use the software. This is especially useful if there is a long period of time between training and actual use of the software.

There are many ways to aid your learners during and following a training session. You can offer reinforcement to learning through effective support materials in many forms. These range from a single-sided page or poster to a guide kept on a bookshelf or in a desk. Job aids typically offer systematic checklists for performing a given task. Some common job aids are listed below.

Examples of Common Job Aids

♦ *Pocket Guides.* These are small reminders of key steps, models, procedures, or important information. They can be in the form of booklets or small laminated cards.

♦ *Online Computer Help Screens.* These pop-up screens allow users to access information by topic to assist in using software features or to refresh their memory of information received in training sessions. Such items are often stored on an organization's intranet.

♦ *Reference Guides.* These resources might range from a few to several hundred pages. They are handy quick-reference guides providing important information when someone needs to perform a task or assignment.

♦ *Foldable Strips of Cardboard.* These job aids (often called templates) are typically the size of a twelve-inch ruler and lists steps, codes, deadlines, or other significant bits of information. Users can tape these strips to the edge of a computer screen, laminate them, or post them nearby in a work area to remind people key points covered in your workshop.

Actual Object, Mock-Up, or Simulator

Other types of static aids are actual objects, mock-ups (models) of an object, or simulators that replicate the item or scenario that a learner might encounter. One of the best ways to explain how to use something is to have the actual item present in the training room. Think of how important this can be for learners to practice with the actual object. Some examples are given in the following list:

♦ Have learners hold and fire a real gun or at least practice with a model or simulator in a session on pistol marksmanship.

♦ Allow an aspiring pilot to sit in an interactive simulator or fly a plane in order to learn to fly a commercial jet.

♦ Permit a surgeon who performs heart transplants to be able to work with model hearts and perform an operation on a simulator or cadaver.

♦ Let a mechanic learn to disassemble, repair, and assemble an automotive transmission by using an actual transmission.

Clearly, there is great value in having access to the "real thing" or something that closely resembles it. After all, this is how many people learn life skills. Think about how many things you took apart as a child (e.g., clocks, dolls, toys, bicycles, and model cars) to see whether you could put them back together. Just as children benefit from learning with real items, so do adults. You can set up displays, pass items around, or have learners work with them based on your learning objectives and the availability of items. If the item is small, you can also project an image of it so that the entire group can view it and discuss it at once.

Handouts

Printed handouts can be a vital accessory for virtually any learning event. Not only do they provide your visual and kinesthetic learners with stimulation, but they also are a valuable reinforcement to what you covered once learners leave the classroom. Learners can use the materials they receive as a reference back on the job or to train others who were not able to attend the workshop.

Typically, you will design handouts in the form of individual sheets that you pass out as you discuss a topic. You may also put handouts in the form of a participant guide or workbook that learners receive at the beginning of the session. In this case, encourage them to follow along and make notes throughout the workshop.

Some trainers like to wait until the end of a program to pass out handouts so that learners will not be distracted and read them during the workshop. The down side of this practice is that they likely will have nowhere to take notes, since many learners do not bring notebooks and writing tools with them. Even if you provide these, you may want to consider giving handouts or workbooks that keep learners actively engaged in the learning process. You can always give supplemental resource information that supports session content at the end of the session. Such information reinforces what you presented and provides a value-added takeaway for learners.

Always make sure that your written messages are accurate, and remember to format them in a manner that addresses brain-based principles and any special needs that your learners may have. Some people in your audience may have vision or learning disabilities (e.g., dyslexia) or difficulty reading certain textual messages. Ask learners to let you know if they have special needs so that you can prepare larger-text documents or make other accommodations for them.

Also related to reading difficulties, use caution when asking participants to read selected information aloud. If someone has a reading or learning disability or is illiterate, he or she will likely not be able to perform the task and will be embarrassed. The result is that the person may shut down and stop focusing on the session. Others may also resent having been put on the spot and embarrassed and they might create challenges for you.

Strategy for Success

The wonderful thing about handouts is that they can provide a comprehensive explanation of a topic and can supplement what you say verbally, especially when used in concert with visual images. When creating your handouts, keep simplicity in mind. Be clear and concise and make sure that you read the final product to check for correct spelling, rather than depending on electronic spelling and grammar checkers. The latter might approve a word from a spelling or grammatical standpoint, but you may have used the wrong word in your sentence. For example, "there" instead of "their" or "our" instead of "your"). When such errors occur, they can reflect negatively on your professionalism and attention to detail. If possible, have someone else read through your handouts before you have copies printed to ensure that you used proper grammar and syntax (sentence structure). This is crucial because what you write sends a message about your abilities and professionalism. Improperly composed messages can actually distract certain personality types who might focus on editing and analyzing your written messages rather than listening to the verbal message that you are delivering. These learners will also be likely to point out your errors on the end-of-session evaluation.

Personalizing What You Have Learned

- What are the most important things that you read in this chapter? Why?

- What are some ways that you can immediately apply concepts covered in this chapter?

- What additional resources or topics do you want to research based on what you read?

Preparing to Share Your Knowledge

 fter reading this chapter, and when applying what you learn, you will be able to:

1. Plan a successful learning outcome by keeping learners informed.

2. Create a positive, nurturing learning environment.

3. Lead by example in the classroom to help ensure that learning outcomes are maximized.

"The one important thing I have learned over the years is the difference between taking one's work seriously and taking one's self seriously. The first is imperative and the second is disastrous."

Margot Fonteyn

Planning for a Successful Outcome

High-risk sports enthusiasts such as race car drivers, sky divers, spelunkers, and SCUBA divers pay a lot of attention to their environment. They do this because unexpected change or evolving conditions could mean success or failure, or life or death. To help ensure a more positive outcome, they constantly monitor their surroundings and look for signs of elements that could negatively affect their performance. The same is true of professional trainers and educators. They plan, organize, and quickly adapt to their environment in order to ensure that learners achieve their maximum potential.

Part of this planning is to keep your learners informed at every phase of the process. To accomplish this, consider the following steps.

Give Learners a "Heads Up" on the Workshop

Let attendees know as much as possible about the workshop in advance through your marketing and registration materials (see Exhibits 8.1 and 8.2). Inform them of anything that might help them to mentally or physically prepare to get the most from the session. This includes:

Time(s). Allow your learners as much time as possible to plan for attendance at the learning event by sending out letters of acknowledgement informing them that they have successfully registered. Tell them the beginning and ending time of the session, and send a copy of the addenda showing the daily schedule, if available.

Date(s). In addition to the timing of sessions, inform learners of the date(s) of the workshop. This will allow them to pass the information along to others who have a need to know (e.g., family, peers, or supervisor). It will also provide adequate time to book airlines, rental cars, or hotels or make any other plans that they need to before the workshop.

Location. Give as much information about the facility as known. If learners get lost on the way to your workshop, you and other learners will ultimately be inconvenienced when they arrive late or do not show up at all. This can disrupt your planned session flow and activities. A simple way to prevent this possibility is to provide the room/ suite number, location, directions, and a map. If the workshop is being held remotely or off-site, providing a list of nearby hotels/motels, restaurants and shopping areas, or attractions can be helpful and will likely be appreciated.

Parking, Entrance, and Security Instructions. In addition to location information, share information that they will need related to parking facilities (e.g., will they need a parking permit and if so how to get one), accessibility, and what entrance to use once they arrive onsite. You may also want to send a reminder like the following about vehicle and personal security when traveling or parking.

Sample Security Guidelines

- Do not travel alone.

- Do not leave valuables in your car or hotel room.

- Protect your valuables.

- Have your keys ready when approaching your car.

- Park in well-lighted areas.

- Lock your car doors.

- Be alert to your surroundings.

- Walk near street and avoid alleyways and dark areas.

- Cross the street if you are suspicious of someone.

- Leave your television or radio on and put a "Do not disturb" sign on your door when you leave your hotel room.

- Never open your door if you do not recognize the person.

Program Description and Objectives. Send a brief overview of the session content, along with workshop objectives. This will allow learners to mentally prepare and to discuss any necessary goals with their supervisors (if the session is work-related). By allowing this advance planning, you may be able to engage their support mechanisms, such as a supervisor or coach, who can then be better prepared to assist and support them as they implement concepts they have learned when they return to their jobs. You also provide an opportunity for learners to do any desired advance topic research or bring along appropriate workshop-related materials.

Identify Academic and Professional Credits. Inform learners of any professional certifications or diplomas that will be obtained or academic credits issued (Continuing Education Units [CEUs]). If you have arranged for learners to receive college or professional credit for attending the workshop, let them know this in your registration correspondence. This is an added-value and may be a selling point for people trying to decide whether the session is worth their investment. It could also be the deciding factor for supervisors who are trying to determine which workshop offers the highest return on investment when their employees attend.

Advance Preparation Requirements. If there are pre-workshop requirements (e.g., assignments, materials to bring, or a need to contact you in advance to confirm registration), get these out to your learners as soon as possible. This can be done through mail, facsimile, e-mail, or other electronic means. If you have a website where you can post information related to the session, do so and direct learners to the website in all correspondence and contacts. This allows them to access information at their leisure.

Restrictions. Let learners know if you have planned activities that might create a challenge for some people due to mental or physical requirements. Encourage them to contact you immediately if they have the need for some sort of accommodation, or just to let you know so that you will be prepared to handle the situation. This will prevent uncomfortable situations and allow you to prepare the environment so that all learners receive maximum benefit from the session. To do anything less might put you and/or your organization in a litigious situation, since the Americans with Disabilities Act of 1990 requires accommodations for people with disabilities in the United States. Similar laws are in effect in many other countries.

Reminders. Make sure that at least one week before the start of the session you send out an e-mail or letter, call all registrants, or otherwise remind them of the time, date, location, details, and pre-work for the event. If the group will be small, using a more personal form of contact, rather than a form letter, can help make attendees feel more welcome and start your interpersonal bonding before they show up for the event. For example, you could e-mail or call each learner to say hello, to let them know you are excited about having them attend and look forward to meeting them, and to encourage them to bring a coat or sweater so that they can dress in layers to their own comfort level. You could also stress expectations of them so that they are mentally prepared for the workshop, for example, the fact that learners are expected to participate in small group activities or give a short presentation to the group.

Description of Any Planned Meals and Refreshments. Since some people might have special dietary needs or might need to meet someone during the scheduled lunch period, send along a description of planned refreshments and meals. This courtesy allows people to plan on their own if they need to bring snacks.

Exhibit 8.1. Sample Confirmation Letter
(External Training Program)

May 10, 2009
Global Performance Strategies
142 W. Lakeview Ave, Suite 1030-1039
Lake Mary, FL 32746

Re: Tapping the Brain for Learning Workshop

Dear (Registrant's Name):

Welcome to the creative trainer workshop! We appreciate your registration for the program and are excited about the opportunity to help you learn creative and dynamic strategies for training adults. The workshop incorporates the latest in brain research related to how adults learn best. You will learn strategies for enhancing any learning environment using such elements as movement, color, sound, lighting, nutrition, novelty, and much more.

To help you prepare, I am forwarding directions and parking instructions, a workshop brochure and a questionnaire about your learning needs. Please complete and return the latter by <u>May 19</u>.

The workshop is scheduled as follows:

Date: Thursday and Friday, June 13 and 14, 2009

Refreshments and registration: 8:00 A.M.

Workshop: 8:30 A.M. to 5:00 P.M.

Location: Global Performance Strategies Training Center

142 W. Lakeview Ave, Suite 1030-1039

Lake Mary, FL 32746

(407) 695-5535

Dress: Business casual

Workshop Facilitator: Bob Lucas, Master Trainer

If you have any questions concerning this workshop, the content, or the facilitator, please contact us at the number above. Additionally, if you have special nutritional or learning needs, please let us know immediately so that we can discuss any accommodations that might be necessary.

Bob Lucas looks forward to meeting you and to sharing exciting learning strategies that he has researched and developed over the past three decades.

Sincerely,

_____

Candace Hartsell

Exhibit 8.2. Sample Confirmation Letter (Internal Training Program)

October 10, 2009

Re: Tapping the Brain for Learning Workshop

Dear (Registrant's Name):

Thank you for registering for the creative trainer workshop! We have an exciting learning event planned and appreciate your registration. The workshop incorporates the latest in brain research related to how adults learn best. In it, you will discover strategies for enhancing any learning environment using such elements as movement, color, sound, lighting, nutrition, graphics, novelty, and much more.

To help you us better prepare for your specific learning needs, please complete and return the attached questionnaire to me here in Training & Development no later than October 19.

The workshop is scheduled:

    Date: Thursday and Friday, November 13 and 14, 2009

    Refreshments and registration: 8:00 A.M.

    Workshop: 8:30 A.M. to 5:00 P.M.

    Location: Conference Center

    Dress: Business casual

    Workshop Facilitator: Bob Lucas, Training Manager

If you have any questions concerning this workshop or its content, please contact me at extension 274 or e-mail me at chartsell@abccorp.com. Additionally, if you have special nutritional or learning needs, please let me know immediately so that we can discuss any accommodations that might be necessary.

Bob Lucas looks forward to meeting you and to sharing exciting learning strategies that you can immediately apply in your own departmental training programs.

Sincerely,

_____

Candace Hartsell

Strategy for Success

Part of any successful learning event is planning and marketing it effectively. To make sure that there are a maximum number of learners in attendance, set up a schedule for marketing your workshop. The amount of time required will be contingent on whether the workshop is done for an internal (within your organization or for a single client) or external (a public workshop or for people from various organizations). Based on your workshop date, create a timeline that shows each marketing tool that you plan to use. For example, you might want to use e-mail, phone solicitation, brochure mailing, personal networking at professional events, trade shows, websites, blogs, and other vehicles. Each strategy will take time to plan, create, and organize, so allow plenty of time to accomplish everything.

Create a Positive Emotional Environment

You read in Chapter 4 about the importance and potential effect of the physical environment and how you can maximize learning through selecting and arranging it to support planned activities. It is equally important for you to consider the emotional or psychological impact of what you do and say related to your learning environment. To set a tone of openness and make learners feel welcome, consider the following elements.

Prepare a Nurturing and Welcoming Atmosphere

You can have all preparation and set-up work completed (see Exhibit 3.1) before attendees start to arrive by being onsite an hour or more prior to the learners on the day of your training program. This is crucial in allowing you to be ready to focus on your learners and in making sure that everything planned is present and in place for the workshop.

Plan Seating Arrangement. One of the common challenges that anyone who trains or teaches faces is how to control side talk or conversations and comments from people who know or work with one another. Often these people can be a disruption and distraction for you and other learners and can detract from the overall session effectiveness because they are more likely to toss out irrelevant comments or joke with one another throughout the event.

Effective classroom management can be one of the biggest challenges faced, especially by newer trainers and educators who are less skilled at this process. A primary role that you have in any session is to monitor and control behavior of learners so that everyone has a positive and powerful learning experience. On one hand you likely do not want to be a disciplinarian, but on the other, all learners, and perhaps your sponsor or boss, look to you to take control and manage the classroom environment effectively in a non-threatening manner. The key is to be fair, but assertive and not let the behavior of one or two distract from the learning of the group.

There are many excellent articles and books on the topic of classroom management that you can check out if you want more ideas on this topic (see *People Strategies for Trainers* in the Bibliography).

Strategy for Success

A simple means of reducing or eliminating disruptions from people who know one another well is to separate them in a nonchalant manner without them even realizing it. To accomplish this, build grouping into your lesson plan by preparing, what appears to be random seat assignments.

In reality, you determine in advance who works together or knows one another by speaking to their supervisors or looking at the roster of attendees once everyone has registered. You then come up with creative strategies for assigning seats apart for friends and co-workers who will likely sit together. The following are some possibilities for separating learners:

Put prepared name tents on tables with the names of learners on them and ask people not to move them as they arrive.

Cut a number of regular playing cards, equal to the number of attendees, in half. Place one-half of each card at a participant location, shuffle the remaining cards to ensure they are not in consecutive order like 2, 3, and 4. As learners enter, give them the second half of a card and have them find their assigned seats. Ask them not to relocate. If by chance friends end up beside one another, you can randomly separate them throughout the day by setting up activities in which they work in teams with others.

Set up tables with enough seats for one team each, for example five or six learners per table. Put a name tent or piece of paper with a number, colored dot, photo of an item or animal, or whatever you choose, in the center of each table. As each participant arrives, give him or her a sheet of paper with a number, name, colored dot, or photo and tell the learner to sit wherever he or she finds a match on a table.

As a variation of the last idea, select a prop type for each table, for example, a stuffed animal, ball, toy, or another item related to the session topic. Pass out strips of paper with prop names on them to all learners as they enter. Have them sit wherever they find their assigned props.

Follow a Plan. Make sure that you use the checklist of learner materials and instructor materials and training aids listed on your lesson plan cover sheet (see Exhibit 3.1) as you are packing for the session and again when you arrive to set up the room. Additionally, follow the Instructor Notes found inside your lesson plan so that you do not forget to take care of details prior to your attendees arriving.

Ensure Adequate Support. Training is a team event, as you cannot be successful without a strong support effort. Good rapport and communication with your support staff can often make or break your learning event. Your support team might include:

♦ Printers who handle your handouts, posters, and other visual aids

♦ Registrar who coordinates marketing efforts, mailings, and registration of participants

♦ Caterer who provides food and refreshments and delivers and sets them up

♦ Co-facilitators who help make the session run smoothly and deliver content or monitor small group activities

♦ Audiovisual staff, if you are recording the event or portions thereof. You should work closely with these people in advance to ensure that they know what you want and so that you have a realistic expectation of what the final product will look like and its availability.

♦ Facility staff who deliver and set up tables, audiovisual equipment, wastebaskets, and other needed items. These people should be on call and you should have a means of contacting them readily when something goes wrong with equipment, lighting, or temperature, or you need additional materials, such as an extension cord.

Focus on the Details. Nothing sends a more powerful non-verbal message to learners than what they see and experience in the first thirty seconds after they arrive. For this reason, make sure that you pay close attention the minutia and that everything is perfect with your room layout and preparation. This comes with planning and practice. Small things can say a lot about your attention to detail and professionalism. When placing handouts, pencils, name tents, and other materials on tables, put them in exactly the same location and order for each participant. If pencils have writing on them, place each so that the letters are up and can be read by learners.

When learners walk in they should see that you have taken time to think about their needs and have given thought to the smallest details. This subconsciously sets high expectations for the session and shows that you are a professional who will focus energy on giving them the best possible learning experience. Other details like having all chairs neatly placed under tables in the same position, having refreshments and training aids carefully and meticulously placed, background music playing, a welcome slide or flip chart displayed, and other related elements are important.

Strategy for Success

Even if you set up your room the night before, get to the location at least an hour before learners to double-check everything. Ensure that training aids are visible from every point in the room and make sure that all training aids still work and are where you left them. Training "gremlins" often sneak in during the night to sabotage your efforts. I have been in locations where someone came in to "borrow" a piece of equipment after I set it up and tested it and did not return it before the next morning. The person also used the room for a meeting or other session and did not rearrange materials as I left them.

Remember: You are the one who will look unprepared when learners arrive if you do not follow this advice.

Make the First Few Minutes Count

You may have heard that people form an opinion of you within the first thirty seconds of meeting. Thus, it makes sense for you to go out of your way to create a powerful first impression and set your workshop up for success. It is hard to recover from a bad initial impression. There are a number of ways that you can project a powerful, professional first impression.

Greet Learners. Be ready to meet and greet all participants at the door or once they are seated. Conduct a bit of small talk to get to know them briefly. In doing so, smile, shake their hands, and use their names as you share information, give any instructions, and point out things like seating assignments (if used) and location of refreshments and restrooms. By talking to learners in advance and shaking their hands, you start to form a psychological bond with them. This can help ease any apprehension they might have. You also begin to set the tone for more positive interaction and participation later. This can help you relax as you become familiar with those in the room.

Part of your greeting should also be to introduce newcomers to those already present, since some people are shy about approaching strangers. This measure can help encourage further interaction and communication between learners and their ultimate involvement in workshop discussions later.

Convey Expectations. One of the adult learning principles that you read about in Chapter 1 was that adults are self-directing and like to feel that they control their learning to some degree. To address this need, you may wish to create a colorful poster or flip-chart page and post it at the door or in front of the room that offers some of your expectations of learners. You can also accomplish this with a revolving slide show. Another alternative is to use a handout (see Exhibit 8.3) that lists possible roles that both you and they have to make the session a success. This gets learners thinking about what they should do throughout the program.

Even though you may have distributed materials that explained learning objectives, spend a bit of time early to review these. This will get everyone focused on what will be covered and the materials to be used.

All of this is done to reduce any confusion so that your learners will be more open to what is offered and potentially become more active participants in the process by offering ideas, challenging things that are said, and contributing their own experiences to help others benefit from their knowledge.

Exhibit 8.3. Sample Training Contract

Please consider this program a "safe" environment. What we say here; stays here.

It's all right to . . .

♦ Express your ideas

♦ Challenge the facilitator's ideas

♦ Make mistakes

(continued)

Exhibit 8.3. (*Continued*)

◆ Offer examples (please keep them generic with no names used)

◆ Question

◆ Relax

Your Role . . .

◆ Be on time (from breaks and lunch).

◆ Participate openly.

◆ Learn in your own way.

◆ Opt out of physical activities or participate to your level of comfort.

◆ Provide honest, open feedback on evaluations.

◆ Enjoy yourself!

Facilitator's Role . . .

◆ Start and end on time.

◆ Professionally facilitate the exchange of information and knowledge.

◆ Allow time for and encourage your input.

◆ Listen non-defensively.

◆ Help you grow personally and professionally.

Strategy for Success

As an alternative to my creating a list of expectations, one activity that I sometimes use as an introductory activity is to have learners form small groups and create a list of "rules" or guidelines that they think should be followed during the workshop. The following are some typical guidelines:

Everyone participates actively.

No cell phones or text messaging during the workshop.

No side conversations.

Come back from breaks on time.

Respect the opinions of others.

Be respectful.

Allow others to speak.

Working together to create a list of guidelines will give participants a chance to get to know one another while addressing their need to be self-directed.

Through a nominal group technique activity, you can further engage learners by having them rank the top ten rules to which the group will adhere during the session. To do this, give each participant three colored dots (any color combination in fine) and have them individually go up to the posted list. They then vote by placing one or more dots next to the three rules that they believe are important. The ten rules receiving the most votes are then copied onto another sheet of paper and posted on the wall. These become the guidelines that are used for the workshop.

Develop an Atmosphere of Trust. Trust is crucial in any relationship. Without it, you have no relationship. The need for trust is especially important in a learning environment, in which you need learners to believe in and take to heart what you share with them. Learners must know that you have their best interest at heart, that you will not deliberately embarrass or mislead them, and that you will do your best to maximize their learning.

An easy way to begin establishing this trust with participants is to use some of the techniques described earlier and to quickly establish your credibility. Let learners know your credentials and past experience related to the topic. Because time is precious, they will want to know that you have something valuable to offer. You can do this in your opening remarks by discussing your qualifications. You can also include a one-page biography in your handouts. The latter allows learners to refer to the information later if they want to share information about you and the workshop with others. Providing written information is good for the visual learners in the group and provides something for learners to read as they wait for everyone to arrive and before the session. Depending on your learners' backgrounds, your credentials may be very important to building trust. For example, in many Asian cultures, educators, writers, and other professionally credentialed people are typically valued and respected.

Another way of introducing information about yourself or sharing background information without "tooting your own horn" is to self-disclose or share personal experiences related to session content throughout the program. This is a great way to appeal to your learners and help them relate to what you are saying while providing examples from which they might pull ideas when they apply what is learned to their own real-world situations. Storytelling is a powerful instructional tool. For example, in a train-the-trainer session, when discussing the need to have a contingency plan when using unfamiliar learning environments, I share several examples of less-than-desirable environments in which I have trained in the past. I also tell of strategies used to adapt to those situations in order to make the learning events a success. This shows that I have "been there" and know some of their challenges and that I also have valuable ideas to share that might help them in their own training efforts.

Remain Flexible. The mark of a true professional trainer or educator is being flexible, being able to come back when things do not work as planned or expected, and being open to other ideas or possibilities. One of the biggest mistakes that trainers make is to come across as rigid, stoic, or autocratic. This can turn learners off and create a barrier to learning. It can also potentially prevent learners from approaching you with questions, alternate thoughts or ideas, and information. You can be serious about your role and session content without seeming to take yourself too seriously. Keep in mind that your learners are the most important people in the room. Without them, you would not be there. Everything you do should be focused on making sure that they have a memorable and effective learning experience.

You have probably heard of "Murphy's law: If something can go wrong, it will." In training there are many things that are out of your control that can make this "law" a reality. Even when you do everything right, unexpected events can throw you off balance, for example, a fire, lighting or climate control failing, or learners getting the wrong information about date, time, and location from their supervisors and not showing up. For this reason, plan for extenuating circumstances and be ready with a backup plan. Being flexible might mean conducting training at alternate venues and times. This might include training offsite instead in an organizational training room as planned, or in the evening or on a weekend instead of during the day or normal work week. When the unexpected occurs, it can certainly be frustrating and cause you to want to say, "Fine, we just won't do the program." The reality is that both you and learners ultimately are the ones to suffer if you have not planned for the unexpected. For that reason, keep your mind open to other options and be ready to use them.

Strategy for Success

In addition to greeting learners and setting an informal environment, as described earlier, one of the things you can do at the beginning of your workshops is to let learners know that, while you take the material seriously, you do not take yourself seriously. Depending on the cultural group, topic, or setting, you might also encourage them to call you by your first name and explain that to enhance learning the group will be taking an informal approach to discussion of the topic. Also tell learners to get comfortable, relax, and do what they need to do to be comfortable. You can model this by saying something like, "We are going to be here for a while so I am going to get comfortable and remove my jacket (as you do so). I encourage you to do the same. Feel free to settle back and do whatever you need to get the most from the session, or even take your shoes off! If your neighbors do not complain and it does not distract from the session, I do not mind." Such an approach helps send a message that they are there for the learning and not to follow some rigid format. It can also add a bit of levity.

Depending on the audience and session content, you might start your session wearing some prop. For example, wear Groucho Marx glasses, an animal nose, or a play arrow through your head, then tie in your opening comments to the prop so that there is meaning to the display. I sometimes start with an activity in my train-the-trainer workshops where I wear a foam Cheesehead® top hat and a foam cheese bowtie to add an air of "formality" to the event. In doing so, I announce who I am and that I am their "master of ceremonies" for the day! All of this is done to lighten the atmosphere and generate a few laughs, which can reduce anxiety for me and for my learners.

Empower Your Learners. Empowering learners is a simple way for trainers to encourage ownership and involvement in a learning event. As you read earlier, most adults like to have a feeling of ownership or control over their learning and over what happens to them. You can help satisfy this need by letting them know early in your workshop that they are empowered to do the following:

♦　Ask questions

♦　Challenge ideas and thoughts (in a respectful and courteous manner)

♦　Call "time out" if they miss a concept or want clarification

♦　Volunteer for tasks or assignments

♦　Voice their concerns when things are dragging or they feel a point being covered has already been made

You can also include them in learning by:

♦　Randomly selecting people to be small group or team leaders and scribes (note-takers) for activities

♦　Assigning individuals to monitor time for events throughout the session or announcing when a specified period has elapsed

♦　Being responsible for small tasks like passing out handouts or posting flip-chart pages on the wall

Strategy for Success

One way to allow learners to "vote" or voice their opinions in class is to pass out Ping-Pong-type Dry Erase paddles and markers (see Kwik Chek Paddles at www.presentationresources.net). Have learners use Dry Erase markers to write terms such as Yes/No, Agree/Disagree, Why?/How?, or Confused/Understand, which you indicate, on opposing sides during your opening remarks or before an activity.

(continued)

Let learners know that when they want to make their thoughts known, they should simply hold up the appropriate term. Such engagement ties to the brain-based concepts of novelty, engagement, and physical activity by raising and lowering the arm, which can help keep people alert and involved throughout the session.

An alternative to the paddles is to use multiple-colored strips of construction paper such as Green for Yes/Understand, Yellow for Possibly/Need More Information, and red for No/Confused.

Whenever a learner feels a need to hold up a card to respond, he or she can do so. You can also be on the lookout for novelty items that have the three colors or that can substitute for the concepts. In the past, I have used hand-shaped fly swatters in the three colors and miniature toy signs in the shape of stop, yield, and proceed traffic signs.

One hint in using the paddles or cards is to pause periodically during the first hour or so and ask for their feedback by having them hold up the appropriate response or card related to something you just said or covered. This gets them in the habit of using the materials, gives you quick feedback on their comprehension level, and encourages them to use the items whenever they feel the need.

Lead by Example

One of the easiest ways to turn your learners off is to say one thing and do another. For example, if you encouraged them to relax and enjoy themselves but you are tense, nervous, rigid, and never smile or tell a humorous story or joke, you send conflicting messages. Your "walking the talk" encourages learners to become active participants in the session. This can lead to elevated learner confidence, a higher number of ideas generated, and a more productive learning experience for them and for you.

One simple way of being consistent in your messages is to take a lead role throughout the session. This can be something as simple as going first when you ask them to do something. For example, after showing a flip-chart page with information that you would like learners to disclose as they introduce themselves, start by modeling the desired behavior and introduce yourself before learners introduce themselves. Another instance might be taking the lead in a role play or demonstration if you are asking them to act out a part afterward. This not only shows them what you expect, but also provides a model and lets them see that you are willing to put yourself out in front of the group.

Project a Positive Personal Image

You have already read about the importance of making a powerful first impression. You can do many things to make this happen. Plan and think about your event. Gain more knowledge related to effectively presenting information and learn how the brain best processes information. By doing these things, you are more likely to be successful in imparting your knowledge and skills to learners.

Have you ever had a trainer who was very serious, focused, and formal? If so, you and your peers likely reacted to that and were also very rigid and serious. On the other hand, if you had a trainer who was professional but was more laid back and took an informal approach by smiling, laughing periodically, telling jokes, and sharing personal stories related to the program content, you likely acted similarly. I am willing to bet that if you have experienced both types of sessions, you probably remember the latter and its content more that you do the former. This is because, as brain researchers have found, laughter, levity, personalization, and other similar tactics tend to grab and hold attention while reinforcing and encouraging learning. To mimic these results, make sure that, before you go "on stage" and start your workshop, you take a deep breath, walk through your opening remarks mentally, and literally relax a bit before stepping in front of your participants. Smile and look for smiling, friendly faces in the group. These people usually sit up front, as those learners are anxious to gain from the session and often sit closer to the trainer. They will recognize and respond to your actions. You smile and they will smile in return, which in turn helps you relax and feel wanted more, so you smile at others, they feel welcome, and the pattern repeats itself. Pretty soon, most people in the room are relaxed and smiling.

Avoid Stage Fright. Stage fright is an issue that plagues many professional trainers, speakers, and educators and it is quite normal. After nearly four decades of speaking to large groups, I am still anxious at times before stepping in front of a large audience or new training group, or when presenting a new topic or workshop to a group. I am not alone. There are numerous stories of how famous stars like Carol Burnett, Barbra Streisand, Donny Osmond, Kim Basinger, Sir Laurence Olivier, and others have struggled with "stage freight" throughout their careers and had to work to overcome it. We all use a variety of techniques to overcome anxiety, fear of speaking, or concern about public rejection.

When people experience stage freight, they often fear social rejection and exhibit symptoms like the following:

♦ Increased pulse rate

♦ Shortness of breath

♦ Tight or constricted throat and cracking voice

♦ Trembling lips

♦ Sweating

♦ Dry mouth

♦ Queasy feeling in the stomach, nausea, or diarrhea

♦ Cold or shaky hands

♦ Shaky knees

♦ Dizziness

In addition to proper planning and taking care of many of the details that you read about earlier in this chapter, some common strategies for helping to overcome stage fright include the following.

Never Apologize. It will or focus attention on the fact that you are nervous or that something did not go as planned, for example, a DVD or video player is not working, hand-outs did not arrive from the printer, or a guest speaker cancelled at the last minute. In instances such as these, your learners will likely never know that something went wrong unless you point it out or have previously announced that those things would be included in the workshop. They do not have your lesson plan and only respond to what you do or say in front of them. If something goes wrong, pause, take a deep breath, think of an alternative to what was planned and move on. Remember that, until you open your mouth, learners typically assume that you are a professional and that they are about to experience a memorable learning opportunity.

Know Your Session Content Well and How You Will Present It. This comes from thoroughly rehearsing your workshop content delivery a number of times until you have a feeling of routine. Getting your timing and movements down in advance can do a lot to relax you when learners arrive. As a rule of thumb, I recommend that you have at least eight hours of subject knowledge for every one hour of session content that you plan to present. This will give you adequate background information to answer questions and to fill in if you find that you need additional material.

Be Familiar with Your Training Venue. Knowing the room size, configuration, and layout in advance can make a great deal of difference in how you plan to deliver information. By getting to your venue early and rehearsing in the actual room where you will conduct your session, you mentally lock in details and do not have to think about them once you start to present your content. If possible, view your room at least a day before the workshop to visualize yourself in it as you plan for delivery.

Envision Yourself Being Successful. Before you arrive onsite, imagine the audience, room layout, how you will handle questions, that participants are attentive and contribute to the session, and that you successfully deliver the program content to learners.

RELAX! Do some simple stretching or isometric exercises. For example, you can place the palms of your hands against the wall, move your feet back several feet and shoulder width apart, and simply push your weight forward on the wall to expend energy. Open and close your mouth and throat. Inhale and exhale forcefully several times to clear your head and get oxygen into the lungs. Breathe normally.

Strategy for Success

Trainers, speakers, and educators have many ways to relax before beginning their programs or presentations. Many have learned what works for them through experience. Some of their secrets might work for you also. Some of the tricks I often use include:

Taking a walk through the hallways or outside in the fresh air for about ten minutes as I rehearse my opening remarks mentally and clear my head before encountering learners.

Greeting learners as they enter and engaging in small talk so that we are not strangers when I actually begin the session.

Taking a deep breath and exhaling before stepping in front of a group.

Having water available on my instructor's table and taking a sip before I begin. I avoid caffeine and milk products, since the former is a diuretic and the latter coats the vocal cords and can make speaking difficult.

Enthusiastically greeting learners, smiling, and genuinely welcoming everyone. For example, I might say in a loud, enthusiastic voice: "GOOD MORNING EVERYONE! HOW ARE YOU DOING TODAY!" This quick burst of energy typically affects my learners and me positively. If I do not receive an enthusiastic response from the group, I simply say, "Oh come on! You can do better than that!" I then repeat my greeting, which typically elicits a more enthusiastic group reaction.

Start on Time. Do not penalize learners who arrive on time because others are not punctual. There may be legitimate reasons why someone is late, such as traffic problems or personal issues; however, this is not your concern and should not be a reason to delay your start time.

By starting at the scheduled time, you send a non-verbal message that you are professional and that punctuality is expected. If you know that a sizable number of your group has been delayed because of a serious traffic accident, weather, or other issues like a bus from the hotel at which they are staying got lost, you can still start on time with those present. You can state, "We'll be starting the content portion of our session shortly; however, let's begin now by doing a bit of networking." Follow that by assigning specific information components for learners to exchange, such as their names, positions, organizations, expectations for the session, or other pertinent items. This informally begins the workshop. When others arrive, simply ask them to introduce themselves briefly and encourage them to network throughout breaks and at lunch to get to know their peers. If there are people still delayed following the networking, go ahead, start the session content portion, and suggest that newcomers partner with others to get notes during the first break or at lunch.

Follow a Structured Process. You read about the importance of having a structured lesson plan in Chapter 3. As part of your preparation, give thought to how you will address the three sections of your session: Introduction, Body, and Conclusion. Through better planning, you can enhance the chances of success in meeting the learning objectives that you developed from your needs analysis and outlined in your lesson plan. Think about how you will accomplish the following in each component of the workshop.

Introduction

You may have someone introduce you or you can introduce yourself at the beginning of your workshop. You normally will base your approach on the workshop design and whether it is conducted internally or externally. In either case, it is a good idea to have a series of points that you want learners to know that will help quickly to establish your expertise and credibility. Some common things to share include:

♦ Name

♦ Organization

♦ Brief professional highlights related to the session, for example, research you have conducted, books or publications, years of experience in the field, or educational background

♦ Any fact about yourself that you might think pertinent or that learners should know

The key is to be brief and not waste time "tooting your own horn." An easy way to cut down on the amount of information that you need to share is to place a brief personal biography as the first or last page of your participant workbook or handouts. You can then simply tell learners who you are and highlight a couple facts and refer them to that page if they want to read more about you later. By placing this page in the materials, you also provide a potential resource for learners and their organization that might be shared with others looking for a workshop in the future. This could be beneficial for generating future workshops or consulting work.

During this portion of your workshop you may also want to have learners in turn introduce themselves or get involved in a small group activity. Your choice depends on what you have planned.

Opening Comments

Your initial comments are normally found in the Introduction section of your lesson plan and include statistics, examples, stories, jokes, or other statements that will motivate learners to actively listen and stay focused on you so that you can provide meaningful information later. You may also want to cover the learning objectives briefly, supported by visual aids or handouts. Let learners know that you appreciate their attendance and punctuality and that you are there to help them enhance their knowledge, skills, or attitudes (KSAs).

Strategy for Success

I often do an activity involving a simple magic trick during my opening comments. During such times, I capture the attention of my learners and tie to learning objectives. To accomplish this, I demonstrate a trick involving a prop called a *Change Bag* (available at www.presentationresources.net) that has an inside hidden compartment.

Before the session begins and learners arrive, I create a list of the session objectives on a single sheet of flip-chart paper, fold the page neatly into a small square, and insert it into one of the bag's two compartments. Learners are not aware of the list or the multiple compartments.

Next, I create an identical flip-chart sheet and cut strips of paper containing one objective each. I fold these strips and place them in a bag, box, or other container on my Instructor's table.

When I am ready to cover the objectives during my introduction, I ask for one volunteer at a time to come forward to select and read an objective. I reward these people with candy or toys or other small prizes related to the session content to begin setting a positive motivational tone to the workshop and encourage future volunteerism.

As each volunteer reads an objective, I explain how we will address that particular point during the workshop. The volunteer then refolds and inserts the objective into the Change Bag (in the second compartment of the bag).

Once all the objectives have been read, I have everyone give the volunteers a round of applause and say something like, "You now know our objectives for the session. Let's review them." At that point, I reach into the Change Bag, extract the full flip-chart page with objectives, open it, tape it to an easel, and review the objectives. Learners are captivated and stunned that the paper has magically reassembled, and I now have their attention and can continue.

Workshop Flow

This portion of a training program is what I call "administrivia." Cover the following points after your introduction in order to let learners know what is going to happen during the workshop. This ties to adults' need to feel in control of their learning. Address such items as the following:

♦ Policies on cell phones and personal digital assistants (PDAs)

♦ Smoking guidelines

♦ Times of breaks and lunch

♦ Handouts and materials that they have or how they will use them

♦ Refreshments (I encourage learners to help themselves)

♦ The reward system, if you are using one. (I stress the fact that contributions or ideas and volunteering will reap stickers, prizes, toys, opportunities, or other incentives.)

Body

The major portion of what you will do or say is included in the Body section of your lesson plan. It is important that you have a firm grasp of session content and that you deliver your message in a creative, dynamic, and meaningful manner. As you read in Chapter 3, the information that you cover must be organized and presented in a logical sequence, using numerous examples, and including suggestions for application. To make sure learners get the most out of the content, use activities in which they discover uses and ideas related to concepts you identify. You must also be able to answer any questions that are asked and counter any challenges from learners. In addition, transitions from one key topic to the next must be smooth and flawless and provide a verbal bridge for learners to cross from one topic to the next. Anything less will likely feel awkward and unprofessional.

Conclusion

In the closing portion of your session, you must briefly summarize key points that you covered in the Body section. You should never introduce new information at this point. This is the end of the session and you should wrap everything covered into a nice neat package. Because people often remember the first and last thing they experience in a presentation, you want to ensure that your learners will walk away with more than they started with. You may want to have learners complete a post-test that consists of the same questions that they answered on any pre-test that you administered. You may also want to build in a final review activity in which key concepts and terms are highlighted.

Strategy for Success

Instead of simply going through a list of key concepts as a review, I have used a simple review activity for years. I form two equal teams that form two circles and randomly select one scorekeeper from each team. These people will keep score for the opposing teams and capture ideas generated by that team on a flip chart.

When I shout go, team members take terms shouting out key concepts, ideas, or terms that they learned during the program while the scorekeeper writes these down. Learners cannot duplicate concepts. At the end of three minutes, I sound a noisemaker to stop the competition.

Scorekeepers eliminate all duplicate terms and tally the remaining ones.

The team with the most ideas, concepts, or terms wins small prizes and everyone gets a round of applause.

As a class, we quickly review each term and I ask questions such as, "What does that mean to you?" "How can that be applied?" and "In what ways can this benefit you?"

Be a Valuable Resource. Most learners attend training to grow professionally and hope to leave with KSAs that they did not have when they entered. Through the process, most people also desire to identify tools, strategies, techniques, and other resources that they can call upon as they need them in the future. Unfortunately, many trainers fall short of helping learners accomplish this goal by not providing resource listings with their handouts or they fail to offer themselves as a future resource. The result is that both trainers and learners miss additional opportunities.

To become a resource to learners, try the following strategies:

◆ Either create a biographical listing of sources used for your session content and include it at the rear of your handouts, or list those sources individually as footnotes throughout the document.

◆ List a series of resources such as organizations, people, items, or other useful content relevant to your session material. This allows learners to follow up on or refer to them after the session has ended.

♦ Pass out business cards and put your contact information on the bottom of all handout pages as a footnote. This provides a way for learners to get in touch with you for questions in the future.

♦ Write articles or compile a list of articles, books, or resources on workshop-related topics. Pass these items out at the end of your session as a value-added product that learners can read, refer to, and pass along to others.

♦ Do not forget to put your contact information at the bottom of handouts so that learners will know where they came from later. This is a great way to generate future training and consulting opportunities, sometimes years later, as someone comes across an article and needs further training or assistance in your specific area of expertise.

♦ Create a website resource in the form of articles, tips, or blogs that offer additional ideas, connections, and information following the workshop. Learners can then log on at their leisure. This is also a great way to promote future learning events to past attendees.

♦ Create audio and video files or short e-books on related content if you are technology-literate. Place them on your website to allow learners access to additional resources. Such products might even become residual revenue streams as people purchase them from your website.

Personalizing What You Have Learned

- What are the most important things that you read in this chapter? Why?

- What are some ways that you can immediately apply concepts covered in this chapter?

- What additional resources or topics do you want to research based on what you read?

PART 4

Making the Workshop a Success

Keeping the Learning Going

After reading this chapter, and when applying what you learn, you will be able to:

1. Ensure learner readiness by starting your sessions on a high note.

2. Manage learner expectations by maintaining a flexible approach to training.

3. Connect with learners through effective feedback strategies.

4. Engage learners through a variety of activities.

"Good teaching is one-fourth preparation and three-fourths pure theatre."

Gail Godwin

Ensure Learner Readiness

Have you ever wondered why, when you go to a rock concert, you see one or two opening acts of groups you may never have heard of before the big-name group appears on stage? And why do you have to sit through a variety of previews of upcoming movies on themes similar to the movie you have paid to see before your movie begins? What's the reason for comedians and magicians "setting up" the coming jokes or tricks by providing a bit of background banter? Certainly, advertising or generating interest in the unknown bands, the upcoming movies, and forthcoming jokes or magic are part of the goal. A more important reason is that the audience is "cold" and needs to get into the right frame of mind. In the same way, as a trainer, you need to think about your "opening act." How are you going to set the learning stage? You must ensure no learner is still thinking about a conversation he or she was having with a peer or a project in the workplace or an e-mail on his or her PDA when you announce the start of the your workshop.

Just like a comedian or actor, if you do not have a receptive audience, your remarks could very easily "bomb." Trust me, once you hit that low, it is very difficult and sometimes impossible to recover quickly, if at all. Remember what you read in Chapter 8 about the importance of first impressions.

Strategy for Success

To ensure that you are in the right frame of mind and ready to open your session successfully, I encourage you to have your opening remarks memorized so that you do not have to keep referring to notes or visual aids. If you plan to tell a joke, but are not a regular joke-teller, make sure you have practiced it on a few people to see whether it is funny to them before using it in training. Otherwise, you may want to think of alternative ways to gain learner attention and start with a bang. If your opening remarks do not grab learners and pique their interest in what you are saying, you are likely to lose them in the first few minutes of the your presentation. Here are two other points to consider related to joke telling:

1. If you could potentially offend ANYONE because of race, gender, body type, ability level, or anything else, do not use the joke.

2. Keep in mind that humor and sarcasm do not always transcend cultural divides. If learners are from other cultures in which humor is not commonly used in training or in which they have no context for the joke, learners will not "get it" and your intend will be lost. For example, humor related to certain sports, politics, or cultural-related issues may have no meaning to someone from another country. Additionally, some people view jokes as a waste of time and as not professional behavior in a workplace environment.

Manage Learner Expectations

Making sure that learner expectations match your workshop objectives will be crucial to your success. It will also help ensure that you do not receive negative remarks on your end of session evaluations.

For a variety of reasons, people may show up for your workshop with differing perspectives on what they will receive.

This may occur because learners did not effectively read workshop marketing materials or because their supervisors did not appropriately inform them what to expect. In these cases, if you do not clarify the objectives of the program early and define how learners will benefit from the workshop content, you may end up with dissatisfied and upset attendees.

To prevent any misunderstandings, build a question like "What do you want to know or be able to do differently at the end of this workshop?" into your opening remarks or icebreaker activity. Based on the responses that you receive, you can proceed as planned or you may have to address any misperceptions. For example, assume that you are conducting an advanced skill workshop titled "Creating Dynamic PowerPoint Slides" in which you will show how to add music, color, sound, film clips, and other creative add-ons to slideshows. In the opening minutes of the program, you ask learners why they are there and several people indicate that they are there to learn how to use PowerPoint. Obviously, there is a mismatch between program content and learner needs or expectations. You must first clarify learning outcomes for this session and suggest that the misplaced learners leave and sign up for a more appropriate session. Failure to do this will cause problems later when you are going through technical aspects of the PowerPoint software. Less experienced learners will require special help. This would detract from your facilitation and will slow down the delivery for everyone else. In the end, none of your learners will likely be satisfied with the workshop, and their evaluation comments will likely reflect that reaction.

One way to deal with the situation would be to have your learning objectives printed on a slide or flip chart and in participant workbooks. Refer to these as you say something like, "It sounds like several folks have a need for more basic instruction on PowerPoint. This is NOT what we will be covering in this session. In this workshop we will focus on. . . . " Following this, begin an icebreaker activity and call the learners who obviously do not belong in the workshop to the front of the room to discuss options of staying if they have enough knowledge of PowerPoint or quietly leaving and signing up for a different workshop in the future. It they opt for the latter, that might be an opportunity for you to design and offer a separate workshop on basic PowerPoint skills.

Connect with Learners

Many people have written about the importance of opening remarks and the first ten minutes of a learning event for guaranteeing the transfer of knowledge and skills. Numerous brain and memory experts suggest that people tend to remember the first and last things they encounter during a conversation or training program. For that reason, it makes sense that you should put some extra effort into making the introduction to your workshop as powerful and meaningful as possible.

Look for ways to engage your learners immediately in the workshop. Many trainers and educators use icebreaker activities designed to help learners quickly get to know one another and share information and to introduce information about the key concepts of the program. Everything that you do, say, or introduce into the workshop should be in some way related to your session topic and add value. Any training aids, stories, jokes, analogies, or metaphors that you will use should be pertinent and help to reinforce session objectives.

Ask for Feedback Regularly

Before you can share your ideas and other information that will help your learners improve their KSAs, you must know what they are thinking and feeling related to you and your workshop. You can find this our by regularly gathering verbal, non-verbal, and written feedback and through observing learners. This can assist you in determining whether learners are effectively absorbing what you have presented.

Seek input from learners from the very beginning of a learning event. Learners are constantly providing clues to their comprehension and level of motivation in training. Be alert and pick up their verbal as well as non-verbal signals. By using rewards or reinforcement of some type when you receive feedback, you increase the likelihood that learners will stay connected and involved. For example, if you ask a question and someone volunteers a response, thank the person and give him or her a piece of candy to reinforce the positive nature of the exchange. Similarly, if learners volunteer to demonstrate steps of a process that you have taught, you can reward them with positive feedback and a small toy or other prize related to the session theme. You can also have other learners give a round of applause for the demonstration.

The following are some of the more common ways to help determine workshop effectiveness and gauge how learners are doing during a workshop.

Watch Non-Verbal Cues

Make eye contact with learners and monitor their responses as you deliver information. If you see the MEGO effect (My Eyes Glaze Over) occurring, change the pace of your delivery, get learners more actively engaged, give a stretch break, or add some sort of sensory stimulus. This includes things like the use of props, sounds, movement, or color. Failure to use one of these strategies can result in lost learning time, since most people will have mentally "checked out" at that point.

Effective trainers continually watch the body language of their learners to gauge learner attentiveness. If you see learners exhibiting any of the following cues, you have likely lost their attention and need to address the issue in a positive manner:

Indicators of Lost Attention

♦ Being caught off-guard and not knowing what is being discussed when you ask a direct question

♦ Checking their personal schedules on their PDAs or personal planners

♦ Doodling, drawing, or writing things not related to the session

♦ Dozing off

♦ Facing away from you or the front of the room

♦ Having quiet, distracting side conversations

♦ Playing excessively with props like manipulative toys that you provided on their tables

♦ Regularly checking their watches or a wall clock

♦ Staring out a window or door or at a wall, ceiling, or floor

Ask Questions

You have already read about the importance of asking the right type of questions periodically in order to gather information and measure learner comprehension. Use this technique often and in various ways throughout your workshop. For example, your questions might be in an instructor-led activity, on a questionnaire or a visual aid, or can be learner-generated,.

Use Small Group Activities

Build in a variety of periodic activities with groups of four to six learners in which you assign them the task of generating lists or solutions. For example, they could develop a list of questions that they might ask their supervisors, peers, or customers related to your workshop topic when they return to their workplaces.

Incorporate Demonstrations

One of the easiest ways to engage learners and determine whether they have a solid grasp of workshop content is to have them demonstrate how they might apply what they have learned. You can involve the auditory, visual, and kinesthetic learning modalities, as well as several of the multiple intelligences, through this technique.

Strategy for Success

When you notice learners losing interest in workshop content; stop what you are doing and conduct a quick physical activity. To accomplish this:

Have learners stand behind their chairs and tell them to use their chairs for balance, if needed.

Explain that, like the children's game "Simon Says" in which they complete a task that they are told, they will simply follow your instructions in a fun exercise. The only difference is that they you will not be saying "Simon Says" before each action.

Tell learners to participate to their own level of comfort and ability. For example, if you tell them to raise their arms to shoulder level and rotate their arms to the front, but they have an impairment that prevents doing so, they can rotate hands by their sides.

Have learners pat themselves on their left shoulders three times with their right hands.

Have learners pat themselves on their right shoulder three times with their left hands.

Have learners raise their left feet behind their right knees and pat their left heels with their right hands three times.

Have learners raise their right feet behind their left knees and pat their right heels with their left hands three times.

Have learners pat their left knees with their right hands three times.

Have learners pat their right knees with their left hands three times.

Have learners lift both arms straight out to the side at shoulder level with their palms down (or to their level of comfort) and rotate both arms in a forward circular motion until told to stop.

Have learners stop the forward motion after fifteen seconds and reverse the circular motion to the rear until told to stop.

Have learners stop after fifteen seconds and rotate their arms in opposite directions at the same time until told to stop.

Have learners stop and give a round of applause, then sit down.

Tell learners that the activity ties to the theory that each side of the brain controls the opposite side of their body. By using body parts from both sides of the body at the same time, they engaged the whole brain. Also explain that the purpose of the activity is to increase their heartbeats and flow of blood to their brains. Since the blood contains oxygen that stimulates the neurons of the brain and increases brain functioning, they become more alert for what you will discuss next. With that statement, move to your next topic.

Provide Feedback to Learners

Your learners expect that you will let them know what you expect from them and how they are meeting expectations during a learning event. When learners receive appropriate, ongoing feedback, their motivation typically will go up.

According to Eric Jensen in his book *Sizzle & Substance,* "Feedback comes in many forms. It may be the single most powerful motivator there is. The research, however, suggests that, when it is learner-controlled, feedback is far more effective." To tap into this concept, use feedback strategies that allow learners to self-assess or to give one another feedback and input during your workshop. This will give them a better picture of how they are doing and will reduce the amount of feedback that you have to provide.

The following are some techniques for ensuring that learners receive feedback:

♦   Form pairs and have learners discuss what they have learned thus far and how they will put the information to use.

♦   Create equal-sized groups in which learners discuss various topics covered and how they relate to the workplace.

♦   Provide self-scoring assessments related to key workshop topics or skills taught.

♦   Have learners work together in groups to generate lists of ideas, mind maps, or other tools that allow them to see what they have learned thus far.

♦   Allow learners to come up with questions that test their knowledge of key concepts learned. Collect these questions and quiz the class on them.

♦ Get learners to do short, impromptu (without preparation) presentations on session-related topics that you have written on cards or a flip-chart page and that you assign to each learner one at a time.

♦ Set up activities in which you form learners into equal-sized teams, then divide each group in two and assign different roles, for example, pro and con. Assign a key concept that one person is to defend based on his or her role. For example, in a train-the-trainer workshop you might assign a group the topic of "brain-based learning in the classroom." One side of a group would argue the importance of applying brain research (pros) and the other side would assume a devil's advocate role and argue why it is not a good idea (cons). In this manner, learners review a key component of the session, give some critical thought to the topic, and come away with varied perspectives that you may not have offered. You also receive feedback on their understanding of the topic.

Repeat Information to Aid Memory

Learning and memory are closely associated, and the terms are often interrelated. Learning refers to the acquisition and encoding of information, while memory relates to the storage and retrieval of that information. Both learning and memory affect your workshop outcomes.

The research that deals with memory points to a need to refresh important information periodically for learners; otherwise, they will lose the data and skills to which they are exposed. Learners obtain information through the various modalities and tie to the multiple intelligences that you discovered earlier in this book. All incoming stimuli arrive in the brain through the five senses and then are held there long enough (milliseconds) to recognize and either pass them along to working memory or discard them.

Learning occurs when information passes from short-term to long-term memory. Additionally, when information is effectively organized or sequenced, it is easier for the brain to find and retrieve it. This is why you should give a lot of thought to how you will structure key concepts when designing your workshop.

Strategy for Success

As an example of how incorrect answers or assumptions can result when you do not present information in a logical sequence, try the following activity with your own learners as an energizer. It also demonstrates the importance of involving multiple senses and encouraging learners to takes notes.

Before beginning the activity, write the following on a flip chart and hide it from the view of your learners:

10	1,000
+1,000	+1,000
+20	+1,000
+1,000	+1,000
+30	+10
+1,000	+10
+30	+20
+1,000	+30
+10 =	+30 =

4,100

Tell learners that they are going to participate in a quick activity to demonstrate the importance of logical planning when they are working on a task or project.

Explain that you are going to provide a list of numbers verbally and that they are to quickly add the numbers in their heads and shout back a running total.

Call out the following numbers one at a time as learners calculate and call out their responses:

10

1,000

20

1,000

30

1,000

30

1,000

10

Point out that most people come up with 5,000. Ask for a show of hands of all learners who got that total. Tell them that this is NOT the correct answer.

Next, have learners take a pen and piece of paper to write down numbers as you call them out a second time.

Call out the following numbers:

1,000

1,000

1,000

1,000

10

10

20

30

30

(continued)

Have learners add the numbers again. Ask, "What total did you get this time?" They should have 4,100.

Explain that the numbers used for both portions of the activity were the same as you show the hidden flip-chart page.

The difference is in the way that you presented the information (numbers) to learners. The brain got into a pattern of thinking 1,000. For example 1010, 1020, and so forth. At the end, their brains transposed that notion to round up to 5,000.

Explain that when working on a project they should consider the sequence in which the workshop will proceed because it can make a difference in the outcome. Also stress that there is value in having information made visual during an activity for visual learners and that learners should be encouraged to take notes to help kinesthetic learners.

Short-Term Memory (Working Memory)

Some researchers believe that the human brain can retain limited amounts of information for a around five to thirty seconds. That makes it important that you not overload your learners' memory and that you chunk material into small bits. This allows learners to process information by matching it to other knowledge they already possess. They can then act on the new information, store it in memory, or discard it. This is where the research by Miller (described in Chapter 1) becomes valuable.

Retaining information in short-term memory for longer periods requires repetition. To get a better idea of how short-term memory works, think of a time when you were trying to remember a telephone number you looked up in the telephone directory. As long as you continued to repeat the number to yourself en route to dial the number on the telephone, you likely accurately recalled it.

However, if someone or something distracted you, you probably forgot and had to look up the number again. Similarly, if you fail to give learners uninterrupted time to practice or rehearse information, they will likely be unsuccessful in memorizing it and will be unable to retrieve it later.

Long-Term Memory

The storage of large amounts of information, procedures, events, and other memories for indefinite periods is called long-term memory. Through this type of memory, participants recall material learned years before. Examples of long-term memory include childhood experiences, workplace examples from throughout their careers, or any other details from their past. These are the memories to which you may want to connect new information, as they are emotion-based. Using techniques that reach learners emotionally can help implant concepts into their long-term memories better.

Scientists differ in their perspectives on how memories arrive in long-term memory. Many believe that information first goes to short-term memory, where it is processed and forwarded on to long-term memory, based on the significance of the information or event. Other researchers believe that short- and long-term memory are parallel, rather than sequential in their functioning. In other words, information received by learners can be stored at the same time by short- and long-term memory.

The value of long-term memory from a classroom perspective is that you can design training that builds on previous knowledge and experience. This will help participants retain new knowledge and skills and strengthen those already in existence. An example could be if you were teaching computer keyboarding skills to learners who used typewriters before retirement and are now reentering the workforce. Many skills, techniques, and principles are the same, so learners just need to have new information about computers and be given the opportunity to practice.

No tool in the world will help participants retain information if you fail to remember that for most adults, information that they receive must be meaningful and something they perceive as valuable or useful. When presenting such information it is helpful to put it into a format or structure that aids in retention and allows participants to connect it to previously received information. The use of analogies and metaphors can assist in this effort, as can short interim reviews.

Make sure that you provide concepts one at a time, with no other distractions, so that learners can focus on retaining what they experience without competing stimuli. For example, if you are presenting a key point for discussion on a flip chart, turn off your overhead projector images.

Present in a manner that allows time for participants to think about and grasp the concepts. Allow ample time for learners to process what they receive and to take notes or ask questions. Slowing your rate of speech and reducing the numbers of points presented in a session can be helpful to learners.

Reviewing and tying points to previously learned concepts every fifteen to twenty minutes can cement them into memory and enhance understanding of the overall scheme of the concept or material.

One finding from memory research that you should think about when designing your workshop is that learners will often recall words or information that is implied, rather than actually presented. For example, if you were to give a series of terms when describing brain-based learning, such as fun, excitement, music, color, balloons, table glitter, toys, and props, then later ask someone to describe the environment of a brain-based learning program, he or she might use the term "party atmosphere." This is because the brain continually stores and recalls information and material. It may reduce all the component parts down to a short descriptive phrase.

Repetition is a key component of learning and memory and is one of the most important ways to help learners transfer information from short- to long-term memory. Through the process of thinking about information, writing it, or saying it aloud, learners can help cement information into their long-term memory. The more times that your learners use multiple senses (sight, feeling, taste, touch, or hearing) to gather information, the more likely they will be able to attain, manipulate, retain, recognize, recall, and use the data. Make sure that you provide concepts in numerous formats to aid learners in accessing the information later. For example, give information visually through handouts and in an auditory fashion through discussions and Q&A. In this way learners' brains can pick out familiar terms or information from a list faster. Once you have introduced ideas or concepts, continue to tie them to previous points throughout the session so that you continually reinforce learners' memory and create neural connections in their brains.

Build in opportunities to revisit as many key concepts from the workshop as time will allow. Then, at the end of the workshop, design a solid review. Remind learners of the original objectives introduced at the beginning of the workshop. Show these objectives and refresh their memory on how you covered each one during the program. Include written, verbal, visual, auditory, and physical reviews so that you address all learning modalities and incorporate as many senses as possible. Make your reviews fun and active!

Engage Learners Through Activity

You have read about the importance of involving learners soon and throughout your workshop in order to gain and hold their attention, reinforce learning, and maximize learning outcomes. There are many ways to do this, depending on the makeup of your group, time constraints, budget, and other factors.

Icebreakers

Trainers often refer to activities designed to help learners feel less anxious about the workshop, learning environment, and other learners as "icebreakers." The term alludes to thawing or clearing a path so that participants are more comfortable, receptive, and open to what will follow in the session. Icebreakers typically involve one or more elements and are not normally time-consuming. Depending on the length of your workshop, fifteen to twenty minutes is probably a good guideline on icebreaker length for a one-half or one-day workshop.

Like any other aspect of your workshop, you should have definitive goals or objectives for what you wish to accomplish with the icebreaker that you choose. Typical activity goals include:

♦ Warm up and relax learners

♦ Facilitate introductions

♦ Help break down interpersonal barriers

♦ Build a sense of camaraderie and community

♦ Create a positive learning environment early in a workshop

♦ Reduce anxiety

♦ Help motivate and energize learners

♦ Build confidence in learners

♦ Help set an atmosphere in which learners think outside the box

♦ Lead into workshop content

Consider your audience and the learning situation when selecting an icebreaker. If you have a short training period, you may have to limit what you ask learners to accomplish. Additionally, some icebreakers may not be appropriate for all groups. Consider, age, gender, position in the organization, experience level, and other demographic factors when deciding what you will do. For example, depending on your topic and audience makeup, you may want to limit physical activity or reduce the use of toys and props.

The following are a few common-sense points to remember related to using icebreakers.

♦ If the activity will embarrass, negatively call attention to, or offend anyone in the room, do not use it.

♦ If the activity does not relate to or contribute to the overall success of your workshop, avoid it.

♦ If the icebreaker involves competition in which there will be losers, you may want to reconsider or restructure it. There should be no losers in a learning environment.

♦ If the activity uses time that you can use more productively or does not add value; shorten or eliminate it.

♦ If budget is a factor, choose exercises that do not involve props and other materials.

Effective icebreaker activities share many of the same characteristics and often include the following:

Relationship to Workshop Objectives. Like every other component of training, icebreakers should have meaning and purpose and not be done simply to get people involved or to add fun to the event. Tell learners the purpose of the activity and how it relates to session content. You can do this before or after your icebreaker.

Learner Engagement. Participants often work in pairs, triads, or small groups during icebreakers. This helps with relationship building and the identification of resources that they can later tap during and after the session.

Movement. Learners often relocate to form groups or to perform a task or reposition themselves for the duration of the activity. Movement ties directly to the brain-based learning concept of incorporating activity into your learning events.

Personal Introduction. Learners often exchange names, professional information, and small details about themselves in order to help build rapport and to encourage friendships and support throughout the workshop.

Specified Time. Since timing of the workshop is crucial to a successful outcome, designation of a finite amount of time for an icebreaker is normal.

Props. Many icebreakers include the use of props or other items related to the program theme. Examples of props and materials you can use include animal noses, hats, puzzles, markers, and flip charts. If using magic, props, or other items, make sure that they support your program theme.

Individual and Group Sharing. Following exchange of information or task completion in small groups, each person or group leader is typically required to share information or report back. This sharing is normally with the entire training group so that everyone has access to the same information, ideas, or results identified or generated during the activity.

Debriefing the Activity. The trainer should bring the activity to formal closure with appropriate remarks, observations, and questions, and tie in to the session content that will follow after learners share their information, comments, ideas, observations, or whatever was required.

Strategy for Success

You can use rubber animal noses in an icebreaker activity when conducting team building, interpersonal communication, customer service, or other workshops that involve a discussion of how people are different but similar. To use the exercise:

Start by obtaining enough rubber animal noses with elastic straps that fit around the back of a learner's head (see Creative Presentation Resources in the Resources section). Ensure that you have an equal number of each type of nose such as pig, shark, toucan, boar, or lion, so that learners can later find a match.

Go to an office supply or rubber stamp store and have a large stamp made that says "Do Not Open Until Told."

Obtain small paper bags like the type some stores put small candy in or that hardware stores use for nails and other small items. Sam's Club, Costco, BJ's Warehouse, and other such stores often sell these types of bags.

Stamp the bags on both sides.

Number the bottom of each bag to identify which noses are contained inside. For example, if you have four of each type of nose, number bags containing the same types of nose with a single number. Put a number 1 on the bottom of all bags containing a pig nose, a number 2 on bags containing a lion nose, a 3 on bags containing a shark nose, and so on.

Put one animal nose in each bag and staple it shut.

As learners enter the room, greet them and pass out bags in numeric sequence. For example, the first person receives a number 1, the second a number 2, and so on. You can use this distribution technique to match learners with someone other than the friends or co-workers who came with them. Thus, networking is more effective. The procedure also precludes the problem of some learners not having a matched nose. This can occur if you put bags on tables in advance and then several people do not show up for the workshop. You then might end up with three people who have a toucan nose and only one with a shark nose.

When ready to start the activity, have learners open their bags, put on their noses, and find one other person in the room who looks "like them." If people do not want to wear their noses because they are allergic to latex or for personal reasons, ask them to hang the noses around their necks or off their wrists so others with like noses can find them.

Group learners by nose type, have them introduce themselves, and share whatever information or task you designate.

Following the activity, have learners introduce themselves and report to the group as appropriate for their assignment.

After everyone has finished, wrap up the activity by tying into session content and transitioning to your next point or workshop section. Part of this debriefing might be to point out that the noses grouped people who were alike and separated those who were different. Think of ways to relate this concept to your session theme of communication, service, or whatever. For example, customer service representatives or employees sometimes feel more comfortable interacting with people with whom they feel comfortable or can relate.

Answer any questions that learners might have related to the activity or how it relates to the workshop.

Have everyone give a round of applause.

Give out small pieces of candy and tell learners it is provided "to help them regenerate all the brain cells that they burned up during the activity."

Allow learners to keep the noses as a reminder of the workshop, since you would not want to reuse them because of sanitation concerns.

Energizers

Researchers know that physical activity makes the heart pump faster and deliver more oxygen via the blood to stimulate the brain. This results in a more alert and focused learner. Short activities known as energizers designed to engage learners physically while tying into workshop concepts can help deliver that valuable oxygen. These upbeat activities sometimes use music, motion, props, equipment, and a variety of other creative tools to get learners up and moving about while they work individually or in a team to accomplish a challenge or goal.

Movement might be nothing more than a Q&A session in which learners are required to raise their hands above their heads in order to respond to questions. It might also require physically relocating to another area of the room in order to work in small groups. All of this stimulates the heart and raises levels of attention and alertness.

The energy level of your learners is dependent on many factors. Some of these include:

♦ *Your level of enthusiasm.* If you do not believe in a game, energizer, icebreaker, or other technique that you are using, your learners will not get excited about it either.

♦ *Your delivery style.* Death by lecture has doomed many trainers and their workshops. Use some of the interactive and more brain-based approaches that you have read about in this book to get your learners actively engaged in the learning process.

♦ *Whether learners volunteered to attend the workshop.* This will make a difference on their dedication, involvement, and level of commitment to learning.

Ongoing problems with equipment, such as computers malfunctioning or visual aids not working properly, can de-motivate and cause learners to lose interest. As they sit by waiting for problems to be resolved, their attention turns to external issues like the workplace and their family responsibilities. Following repair or replacement of the equipment, you then have to start over to regain their attention.

Workshop content or topic can affect the level of enthusiasm that learners bring to the workshop. For example, a common perception is that technical and regulatory training is dry and boring. Thus, many learners attending such a workshop will come expecting those types of experiences. This will result in your having to overcome negative stereotypes, just to get learners to engage and to listen.

Whether learners have attended sessions similar to the one you are conducting in the past can influence how they react to you. For example, certain mandated regulatory, safety, or legal training is required periodically. More experienced employees may have attended such workshops numerous times throughout their career in order to meet requirements or maintain professional certifications. Based on their experience, learners may anticipate what will be covered or have a preconceived idea of how the session will be conducted. In such instances, you could be in for a challenge unless you open with a brain-based approach and quickly grab their attention.

The environment can negatively affect learner enthusiasm if it does not comply with some of the brain-based concepts that you read about in earlier chapters regarding room temperature and other factors. Examples of potential environmental problems include a room that is too hot or cold, not enough refreshments, or nowhere to take comfortable breaks.

Even if learners are excited about attending your workshop, their energy level will likely rise and fall during the event. Unless you plan for ways to reduce or prevent a drop in energy level at various points, there is a danger that learning outcomes might suffer. One of the easiest things to help prevent this is to build energizer activities into your workshop at various points. Typically, such activities follow breaks to help refocus learners or to transition into a new topic area. Energizers are also useful when learners seem to be in an energy slump. Such activities mentally and physically engage learners and refocus them on session content.

Strategy for Success

Here is a fun activity that can get groups of up to one thousand learners moving, help them learn more about one another, and tie to a variety of session topics. You can do the latter by changing the categories to characteristics related to the session. For example, in a workshop on communication skills, the categories might include someone who has attended a program on communication in the past, someone who has recently experienced a breakdown in communication with a service provider, or someone with a college degree in communications. This activity can also be used as an icebreaker.

Prepare a flip-chart page or slide with the following list of five numbered categories. Hide the page from the view of your learners until ready to begin the activity.

1. Someone who has traveled on a cruise ship

2. Someone who can raise one eyebrow at a time

3. Someone who speaks two or more languages

4. Someone who owns more than one pet

5. Someone who has more than three siblings

Hand out blank sheets of paper and a pen or pencil to each learner.

Have learners draw five equally spaced horizontal lines numbered from one to five on their paper.

When ready to begin, display the prepared flip-chart page or slide.

Explain that they will have five minutes to move about the room to introduce themselves to other learners and to identify one person from each category.

Once they find someone for a category, they should have that person print his or her name on the paper on the appropriate line.

Once they have all five lines filled, they should sit down.

Once any learner has returned to his or her seat, ask everyone to sit down.

Announce the winner, have everyone give a round of applause, and reward the first person with a small prize or candy.

Ask everyone who fits into one of the categories on the list to raise a hand as you read the list.

Interim Reviews

By engaging multiple senses regularly, you can help ensure the acquisition, retention, and use of what is learned. To help accomplish this, build in multiple opportunities for learners to reflect upon and review key concepts. Through this concept of giving a bit of material or an idea, reviewing it, then adding more information to what was learned, you can effectively guide learners to your announced learning objectives. You can also help ensure that they "get it" and that they walk away from the session with usable KSAs.

Use your imagination to develop creative interim reviews for use in your workshops. Here are some examples of interim reviews to consider:

♦ Put strips of paper with key ideas or concepts written on them inside colorful balloons that you tape to the wall before learners arrive. The balloons add color to the environment and tie to brain-based research. When ready to review material in your session, have volunteers remove and pop the balloons, recover, and read their strips of paper. Have other learners define or discuss what they heard.

♦ Similar to the balloon idea, put strips of paper inside colorful, plastic eggs and put these in a basket. When ready to review, pass the basket and have learners each take one. In turn, have them open and read their papers and have others define and discuss what is read.

♦ Form circles of six to eight learners, have a volunteer shout out a concept covered up to that point in the session and have someone else define or explain the concept. Continue clockwise until no one can think of any more concepts. If someone cannot think of something, he or she can opt out and the next person goes. This process adds movement, sound, fun, and novelty to your workshop.

♦ Form groups of eight to ten learners and give each group musical Hot Potato toy or ball (available at Creative Presentation Resources in the Resources section) or some other similar prop. When ready to begin the activity, have someone push the button on the bottom of the potato to start the music. Have the person holding it shout out a key idea or concept that you addressed up to that point in the program, then quickly pass the potato to the person on his or her right. Continue this process until the music stops. Whoever is holding the potato when the music stops shouts out a concept and then sits down. The review process continues until a single person remains standing in each group. Reward the winners from each group with prizes and have all the winners assemble into one group. Continue the review activity until there is only one person left standing. Reward the last person and have everyone give a round of applause for the entire group effort. Finally, review all key points to ensure that learners did not omit anything. Such activities incorporate a number of brain-based learning concepts, including use of movement, sound, color, novelty, and repetition.

- Model a review activity after the classic television and board game "Concentration" and have learners work in pairs. Create enough sets of 3-by-5 cards so that each pair of learners (dyad) has a one. Write one key term or concept from the session per card and then create an exact duplicate set of those cards. You now have one complete set of cards consisting of duplicate terms for each dyad.

- When ready to review, give each dyad a set of cards. Have one person in each dyad act as the controller while the partner guesses the location of terms. The controller spreads the cards out randomly in even rows so that terms are face down and mixed so the partner cannot see the terms. When you say "Begin," the person who is not the controller guesses the location of cards by pointing to two cards. The controller turns those cards face up. If the guesser was correct, leave the cards face up and the person guesses again. If incorrect, turn the cards over and continue the process. The object is for each guesser to find matches for all terms or concepts within the time you allot. The first dyad with all cards matched (turned upright) shouts "Done!" and both team members receive prizes. Learners then switch roles, cards are shuffled and repositioned, and the former controllers then try to find term matches. The object of the activity is for learners to view the key concepts or terms multiple times in order to help reinforce and lock into memory what they have learned in the workshop. It also injects a bit of fun, novelty, and mental stimulation into the workshop.

Personalizing What You Have Learned

- What are the most important things that you read in this chapter? Why?

- What are some ways that you can immediately apply concepts covered in this chapter?

- What additional resources or topics do you want to research based on what you read?

Ending on a High Note

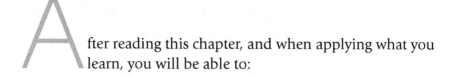fter reading this chapter, and when applying what you learn, you will be able to:

1. Discuss the importance of effective closure to your learning event.

2. Use strategies that help participants transfer what they learned back to the real world following training.

3. Creatively review key learning concepts in your training programs using strategies read.

4. Evaluate learning outcomes using the techniques shown.

5. Apply the "Four Levels of Evaluation" to your own learning events.

6. Effectively follow up with learners after training to ensure you met their training needs.

7. Creatively close your sessions with brain-based strategies that involve movement, music, props, and other creative tools.

"Education is not the filling of a pail, but the lighting of a fire."

William Butler Yeats

The Importance of Closure

Most things in life have closure. It is a way of mentally moving from one phase to the next or bringing events to a conclusion. Think about your own typical day:

♦ Sales transactions are typically closed with some form of thanks for the customer's business and an offer to assist again in the future.

♦ You say goodbye on the telephone.

♦ You tell guests leaving your party, "Thanks for coming."

♦ Casual encounters with friends and acquaintances at the supermarket close with something like, "It was good seeing you; let's get together soon."

♦ You say good night to family members or significant others.

Not only are closures a polite courtesy, but they also help reinforce value of relationships, an encounter, or effort put forth by someone. In your learning environments, a solid closing statement or event accomplishes similar things. For example, if you are conducting a multiple day workshop, you can close each session with one of the following.

A statement of appreciation for learner contributions: "Thank you for all your valuable input and great ideas today. They really added value to the content we discussed. Tomorrow. . . ."

A review of what you covered in the session and a preview of the content for the next session: "When we get together again, we will be examining. . . ."

A teaser about what will happen in the next session: "In the next session, how would you like to learn five steps to increasing your salary? Well, that is what we are going to address along with many other tips for achieving professional success."

In a good session closure, you should include the following:

- ◆ Reinforcement that what participants learned was important and useful. Remember that adult learners need to see immediate value and application for their investment of time, money, and energy in a learning event.

- ◆ Validation that learners have a grasp on key concepts and will be able to recognize or recall and use them later.

- ◆ An opportunity for learners to clarify any misperceptions or confusion over something covered in the event.

- ◆ Overview of next steps or what learners can expect in future sessions or as follow-up.

- ◆ A solid conclusion in which learners recognize that the event has officially adjourned.

Look at your workshop conclusion or closing as a ribbon on a present that you give your learners. When you give a present, you probably wrap it neatly in pretty paper based on the occasion. When you finish wrapping it, it looks nice, but you probably realize there is still something missing—a bow. The workshop closing is the bow on the present of knowledge that you just gave your learners. Your goal in your conclusion is to make sure that learners got what your outlined in your opening remarks and learning objectives. Through a closing activity, you can reinforce key concepts and encourage learners to further their study of the topic. For example, if your goal in a session on behavioral styles and interpersonal communication was to help learners identify their strengths and areas for improvement related to their style(s), you could ask a series of questions that would help.

By helping learners arrive at closure on your workshop content and plan next steps, you can better ensure that they will apply what was learned. Here are some questions that you could have learners address in a closing activity to accomplish this:

♦   How will I immediately apply what I have learned?

♦   In what ways will the concepts learned aid in making my job/life different?

♦   What additional information do I need to research related to the workshop topic?

♦   What additional training workshops should I attend to learn more about the topic?

♦   How does the workshop content add value to what I already know about the topic?

- What resources do I have in the form of people, information, or materials that will aid in successful implementation of workshop concepts?

- Do I know anyone else who would benefit in my sharing what I learned with him or her?

Ensure Transfer of Training

You can increase learning effectiveness in your training workshops by thinking about the concepts of brain-based learning that you have read about in this book. There is no one quick answer to help ensure that learners apply new knowledge and skills on the job. Instead, transfer of learning is a culmination of strategies and activities that you start using before your session even begins.

Internalization by Learners

Learners have to embrace the concepts learned and make them their own before they will consciously apply them outside of the workshop. You can use a number of techniques at the end of your workshop to help them accomplish this. Some of these include:

Visioning. Use the visualization technique format described in Chapter 5. Put on some relaxing instrumental music, reduce lighting, and have learners close their eyes and imagine a workplace in which they are applying the knowledge and skills gained in the session. Develop a series of questions to facilitate their thinking.

Journaling. If you have been asking learners to write down ways that they will apply certain concepts learned in their workbooks, have them do so again at this point.

Ask them to reflect on everything they have heard, review their notes briefly, and jot down any additional thoughts they have related to application of workshop content.

Goal Setting. Have learners write down three goals that they have related to changes they can help make in their behavior, their workplace, or others by using what they have learned.

Enlisting the Assistance of Others. Have learners write down the names of at least two people they can approach to share what they have learned in the workshop. They can then form partnerships with these people to implement improvement strategies based on workshop concepts.

Role of Organizational Support

Organizations spend millions of dollars each year sending employees to various internal and external training and educational programs. Unfortunately, much of this money is wasted simply because employees are not held accountable for applying what was learned or do not receive the support they need on the job. Outside influences often interrupt a learner's intentions to use what was learned in your workshop. In other instances, learners simply do not possess the personal motivation to apply new knowledge and skills until they become part of their normal behavior.

Research shows that it takes approximately twenty-one to thirty days for behavior to change. For this to occur learners must:

♦   Recognize the need to change their behavior.

♦   Want to change the behavior.

- Know how to change their behavior through new knowledge or skill attainment.

- Practice the learned behavior consistently for the needed period of twenty-one to thirty days.

- Have their behavior supported through positive feed-back or reinforcement from others.

Unfortunately, one or more of these factors is missing for many learners, mainly because their motivation for attending training can differ significantly. Typically, employees end up in training in one of three ways:

1. The organization decrees that certain training will occur and that it is required by specific employees. For example, new-hire orientation, new supervisor training, or computer software training may be required.

2. An employee asks to attend a program to strengthen knowledge or skills because of a desire to grow personally and/or professionally.

3. Federal, state, or local regulations require that employees attend certain training programs, for example, Equal Employment Opportunity (EEOC) or Office of Safety and Health Adminis-tration (OSHA) training.

Effective coaching and management are key elements in helping trainees successfully transfer the theory they learn in your session to the workplace or other areas of their lives. Prior to sending someone to training, supervisors should help employees identify performance gaps in knowledge, skills, or attitude. Then they should jointly establish learn-ing goals with the employees prior to the program.

Some ways that you can help increase learning effectiveness and encourage learners to use of workshop content after training follow.

Get supervisors and managers involved in the learning process early on. Too often, employees are sent to training to be "fixed" because something is not going well in the workplace. In truth, the issue is often more of a management or organizational issue. Some common causes are lack of regular effective coaching and feedback and confusing or conflicting policies or procedures.

By actively involving supervisors in the training process, you can help them take ownership in supporting transfer of learning to the workplace. The following are some ways to involve learners and their supervisors in effecting transfer of learning.

Prior to Training. Distribute a brief memorandum to attendees and copy their supervisors, stressing the importance of the training. It should also encourage participants to focus attention on obtaining specific ideas and strategies for application on the job following training. Participants can do this by coming prepared to discuss specific types of generic and/or specific workplace or personal situations related to the training topic and to express questions and concerns. They can also actively participate in program activities.

Front-line managers/team leaders can assist in mentally preparing attendees. They can do so by reinforcing precepts outlined in the memorandum they receive from you before the workshop and by discussing how to relate the upcoming training to personal and job success with attendees.

During Training. Make learning fun and interactive while engaging learners continually throughout the workshop.

Where appropriate, encourage members of upper management to observe segments of the training and participate or assist the facilitator. This will send a non-verbal message about the importance of the training and that management supports the initiative. If nothing else, try to get a CEO or high-ranked member of management to address learners at the beginning of the workshop. He or she should welcome learners and stress the importance of the training.

Also ask someone from higher management to close the session by awarding certificates and again stressing the importance of training and application of what was learned.

After Training. Supervisors and employees should discuss the concepts that were learned in the workshop and how they relate to the workplace. Supervisors should also observe employee behavior following training and provide feedback on situations in which the concepts learned are applied. Additionally, they should provide constructive feedback for improvement when they see concepts ignored or misapplied.

Workshop learning objectives should be linked into individual performance goals for training attendees. By connecting these, supervisors encourage learner accountability for use of the information, knowledge, and skills learned in training.

Review of Key Concepts

If you fail to conduct one final review of key workshop concepts before learners leave, you will miss a crucial opportunity to reinforce learning and cement session content in their memory. A final review is one more chance to find out whether learners have grasped key elements of your workshop.

Remember what you read about the importance of using the five senses to engage the brain and help ensure learning. You can create a review activity that incorporates multiple modalities and is fun and engaging at the same time. Unfortunately, many trainers and educators only do a cursory review of session topics and call that a review.

Depending on the length of your workshop, use a review that ranges from twenty to thirty minutes in length. It is that important. For a shorter program of a couple hours, five to ten minutes should be sufficient. For a workshop of one or more days, a solid review could take at least thirty minutes and include an activity involving learners.

During your review, you should reexamine key concepts without introducing any new content. Have learners reconsider learning objectives and provide specific examples of how you covered each concept.

Final Concept Review Activities

The following activities are simple ways to engage learners, encourage recall and reflection on key points covered in the workshop, and tie into a variety of concepts related to brain-based learning.

Here is a simple activity that reinforces and reviews key concepts, appeals to all three learning modalities, focuses on several of the multiple intelligences, and ties to such brain-based concepts of novelty, movement, learner engagement, color, and repetition.

Learning Reflections

Hand out blank sheets of paper to each learner.

Tell learners that they have five minutes to write down as many key concepts covered in the workshop that they can remember.

At the end of five minutes, form equal-sized groups with no more than six participants each.

Give each group a marker and sheet of flip-chart paper.

Tell learners that they have ten more minutes to compile their individual lists into a single list of all the concepts covered in the session.

After ten minutes, have groups post their lists on the wall.

Compare the lists and reward members of any group that listed all the key session concepts on their list with small prizes.

Give pieces of candy to the remaining learners so there are no losers.

Review any additional key concepts that learners omitted from their lists.

Ask all learners: "Which concept do you think will be most useful to you? Why?"

Reward volunteers who answer the question.

Have everyone give a round of applause for individual contributions.

Tree of Learning

Draw an image of a large tree, showing its trunk, roots, and limbs (see Figure 10.1) on a sheet of flip-chart paper with colored markers.

Spray the page with repositionable spray artist adhesive (available at art supply stores or Creative Presentation Resources in the Resources section).

Count the key concepts covered in your lesson plan and multiple that number by the number of learners in your workshop.

(continued)

Tree of Learning (*Continued*)

Figure 10.1. The Tree of Learning

Cut a number of pieces of different colored construction paper in the shape of leaves (see Figure 10.2) equal to the total from the last step. Leaves should be at least four inches (109.22 cm) long and three inches (7.62 cm) wide.

When you are ready to conduct the review activity, give each learner the number of assorted colored leaves to match the number of key concepts from the session. For example, if there were twelve key concepts, each learner would receive twelve different colored leaves.

Explain to learners that they are to print all the key concepts that they can remember on the leaves (one per leaf).

Allow five minutes for learners to print the concepts and then ask volunteers to read one concept each and explain how they might apply it.

Figure 10.2. Sample Leaf

After reading their concepts, the volunteers should go to the tree and stick the leaves that they read on one of the limbs.

Continue this process until participants have covered all key concepts and everyone has posted a leaf (there may be duplicates depending on the number of key session concepts).

Have everyone give a round of applause for participation and reward volunteers with small gifts or pieces of candy.

You should then do a summary of the key concepts, cover anything that learners missed, discuss the importance of each concept, and offer any summary remarks.

Story of the Day

Have learners pair with someone else.

Explain that, when told to begin, they are to work together to alternately tell a story of their day in the workshop.

Tell learners that the goal of this activity is to discuss what happened, what they learned, and how to apply what they learned.

(continued)

Story of the Day (*Continued*)

One person will start by explaining the first thing that the class did at the start of the workshop, what was covered, and how they can use it. For example, "We started with an icebreaker activity in which we worked in small groups to. . . ."

The partners will then pick up the story line with the next thing done in the workshop, for example, "And then we discussed the four learning objectives" for the workshop and talked about how we would be able to apply them.

The first learner would take over with the next phase of the workshop, for example, "Following the introduction, we examined the first step of the process, which was _____ and talked about how were could incorporate it into our workplace."

The process continues until each pair has reviewed the entire day.

Do not tell learners that they cannot refer to notes. If they do so, allow this since it visually reinforces the concepts as they look through their workbooks again. The key is that they pull what they have learned from memory, actively think about it, and think of ways to apply it once they leave the workshop.

After everyone has finished, ask volunteers to share one important thing that they learned in the workshop that they can immediately apply once they leave the workshop.

Reward volunteers with small prizes or candy.

Have everyone give a round of applause at the end of the activity for contributions that all learners made.

Strategy for Success

Use floating rubber ducks (available at Creative Presentation Resources in the Resources section) to add fun and novelty to your end of session reviews. Write consecutive numbers on the bottom of these cute little rubber ducks, float them in a container of water, and allow learners to randomly choose one. The numbers correspond to a list of key concepts that you have written out in your lesson plan. Based on the number drawn, you read that concept aloud and the learner attempts to explain what it is or answer a question you pose about it. If successful, the learner wins a prize and someone else chooses another duck. If a learner is incorrect, other learners can try until someone has the correct answer.

Evaluate Learning Success

Do not forget to elicit input from learners on their perceptions of you and the event following your workshop review. This will aid you in determining changes needed before you conduct the session again for another group.

Unfortunately, many trainers handle evaluations as an afterthought. Think of times in classes or workshops you have attended when the trainer shouts as you are picking up personal items to leave, "Wait, before you go, please take a moment to provide some feedback on your experience here today." This approach does not send a very powerful message about the importance of that feedback, does it?

To obtain feedback that will be meaningful and actually provide you with some information that you can use to enhance the workshop for future groups, plan the manner in which you will gather it.

In earlier chapters, you read about how to use interim reviews to gather information from learners during your workshop(s). A perfect time to gather feedback on your session evaluation form is immediately following an interim review. To do so, pass out evaluation forms at the start of your workshop and encourage learners to write down their thoughts throughout the session. After each review, have learners take out their forms and jot down any thoughts related to what they like or dislike about the workshop at that point. Have them write this in pencil, since you may later cover something they suggest early on and they can then erase their comments at the end of the day. As part of your closing activities, have learners finalize comments and rate elements of the workshop on their evaluation forms. Some areas for comment might include your delivery style, the training environment, materials, or whatever else you would like feedback on.

As you read about in Chapter 1, many organizations use the Four Levels of Evaluation developed by Donald Kirkpatrick to determine the degree of training effectiveness reached following a learning event. Because most organizations do not move beyond Level 3 due to the cost and effort involved in doing so successfully, you will likely follow this pattern.

There are generally three types of evaluations or strategies. You can employ them to help determine the degree to which training met intended objectives and learner needs.

1. *One-on-One Evaluation.* In this category, you obtain feedback obtained directly from your learners or possibly from others in their workplace. These might be peers, supervisors, or customers.

2. *Small-Group Evaluation.* Often you can hold meetings with small groups of learners or others with whom the learners interact in order to gather information about how well KSAs are being transferred back to the workplace. Focus groups are the most common type of small group evaluation.

3. *Field Evaluation.* If you are an internal trainer or an outside consultant with access to learners in the

workplace, you can visit them on the job and observe how well they use the KSAs that were addressed in the workshop.

Active Evaluation

In order to tie into brain-based learning concepts related to movement, learner engagement, fun, and novelty, you can obtain feedback from your learners in several novel ways. This is in addition to written evaluations. Such techniques work best when the session has gone well and learners are satisfied with the results. You would not want to use them if there is a chance of having displeasure or dissatisfaction surface, since you want to end the workshop on a positive note.

The following technique can help gain input and add to a light-hearted evaluation to the session.

Live Voting

Prepare flip-chart pages in advance using large letters with one key concept from the workshop on each page.

Post your pages around the room on the wall.

When ready to begin the evaluation, have learners stand up.

Explain that you are going to ask a series of questions to which they will respond by moving in front of the concept that is most appropriate for them.

Questions to ask:

♦ What key concept do you feel that you now know the most about as a result of this workshop?

(continued)

Live Voting (Continued)

♦ What concept do you know the least about?

♦ What concept do you think you are most likely to immediately apply when you leave the workshop?

♦ What concept do you think you are least likely to use when you leave the workshop?

As learners assemble at each flip-chart page, ask a couple of people in each group to explain why they stood at that location.

Reward volunteers with small prizes or candy.

Following the activity, have everyone sit down, give a round of applause for their contributions, and complete their written evaluation forms for the workshop.

Four Levels of Evaluation

There are numerous ways to gather feedback and information regarding workshop effectiveness and transfer of knowledge following your session. These methods are based on Kirkpatrick's Four Levels of Evaluation, discussed below.

Reactions of Learners

This level of evaluation seeks to determine to what degree your learners liked what was offered in terms of the facilitator, learning environment, materials, food and refreshments, and other elements of the learning event.

End-of-session "smile sheets" are the most common form of evaluation used by trainers to gain the reactions of learners related to what they experienced in a training session. These forms typically are a combination of quantifiable scales and open-ended (discussion) questions. Exhibit 10.1 provides a sample end-of-session evaluation.

Exhibit 10.1. Sample End-of-Session Evaluation

Program: Enhancing Your Credibility

Presentation Date: _____ Location:

To help us evaluate this program's effectiveness and value to you, please take a few moments to objectively respond to the following questions. ("1" is to a low degree and "7" high.)

Based on material presented, I have a gained new insights and ideas for enhancing my presentations.

1	2	3	4	5	6	7

As a result of activities and discussions, I am aware of a variety of strategies and techniques for creating and sustaining credible relationships.

1	2	3	4	5	6	7

The participant workbook provided will be a valuable future resource.

1	2	3	4	5	6	7

The program format allowed for participant involvement and an exchange of ideas.

1	2	3	4	5	6	7

Information was presented in a clear, concise manner that aided understanding.

1	2	3	4	5	6	7

(continued)

EXHIBIT 10.1. (*Continued*)

What were the strengths of the program you just experienced?

_____

_____

_____

_____

Were there any areas you would recommend modifying/deleting? If so, please explain.

_____

_____

_____

_____

Please provide any general comments concerning the program (please use reverse side if necessary).

_____

_____

_____

_____

Would you recommend this program to others? _____ Yes _____ No
_____ Possibly

May we use your comments to publicize future programs? (If yes, please provide your name and title below.) Yes_____ No _____

_____

Name (Optional):

Thank you for your participation, time, and feedback.

_____

Strategy for Success

To obtain feedback at the end of each day of a multiple-day workshop, have learners participate in a brainstorming activity that you lead to gather their reactions to the events of the day. Use the results to modify the strategies planned for the following day and your materials for future use.

Draw a "T" chart with any two questions similar to those shown in Figure 10.3.

Figure 10.3. Sample End-of-Session "T" Chart

What could we have improved today?	What did you like about today?

Learning

At this level of evaluation, you are trying to determine what your learners actually gained in terms of KSAs. By using written and oral pre- and post-tests, demonstrations during or at the end of the program, and interim and final review activities in which learners regurgitate key concepts, you can identify their level of understanding.

Behavior

Your focus in training others is to help bring about learning of new knowledge and skills and to positively influence their attitudes toward a variety of issues. By gathering information and data on these three areas and observing learner behavior following your training, you will be able to determine its behavioral impact. Some of this information gathering can be done as part of your needs analysis followed by on-the-job observation of behavior after training. Ask whether there are visible changes. If so, you may deduce that the changes are at least partially a result of the content, format, and learning strategies experienced during the workshop.

Results

At Level 4 of Kirkpatrick's model, you are attempting to figure out whether the learning made a difference for the individual and organization and to what degree. Most importantly, you must determine whether the investment of money and time resulted in any meaningful return on investment (ROI).

Session Follow-Up

The mark of a truly committed and professional trainer or facilitator is to ensure that you have met the needs of learners. If you are an internal trainer who wishes to remain employed and to have employees register for future learning events, this is imperative. If you are an independent trainer or consultant who wants repeat business or to have people recommend your sessions to others and return themselves; this is a must.

One simple way to help determine the effect that your training had on learners is to build in some type of follow-up with them when planning and designing your workshop. Think about ways that you can contact your attendees at various points after the session has ended in order to act as a resource and answer any questions that they might have. At those times, you can also gather additional feedback on what works and what does not work for them from the session. The following are some strategies for accomplishing this follow-up.

Mail Follow-Up

Statistically, when people put their goals or intentions in writing, they have a higher chance of implementing and successfully attaining them. As part of your closing activity, have each learner create a "letter to me." In their letters, they should list three things that they learned in the session, along with how they intend to use them. Each learner should also list the name of at least one person that he or she plans to ask to help institute any implementation ideas. Finally, have learners self-address envelopes, insert their lists, seal them, and give them to you. At the end of four weeks, put stamps on the envelopes and sent the lists back to learners. When they receive their lists, it will be a quick reminder of the workshop and key ideas they experienced along with three ways to use the information.

Through this activity, you cause one more review of key concepts in the minds of learners as they read access information from memory. Thus, learning is once more reinforced.

E-mail or e-Group Contact

Make sure that you collect e-mail addresses during registration or before learners leave the workshop so that you can contact them easily by e-mail once the session ends. Create an e-mail group (e-group) listing of names with e-mail addresses on your computer to use for future contact with your learners.

You can send a follow-up e-mail immediately after the workshop to thank learners for attending, elicit any additional questions they might have about the content or application, and ask for any additional feedback that they might want to offer for improving future events. You can also encourage them to write to you if a question or thought comes up later.

If you used the "letter to me" idea above, you might mention it in the e-mail and encourage them to get started with their ideas, if they have not already done so.

Strategy for Success

One strategy that I use following a learning event is to set up an e-group on my computer and send out a "Tip of the Week" related to implementation or application of session content. I send this out for six weeks and include an "opt out" option at the bottom of each message. The opt out is a link at the bottom of the e-mail that allows recipients to notify me that they want to be removed from the distribution.

After six weeks, I invite learners to join my free monthly e-newsletter distribution list (see Robert W. Lucas in Resources section) to receive a publication that has tips, games, activities, resources, and articles for trainers, educators, presenters, and others in the workforce. This provides learners with an ongoing resource and gives me a marketing list to notify them of future training opportunities.

One-on-One Coaching

If you are an internal trainer or consultant, you might work out a schedule that allows learners from your workshop to meet with you periodically in order to gain new insights into the application of the KSAs provided in the session. This could be a "Lunch and Learn" mini-seminar format or a one-on-one coaching format.

Group Coaching

If you have multiple learners at one location, you may want to offer an opportunity to gather after four weeks or so to review key concepts learned briefly, answer any questions, and offer tips on how to maximize the application of KSAs from your original workshop.

This could even lead to a support network that meets periodically for which you charge a fee.

Telecoaching

You can also coach via the telephone if it is more convenient for you and your learner(s) or if they are at a remote location.

Teleseminar or Teleclass

If you have a group of learners needing follow-up coaching or additional information related to your session, you can hold a session via the telephone. Many companies provide teleconferencing plans relatively inexpensively. Such plans allow individuals to call in to your assigned telephone number and log in to join the class.

You can market the fact that they receive a free follow-up session with you via the telephone for attending the workshop. If you need to pass the cost of time and equipment needed for dedicated telephone lines to learners, you can build it into your workshop registration cost.

Close with a Bang

Celebrations

By including fun celebratory activities at the end of your workshop, you can help turn on the brain's "pleasure center." In doing this, you cause the brain to emit dopamine in the brain. This hormone acts as a neurotransmitter (chemicals that relay or amplify signals between neurons and other cells) and is related to attention and learning, according to some researchers. When rewards or fun occur, dopamine is released, which creates a "good" feeling in your learners. This sensation ties to pleasant memories and helps reinforce their learning. This is one reason that you remember fun events from your childhood. By including celebrations in your learning events, you help learners associate pleasant memories with you and the workshop, thereby reinforcing that the event was worthwhile.

There are many things that you can do to help end your workshop in a memorable fashion. The following are a few strategies to consider:

Create a Festive Atmosphere. By passing out party confetti poppers or streamers; putting metallic confetti on tables; using decorative party tablecloths, noisemakers, and party favors; having upbeat music playing (see the list later in this chapter for some suggestions); and serving cupcakes, fruit, and drinks. If you have a second room that was used during the workshop, you can set the area up with the party decorations during breaks or have an assistant do it before the end of the workshop. If you do not have this luxury, you might be able to take a short break before the final review and send learners out of the room or have an assistant bring in a cake or refreshments when you are ready to celebrate.

Group Photographs. Use a digital camera. To ensure that you and all learners are is in the photo, use an autotimer or ask someone to come in to take the image. Following the workshop, e-mail a copy of the picture to learners. You can encourage them to continue to network with one another and share what is working and not working in their efforts to use concepts learned in the session. If you write a newsletter, you can also attach a copy and suggest they sign up for future issues to gain additional ideas and resources related to the workshop, share your website address with them, and encourage them to use you as a resource in the future. Your goal in doing all this is to reinforce content and remind them about the workshop, encourage future application of what they learned, and stay connected with learners. This will help when you want to market future workshops.

Praise. Most people appreciate praise, but rarely get enough of it. To remedy this at the end of your workshop, have learners pair up with the person to their left or right and each share one thing that they appreciate the other person doing during the workshop. For example, someone might offer a partner, "I appreciate the fact that you asked a question to clarify _____. I really did not understand that either, but was reluctant to ask the question."

Drawings. Hold a drawing to allow learners to win door prizes. You can base drawings on incentives accrued by learners during the workshop. For example, if you have given out incentives such as numbered coupons, strips of colored or numbered paper, or playing cards, draw or call out the name/number of one. The person holding it can select a small toy or other item off the "prize table" in the rear of the room. Continue until all prizes are distributed.

Games. Play a carnival game. Games can provide an equal opportunity for everyone to win something, since they all contributed to the success of the workshop. For example, you could have learners play Plinko (see Creative Presentation Resources in the Resources section). In this game, learners get to drop large flat plastic disks into the top of the game frame and watch them move down the board bouncing off pegs. Based on where they land, they might win prizes.

Some typical ways to randomly determine who gets prizes at the end of your workshops include:

♦   Pass out playing cards first thing in the session to those learners who arrive on time.

♦   Additionally, randomly give cards for volunteering as scribes (note-takers) or group leaders, for contributing information during the session, and for returning from breaks and lunch on time.

♦   Explain in your introductory remarks that the person with the highest (or lowest) card score at the end wins a prize. Aces count as 1 point, 2 through 9 are at those values, and 10, jacks, queens, and kings are 10 points each. Jokers can be used as whatever points you desire if you want to add a bit of extra value (15 points) to help break any ties in score that might occur.

♦   Use the double carnival tickets that come on a roll, instead of playing cards. These coupons come in pairs and have the same number. Learners receive one coupon and you retain the second for a drawing at the end of the workshop.

♦   Tape one of your business cards or other item, such as a strip of paper that says "Winner!" under a few chairs in the room.

♦   Put a colored dot inside the back cover of participant workbook, under someone's coffee cup or saucer (if tables are pre-set with these), or on the underside of a few name tents.

♦ Use smiley-face stickers on name tents. The learner who has the most, or least, stickers at the end of the session wins a prize. Stickers are given for the same reasons as the playing cards and coupons.

♦ Pass out pennies that all have the same year to reduce the chance that someone will use his or her own coins, instead of other incentives. The person with the most or least wins. They receive pennies for the same reasons as described above.

Strategy for Success

Use carnival-type games to provide a fun, festive means of awarding prizes. Such activities actively engage people, the noise level goes up, color and novelty are injected into the closing, and learners are stimulated by the emotional excitement of the event. Most of the games mentioned below are available at Creative Presentation Resources in the Resources section at the end of the book.

Baseball Game. Here's a great activity that uses Velcro balls that stick to the fabric background with an image of a baseball catcher on it and a target format showing different "hits." Allow learners to toss one of the Velcro balls and award prizes to the best or specified "hit."

Milk Bottle Game. If you have an area that allows a backstop to throw rubber balls, you can incorporate this classic game. Learners each throw three balls in an attempt to knock the balls off a table. Successful competitors win a prize.

Dart Ball Game. This soft, hanging dart board has various numbers that learners attempt to hit with soft Velcro balls. You can use this to award prizes, to determine members for each team, or to pick who goes next in an activity during the workshop.

(continued)

Prize Wheel Spinner. Use a large game spinner that has a series of comments. Some sample categories might be:

Sorry—Not a Winner

Pick a Grab Bag

Select Any Prize

Win a Smiley Face Ball

Spin Again

Learners spin based on criteria you establish at the beginning of the session. This device can also be used to randomly select team members or for other purposes during the workshop. You can change the categories on the wheel before the conclusion to allow for its use as a prize wheel.

Closing Rituals

Have learners offer verbal or written feedback to one another.

Use Music. Most people enjoy music. Because of their experience with television, radio, and movies, they probably have many emotional memories connected to various songs. You can tap into their connection with music, add a bit of novelty, tie to their musical intelligence, and literally end your session on a high note if you choose appropriate music to close your session.

When choosing music, select songs that are festive and tie to the workshop theme. A number of popular upbeat tunes are listed below. You can also find several books that will help in finding appropriate music in the Resources section of this book.

Some fun and upbeat songs that you can use to set a positive tone when closing your workshop include:

"1999"—Prince

"Celebrate"—Three Dog Night

"Celebration"—Kool and the Gang

"Footloose"—Kenny Loggins

"Fly Like an Eagle"—Steve Miller Band

"Gonna Fly Now" (Theme from *Rocky*)—Bill Conti and Maynard Ferguson

"Happy Trails to You"—Roy Rogers and Dale Evans

"Heigh-Ho" (from Disney's *Snow White*)

"I Just Want to Celebrate"—Rare Earth

"I'm So Excited"—The Pointer Sisters

"I Thank You"—Sam and Dave

"I've Had the Time of My Life"—Bill Medley and Jennifer Warnes

"Jump"—Van Halen

"Na Na Hey Hey Kiss Him Goodbye"—Steam

"Pomp and Circumstance Military March No. 1"

"See You Later, Alligator"—Bill Haley and the Comets

"Tomorrow" (From the play *Annie*)

"We Are the Champions"—Queen

"What a Wonderful World"—Louis Armstrong

"Who Let the Dogs Out?"—The Baha Men

As discussed earlier in the book, do not forget to obtain appropriate copyright permission.

Strategy for Success

When closing a workshop, review your session objectives, engage learners in a fun review activity, then have a member of upper management, such as the CEO, president, a vice president, or the managing director come in to speak. Following his or her speech, have the senior manager pass out certificates. As learners come forward to receive their certificates, play "Pomp and Circumstance." This adds a bit of novelty and humor into the ceremony.

Following awarding of certificates, hold any drawings for prizes that you planned, share parting or closing remarks, and have everyone give themselves a round of applause for all the great ideas and contributions they made during the workshop.

Thank Your Learners

Your learners have spent time, effort and, in some cases, money to attend your workshop, participate, and help make it a success. The least you can do is thank them. Instead of just saying the words "Thank you," make your expression of gratitude a visual, group event. To accomplish this, prepare a series of closing slides in large multicolored font as follows:

Slide 1—T

Slide 2—H

Slide 3—A

Slide 4—N

Slide 5—K

Slide 6—S

Slide 7—THANKS

After any speakers have concluded, you have conducted your review and closing activity, learners have completed and turned in their evaluations, and you are ready to end your program, prepare to use your slides. To do this, explain to learners that learning is a joint venture between you and them and that throughout the workshop they have provided valuable input. Stress that THEY have made the event a success. Tell them that, in closing, you need their assistance one more time for a final team activity. Explain that you will show a series of slides and that you would like them to read what is on them aloud with you. In enthusiastic voices. Get a verbal commitment from them to help by asking, "Can you do this?!" If necessary, repeat the question louder to emphasize that they should also shout. Once they yell "Yes," say, "Then let's get started." Show the slides you created one at a time as everyone reads them loudly. At the end of the slide show say, "Thank You!" as you gesture toward them with open arms. Wish them well as you remind them that you are a continuing resource that they should call if they need additional information about the workshop content.

As learners gather their personal items to leave the room, play the song "Happy Trails to You" by Roy Rogers and Dale Evans, or one of the other recommended songs on the list earlier in the chapter.

Personalizing What You Have Learned

- What are the most important things that you read in this chapter? Why?

- What are some ways that you can immediately apply concepts covered in this chapter?

- What additional resources or topics do you want to research based on what you read?

BIBLIOGRAPHY

Brewer, C.B. *Soundtracks for Learning: Using Music in the Classroom.* Bellingham, WA: LifeSounds Educational Services, 2008.

Campbell, D. *The Mozart Effect: Tapping the Power of Music to Heal the Body, Strengthen the Mind, and Unlock the Creative Spirit.* New York: Avon Books, 1997.

Embry, D. "The Persuasive Properties of Color." *Marketing Communications*, October 1984.

Gardner, H. *Multiple Intelligences: Frames of Mind.* New York: Basic Books, 1983.

Jensen, E. *Brain-Based Learning.* Del Mar, CA: Turning Point, 1996.

Jensen, E. *Sizzle & Substance: Presenting with the Brain in Mind.* San Diego, CA: The Brain Store, 1998.

Johnson, V. "The Power of Color." *Successful Meetings*, 41(7), 87, 90, June 1992.

Kirkpatrick, D.L. *Evaluating Training Programs: The Four Levels.* San Francisco, CA: Berrett-Koehler, 1994.

Knowles, M. *The Adult Learner: A Neglected Species* (3rd ed.). Houston, TX: Gulf, 1984.

Liberman, J. *Light: Medicine of the Future.* Bear & Company, Santa Fe, NM: Bear, 1991.

Lucas, R.W. *The Big Book of Flip Charts*. New York: McGraw-Hill, 2005.

Lucas, R.W. *People Strategies for Trainers: 176 Tips and Techniques for Dealing with Difficult Classroom Situations*. New York: AMACOM, 2005.

Mager, R.F. *Preparing Objectives for Programmed Instruction*. San Francisco: Fearon, 1962.

Miller, G.A. "The Magical Number Seven, Plus or Minus Two: Some Limits on Our Capacity for Processing Information." *Psychological Review, 63*, 81–97, 1956.

Society of Neuroscience. "Music Training and the Brain." *Brain Briefings*. Available at, www.sfn.org/index.cfm?pagename=brainBriefings_musicTrainingAndTheBrain. May 2000.

Pluth, B.P. 101 *Movie Clips That Teach and Train*. Excelsior, MN: Pluth and Pluth, 2007.

Wichmann, F.A., Sharpe, L.T., & Gegenfurtner, K.R. "The Contributions of Color to Recognition Memory for Natural Scenes." *Journal of Experimental Psychology: Learning, Memory and Cognition, 28*(3), 5, May 2002.

Yaman, D., & Covington, M. *I'll Take Learning for 500: Using Game Shows to Engage, Motivate, and Train*. San Francisco: Pfeiffer, 2006.

Zelancy, G. *Say It with Charts: The Executive's Guide to Visual Communication* (4th ed.). New York: McGraw-Hill, 2001.

The items and vendors listed in this section are provided for your reference and possible use only. Information about these resources was accurate at the time of publication. The author and publisher are not responsible for changes, since organizations frequently revise their business strategies and operational processes.

The author and publisher do not endorse these organizations or their products and services. Creative Presentation Resources, Inc., is the exception, in that it is owned by the author, who stands behind its products and services.

Button/Badge Makers

Badge a Minit
345 North Lewis Avenue
Oglesby, IL 61348
(815) 883-8822
(800) 223-4103
www.badgeaminit.com

Button/badge making equipment and supplies

Creative Training Products/Sessions

Creative Presentation Resources, Inc.
P.O. Box 180487
Casselberry, FL 32718-0487
(407) 695-5535/(800) 308-0399
www.presentationresources.net

Toys, games, ribbons, chicken pointers, pencils, erasers, videos, books, copyright-free music, and props. Also creative training, train-the-trainer and other workplace skills workshops.

Robert W. Lucas
(800) 308-0399/(407) 695-5535
Fax: (407) 695-7447
blucas@robertwlucas.com
www.robertwlucas.com

Internationally known consultant, speaker, and author or contributing author of twenty-eight books and hundreds of books and training programs.

Disability Advocacy Groups and Organizations

**American Association of
People with Disabilities (AAPD)**
1629 K Street NW, Suite 503
Washington, DC 20006
(202) 457-0046/(800) 840-8844
www.aapd.org

American Council of the Blind (ACB)
1155 15th Street, NW, Suite 1004
Washington, DC 20005
(202) 467-5081 (800) 424-8666
www.acb.org

Disability Resources on the Internet
www.disabilityresources.org

National Association of the Deaf
8630 Fenton Street, Suite 820
Silver Spring, MD 20910
(301) 587-1788
www.nad.org

National Organization on Disability
910 16th Street, NW, Suite 600
Washington, DC 20006
(202) 293-5960
www.nod.org

Fancy Paper/Presentation Supplies

Paper Direct
1025 East Woodmen Road
Colorado Springs, CO 80920
(800) 272-7377
www.paperdirect.com

Fancy paper and presentation equipment

Games and Activities

Creative Presentation Resources, Inc.
P.O. Box 180487
Casselberry, FL 32718-0487
(407) 695-5535/(800) 308-0399
www.presentationresources.net

Toys, games, ribbons, chicken pointers, pencils, erasers, videos, books, copyright-free music and props. Also creative training, train-the-trainer, and other workplace skills workshops.

The Thiagi Group
4423 E. Trailridge Road
Bloomington, IN 47408-9633
(812) 332-1478
www.thiagi.com

Training workshops on designing and using games and
activities. Game development information.

Music

**American Society of Composers, Authors and
Publishers (ASCAP)**
One Lincoln Plaza
New York, NY 10023
(800) 952-7227/(212) 621-6000
www.ascap.com

License agreements for use of copyrighted songs and music

Broadcast Music Incorporated (BMI)
320 West 57th Street
New York, NY 10019
(212) 586-2000
www.bmi.com

License agreements for use of copyrighted songs and music

The Classical Archives LLC
200 Sheridan Avenue, Suite 403
Palo Alto, CA 94306-2041
(650) 330-8050
www.classicalarchives.com

Purchase rights to use classical music

Music Publishers' Association (MPA)
243 5th Avenue, Suite 236
New York, NY 10016
(212) 327-4044
http://mpa.org

Music Copyright information

Party Supplies and Decorations

M&N International
P.O. Box 64784
St. Paul, MN 55164-0784
(800) 479-2043
www.mninternational.com

Party decorations, hats, and favors for various holiday
celebrations

Self-Study Courses

American Management Association
1601 Broadway
New York, NY 10019
(877) 566-9441
www.amanet.org/selfstudy/

Self-paced learning workshops

Seminar Companies

American Management Association (AMA)
(212) 903-7915/(877) 566-9441
www.customerservice@amanet.org

Fred Pryor Seminars
(800) 780-8476
www.customerservice@pryor.com

National Seminars Group
(800) 258-7246
www.nationalseminarstraining.com

NTL Institute
(703) 548-1500/(800) 777-5227
www.ntl.org

Websites

The following websites are additional resources. These sites were active as of date of publication.

Accrediting Council for Continuing Education and Training
www.accet.org

American Management Association
www.amanet.org

American Marketing Association
www.ama.org

American Society for Training and Development
www.astd.org

Association of Supervision and Curriculum Development
www.ascd.org

International Association of Facilitators
www.iaf-world.org

International Alliance for Learning
www.ialearn.org

International Association of Correctional Training
Professionals
www.iactp.org

International Customer Service Association
www.icsa.com

International Personnel Management Association
www.ipma-hr.org

International Society for Performance and Instruction
www.ispi.org

International Toastmasters
www.toastmasters.org

National Council for Continuing Education and Training
www.nccet.org

National Speakers Association
www.nsaspeaker.org

National School Board Association
www.nsba.org

National Staff Development Council
www.nsdc.org/

North American Simulation and Gaming Society
www.nasaga.org/

Training Officers Consortium
http://trainingofficers.org

Page references followed by *fig* indicate illustrated figures; followed by *t* indicate a table; followed by *e* indicate an exhibit.

TRAINING INFORMATION

Bob Lucas has over three decades of experience training trainers and adults in a variety of workplace topics. His learner-centered, brain-focused training events have been a hit at local ASTD chapter meetings, ASTD International Conference, ASCD National, the Leaning Brain Expo and many other venues for years. To bring Bob and his team of knowledgeable and creative trainers to your location, please fill out the form on following page and forward it to Bob or contact him directly via email.

Name: _____

Position: _____

Organization: _____

Address: _____

_____

_____

Phone:_____ Fax: _____

Email: _____

I would like information about:

❑ In-House Train-the-Trainer Skills Workshops

❑ In-House Presentation Skills Workshops

❑ In-House Brain-Based Learning Skills Workshops for Trainers/Educators

❑ One-on-One Telephone Training Skills Coaching Sessions

❑ Workplace Skills Training Workshops in the following areas:

   ❑ Interpersonal Communication

   ❑ Front-Line Customer Service Skills

   ❑ Team-Building Skills

   ❑ Supervisory Skills

❑ Customized teleseminars for my staff on any of the topic area listed above

Mail to:

Bob Lucas

P.O. Box 180487

Casselberry, FL 32707

USA

Phone: (800) 308-0399 or (407) 695-5535

Or fax to: (407) 695-5535

Or email to: blucas@robertwlucas.com

ABOUT THE AUTHOR

Robert W. Lucas holds dual roles as president of Creative Presentation Resources—a creative training and products company—and as a founding managing partner for Global Performance Strategies, LLC—an organization specializing in performance-based training, and consulting services.

With almost four decades of experience in human resources development, management, and customer service, Bob has gained valuable insights that he shares with client organizations. He has designed, marketed, and delivered hundreds of learning events on various workplace and personal development topics to thousands of adult learners from around the world. Bob uses an interactive, experiential approach to assist organizations and individuals in developing innovative and practical strategies for improved workplace performance. Some of his areas of expertise include presentation skills, creative training and management program development, train-the-trainer, interpersonal communication, adult learning, diversity, customer service, and employee and organizational development.

In addition to training and consulting, Bob is actively involved professionally and has served on a member of numerous boards of directors. He was formerly the president of the Central Florida Chapter of the American Society for Training and Development and the chairman for Leadership Seminole in Florida. Bob also serves as an adjunct faculty member for Webster University.

An internationally known writer and trainer who is listed in the *Who's Who in the World, Who's Who in America, and Who's Who in the South and Southeast,* Bob has written and contributed to twenty-eight books and written hundreds of articles on training and workplace-related topics. Previous books include: *Creative Learning: Activities and Games That REALLY Engage Learners; The Creative Training Idea Book; People Strategies for Trainers;* and *The Big Book of Flip Charts.*

Bob has earned a master of arts degree with a focus in human resources development from George Mason University in Fairfax, Virginia, and a second master of arts degree in management and leadership from Webster University in Orlando, Florida.

Printed in the United States
By Bookmasters